Cedric Cullingford

Prejudice

From individual identity to nationalism in young people

KOGAN
PAGE

To Gill

First published in 2000

Apart from any fair dealing for the purposes of research or private study, or criticism or review, as permitted under the Copyright, Designs and Patents Act 1988, this publication may only be reproduced, stored or transmitted, in any form or by any means, with the prior permission in writing of the publishers, or in the case of reprographic reproduction in accordance with the terms and licences issued by the CLA. Enquiries concerning reproduction outside these terms should be sent to the publishers at the undermentioned address:

Kogan Page Limited	Stylus Publishing Inc.
120 Pentonville Road	22883 Quicksilver Drive
London N1 9JN	Sterling, VA 20166-2012
UK	USA

© Cedric Cullingford, 2000

The right of Cedric Cullingford to be identified as the author of this work has been asserted by him in accordance with the Copyright, Designs and Patents Act 1988.

British Library Cataloguing in Publication Data

A CIP record for this book is available from the British Library.

ISBN 0 7494 3302 7

Typeset by Kogan Page
Printed and bound in Great Britain by Clays Ltd, St Ives plc

Contents

Preface

After a century of unprecedented violence we should allow ourselves the question: Why? Why should the development of worldwide communication and knowledge seem to foster rather than prevent barbarous behaviour carried out through political, concerted actions? What is it about people, civilized in their own terms, that makes them behave with such brutality to each other? And then, why is this statement true only of some people, particular individuals in particular conditions? Is prejudice a condition of the human experience?

This question might seem to some naïve and to others too innocent. We know of many descriptions of human behaviour, of tribalism and ethnic cleansing, of hatred and torture. The newspapers daily bring the horrors of human interaction to our attention. Were I to mention any – Rwanda, Kosovo, East Timor, Northern Ireland, Chechenya – the list would have changed between writing and publishing but the principle would remain. We try to deal, insufficiently, with each new crisis, but do we try to understand it sufficiently to try to prevent it?

'We'. This, in a sense, is the most ambitious word in the research that informs this book. 'We' are human beings. Sometimes, when we look at the cultural inheritance that we share, the collective prejudices and attitudes, as well as the shaping language, seem inevitable and overpowering. But I am after the more general 'we', not those barriers that are half-way towards understanding, whether class, religion, race or nationality. What makes human beings behave in the way we do? It is easier to describe cultural norms, or individual differences, than the way in which the two connect.

Such a question tends to remain unexamined because on the one hand it seems so vast that we cannot begin to contemplate the answer. At the same time and in the same mind a contradictory reaction will arise: we already know the answer. 'It is because of...' and here follows a series of almost atavistic reactions that overwhelm reason whilst appearing rational, at least in the circumstances of the expressor. It is a label that invokes distinctions and easy, generalized explanations that are almost inevitably political, spiritual or genetic.

There are explanations of cultural inheritances, of religious divides, of national hegemonies to do with land and power, with ownership and control. But underneath all this, do people accept that it is a genetic inevitability that 'people' are biased, narrow-minded, prejudiced and full of hate? The reader will react 'that is not true of me'. And yet the reader will also say, 'that's the way *people* are'.

One of the first premises of this book in its search for answers is the contradictory nature of human beings at their best and their worst, upholding civilized instincts and retaining the most crude prejudices. One question that pervades this research and which is an underground theme is the fundamental question: how could people, individuals, uphold religious values, and listen to Mozart, and at the same time kill helpless others in cold blood, as in the case of Auschwitz or Buchenwald.

Perhaps this question is the main driving force behind my research. I want to speculate *why*. I know there are no rewards for such a question. For most people description and cultural explanations are more fun. I want to know why people are so diverted from curiosity that they feel they know the answers before they even begin to contemplate them. That, of course, is such a part of the dilemma of being human that it already suggests part of the answer. The desire for some kind of security remains with us: essentially an intellectual security, a frame of mind that defines us against others, and helps us to understand them through labels.

This book has been years in the making. It is born out of pain, of seeing icons of peoples suffering, of gazing on the generalized and widespread anguish without dismissing it. There are many things to distract us. We seek distractions. One is to witness nation competing with nation on the sporting field. We become passionate about 'our' side. As Orwell pointed out, there is probably more nationalist passion in the improbable circumstances of a game that involves a few people kicking a ball around than in any more rational activity.

Most searches for answers about the curiosity and fallibility of human nature have tended to rest on a hypothetical explanation. It lies in the genes, or environment, or religion, or race, or gender. The 'proofs' have therefore been the search for support for an established opinion. I conclude with an attempt at an explanation. This is not a technical hypothesis but the result of a lot of painful speculation. Instead of establishing a theme and 'mastering' it I have sought to try to understand, which is itself a provocation to researchers. I know there are many descriptions of what goes on. History books are full of examples, so many that in choosing one or two I would beg questions of all the others. This book is about what it is in the mind of each individual human being that makes him or her prejudiced. And why? Is it necessary? Why are not all people the same?

Each individual is complicated. But good people, tolerant, sensitive, concerned for others, loyal, strong, disinterested, gentle, understanding, are the same all over the world. The question is what makes people turn virtue into hatred, and what are the limitations that drive people to do unnatural things to each other. Research that addresses this subject focuses on outcomes and manifestations, on the cultural expressions that are supposed to be either the height of collective identity in music or literature, or the depths of atavistic passion. Books on the manifestations of nationalism abound, and there are many who give the religious and political excuses for such expression. But all seem to take for granted that prejudice is a 'natural' human phenomenon. Few question why it is that there are some people who, whilst focused on their own cultural values, are not confined by them.

There are a number of personal impulses that underlie this book. At one level is the early memory of the years after the second part of the Great War: of bombed buildings, of soldiers returning from years of captivity, of the association of the sound of aeroplanes with bombs. And this was all from the point of view of the English, in a foreign country, in the Control Commission in a divided and defeated land, in chauffeur-driven cars watching the very poor in their shattered, pot-holed land, bewildered, cold and made to feel ashamed. This point of view also includes driving up, in the same large car, to a heap of rubble with the almost inevitable symbolic enamelled pot on top of it, and being told 'That was where your relations lived'.

The other personal strand comes from reflecting on all the research I have done, trying to understand what young people think and why. I have been told by many of a great deal of unnecessary cruelty, teasing and bullying, making others feel isolated and inadequate in order to avoid feeling inadequate in their turn. Even children on holiday by the pool are seen at their psychological exercises: who is to be the leader? If one pushes another into the water is it a joke, a game or an attack? Older children dominate and are fascinating to the rest, but not all older children and not all are fascinated. There is a constant battle of wills, about who is to be feared, or respected, or despised. Just as people learn acquisitiveness for food – and in animals this dominates – so human beings crave social status. How does this translate itself into the imagined communities of anonymous cultural identity?

I recognize the ambition. I am therefore grateful for the comments and example of my friends and colleagues. I am especially grateful to Dinah Ballance, Roy Fisher, Peter Mackenzie, Philip Mudd, Lew Owen, Matthew Pearson and Sue Smith.

1

Prejudice as personal definition

The inevitable human condition?

The good all over the world are very similar, but each group or nation has its own way of being wicked. Of all the problems that face humanity, the greatest is how to deal with the hatred and antipathy expressed and acted upon by some people against others. Concern for the environment, for treating global warming and pollution might seem at some times paramount, but the 20th century was overshadowed by mass destruction based on prejudice and hatred. Whilst the First World War seemed dominated by nationalism, sometimes disguised as patriotism, sometimes as competition, the Second was more clearly revealed as the manifestation of racial hatreds, both in Europe and the Far East. The last years of the 20th century were expressed in different forms of brutal ethnic antipathies, from Rwanda to Kosovo, from East Timor to Chechnya.

The question is whether hatred is part of the human condition. If it seems inevitable in certain circumstances, can this be explained in general terms, in the political or religious conditions that arise from history? Do all people have the capacity for hatred and for injuring their fellow human beings, and are only prevented by the conditions in which they live? To what extent are phenomena covered by sickeningly bland terms such as 'ethnic cleansing', an outbreak of humankind's 'inhumanity', or the result purely of local conditions, of rivalry or fear, of political opportunity or religious fanaticism? The fundamental question is age old and almost naïve. Why are people as they are? To what extent are they conditioned by their particular environment?

This is an open question which requires an answer. Most attempts are literary and philosophical. The question drives the great plays, poems and novels, at least beneath the surface.[1] And yet most of the explanations are at a general level. They

1

talk in terms of whole nations, of cultural identity, of large ethnic groupings, of prejudice against certain tribes or people. They explain in terms of threat, of political or religious intolerance, of rivalry and of fear. Rarely is there an exploration of the personal aspirations and personal histories of the individuals caught up in these confrontations. The tendency to describe, which is easier than the attempt to explain, tends to draw up all the generalizable faults as political circumstances rather than as the circumstances of the individual. Whilst implicitly acknowledging the fact that there is no genetic impulse towards mutual antipathy, the cultural explanations do not delve into those human tendencies that mean that some people are intolerant and others are not. Here we are concerned not so much with the cultural manifestations of the phenomenon of nationalism as with the development of individual consciousness. We seek to explore the inner characteristics that lead to the actions of prejudice.

It is because of the contrast between those parts of the world where prejudice becomes a political act, and those where people live in harmony together, that so much attention is paid to description. The time, the opportunity, the causes of hatred, the rivalries, the threats: all these seem to be circumscribed by place, the particular factors that make the news. Individuals are generalized as phenomena, as well as a number, placed in a political or cultural group: this is of no use in finding out why they should act in the way they do. The study of prejudice reveals that whilst each country has its own way of presenting its nationalism as patriotism, the tendency to adhere to a particular point of view is universal.[2] On the one hand we have a devotion to a way of life; on the other an attempt to improve the way of life of others. There can be many sophisticated means of justifying particular social arrangements and conventions and of sanctioning political actions, but these are all clever and particular – even discriminating – uses of history.[3] Symbols of prejudice fascinate but they have their origins in the tendency to collect, to put up markers of personal identity and make distinctions between the collective self and others.

The phenomenon of discrimination is complex because it has so many different types of manifestation. It is at the heart of politics. Class distinctions, national differences, the hold on power, let alone political parties: are all group identities, defined against 'others'. Self-identity, not as an ontological given, but as a fragile and constantly re-defining state, is crucial. The more febrile, the more weak this sense of identity, the more the sense of the 'other', the defining outsider, is necessary. Tolerance and understanding do not always appeal. The fearful and the insecure seek antipathies. Many of these minor hatreds are contained within communities, but politicians relish the chance to extend them to more global manifestations. As people tend to vote *against* a political party rather than *for* one, so politicians like to define their national and international status against others. It helps to define themselves and what they, as cultural symbols, stand for.

Each person is defined as an individual against others. This is true in the family as in the social group. Gradually the difference between the personal self and the shared norms and beliefs become both more complex and more simplified. They are the more complex because there are so many social forces that impinge on the individual's sense of identity. They become simplified because it is a way of coping with actuality: if a person can be defined as a part of a 'group', of a generalizable identity, then all complexities can be made to seem less intellectually and emotionally threatening. This desire for self-definition in a social sphere can be simplified in terms of class or religion, possessions or politics. But one of the most curious, if most recent, manifestations of this desire for ontological security, is nationalism.

The psychological institution of nationalism

The wish to be part of a collective group, of belonging, is very strong. The very first instinct is to cling to what is known and familiar. This by definition creates an 'other', an outside, personally alien, world. The family, the group, the class and the school are all early examples of a collective or 'tribal' identity.

The distinction between tribalism and nationalism is a comparatively recent one, in terms of human organizations. 'Blood is thicker than water', the sense of personal belonging and identity to and with a family, can be extended widely, and in different layers. Personal ties are not just a chance of birth, but of opportunity. Friendships, networks and clanships are all an almost deliberate attempt to make use of the extension of intimate relations, of disseminating influence without conflict. But these ties are made the more important the moment there is a sense of opposition, or of antipathy. The idea that someone will 'stick by you' without question, as a family does, is made necessary or attractive only when there is a threat. Thus families become widened into groups, groups into collections of interest, in terms of taste or money, and such collections turn into cultural items, like people of a 'like mind'.

Nationality can be defined as both a cultural and a political phenomenon. A nation-state, a political invention, can define a particular territory full of different traditions and inheritances. But it usually defines itself in terms of a common cultural interest. This in itself can be complicated. When, for instance, do people define themselves as British, or English, Welsh or Scots, let alone Irish? At a number of levels, such as patriotism and chauvinism, the belonging to a nationality can be very important. Superficially it is a matter of flag waving, of supporting one group of sportsmen or women on the playing fields against another. The belonging to a group, like a football team, can become a dominant factor in self-identity.[4]

It can also encourage extreme aggression: the sense that some other group is an enemy and always in the wrong. Transferred to the international stage the national team can lead to strong feelings of prejudice as well as support. The team supported is not just a matter of choice, for some feel that their support was thrust upon them. It is a given, a matter of political and cultural chance.

We live in an age in which, despite international communication systems and globalization, nationalism is thrust upon us, usually through sport. The celebration of victory involves a national anthem. But nationalism, in the present sense of the term, is still quite new. The power of the state as a collective force, as opposed to personal ownership, or personal ties, is an invention that was only clearly expressed within the past 200 years. A glance at the maps in the world of 200 years ago, with small patches of tribes or principalities, demonstrates the recency of the phenomenon of people defined blandly and collectively as nations, coupled with a flag, and people defined as enemies. The spread of nationalism all over the world, as defined in European terms, is also recent.[5]

The idea of nationalism as some kind of ideal or perfect state is a comparatively new one. Whilst there are many tribal and religious divisions, inculcating loyalty to a particular cause or creed, the political issue of nationalism, especially in times of war, has only been developed essentially since the idea of a nation-state was formulated. To take the most extreme example of nationality as racial identity, the rise of National Socialism in Germany was the outcome of defining different races in a kind of rank order. Kerdourie traces the idea of the collective state as a group of 'pure' people – *Volksverein* – to the unlikely source of Immanuel Kant.[6] In *Kritik der Reinen Vernünft* Kant expounded his idea of the spiritual ideal, the wholeness of the individual.[7] This was then developed by Herder into a collective ideal state, at a time when Germany was still a series of small territories and petty principalities, with only Prussia demonstrating the idea of a unifying will. From this idea the notion of the nation-state as not just a political or linguistic or cultural entity but somehow something more developed became turned into the gross manifestations of chauvinism expressed in the Nazi rallies.

Nationhood and nationality

Explanations for the rise of nationalism, including its causes and uses, are many. It is, after all, a complex subject since there are so many ways in which it is expressed. It is not only one of the most public and powerful expressions of group identity in terms of both fear and assertion, but a mass feeling which is often exploited. It demonstrates clearly the tension between a sense of superiority and a sense of threat that is at the heart of prejudice. The two cannot easily be separated. One of the root causes of the German expression of dominance that led to the Second World War was collective insecurity in the aftermath of the Treaty of Versailles. Nationalism was constantly exploited, especially in the latter part of the 19th century; and, of course, it still is. It is therefore tempting to explain it in terms of the desire for more land, or the threat of losing land, the political hunger for control and dominance that still causes the tension seen for example in Israel and Palestine.

Nationalism is itself a complex phenomenon. It is distinct from the idea of nationhood. Nationhood, as defined in the French Revolution, was a matter of citizenship, of including all people, regardless of the arbitrary circumstances of birth.[8] Nationalism, in contrast, defines itself assertively against others, based often on traditional divisions of land and culture and history. Most of the time nationalism is quiet. But in a crisis or during a social or political change, nationalisms surface as a powerful surge of feeling. Nationalism then draws on problems like the uneven distribution of land or rights, or, as in Kosovo, memories of past glories. These lead to the political myths of ethnic purity, and the power of sacred sites and homelands.[9] Going a cultural stage beyond the tribal antipathies, as seen so often in Africa, and even beyond what began as a functional distinction between the Hutu and the Tutsi, nationalism draws on people's atavistic sense of cultural and group distinction. It is not just about land but about identity.

At its extreme form nationalism is a powerful force, poignant in the suffering of the First World War, manic in the demonstrations of National Socialism, absurd in the antics of the 'far right'. The question is whether nationalism is part of an age-old primordial condition. Most historians and commentators would argue like Kerdourie that it is essentially an invention of the modern nation-state. Clearly it is most obviously expressed in times of war, but it is not a condition that depends on critical moments to exist. It might be unnatural in the sense that it is arbitrary and not dependent on any obvious social division like language, but it is also pervasive.[10] We have noted the 'banal nationalism' of sporting events such as the Olympic games where national anthems and medal counts invoke vast public attention. Flag-waving, or saluting the flag, as in the United States where the Stars and Stripes is ubiquitous, is an almost automatic habit, taken for granted. Nationalism is a concept so fostered and exploited that it appears to many people to become a matter of common sense. That does not make it part of the natural condition of human beings.

Neurotic rationality: nationalism and race

One reason that nationalism is of such significance is its connection in people's minds with race. To be patriotic, to defend the cause, to realise that 'Gott ist mit

Uns' appears to be a good thing. To be a traitor to one's country is despicable. This is not so much because traitors are giving away secrets for a cause they believe in, but that they are 'fouling their own nest'. It is a betrayal of the sense of a large family, of blood and kinship, that creates such strong feelings. In any multi-cultural society the tension between chauvinism and racism becomes significant, and nationality becomes an all-embracing concept, as in the definitions of new nationhood developed in the United States in the 19th century. But until the recent diaspora of peoples, particularly at the end of empires, the connection between nation and peoples was an automatic one. In was considered both natural and necessary to assert the superiority of one's own country over others. In the popular literature of the early years of the 20th century the very plots, as well as the ethos, were dependent on the notion of hierarchies of difference.[11]

During the 19th century nation and race were popularly regarded as synonymous. Books extolled the wonder of Englishness even if that pure essence was the result of a mongrel mix of bloods.[12] People could talk with open contempt and superiority about the 'Blacks' as if they were by nature not only different but somehow less human.[13] Hitler's typology of peoples had a clear sense of hierarchy, making it explicit that some were less human than others, like Slavs or Gypsies, let alone the Jews.[14] This was a way of thinking typical of its time, even if extreme. Taking just one example, the novels of a popular writer like Percy Westerman, it is possible to see not just the ineffable superiority of the English – with heartier cries, more dutiful, more honourable, more self-controlled – but unexamined distinctions between different peoples within Europe and beyond.[15]

A few phrases give the flavour of the dictums of nationality, expressed as chauvinism.

> As a rule the farther north the better the strain… what I kick against is the mongrel with negro or Indian blood…[16]

> It has taught him the futility of using his fist against the armour-plated skull of a nigger.

> The South American habit of procrastination was… deeply rooted.

> Take my word for it, the Belgians are not a fighting race.

> He never had a high opinion of the modern Greek…

> Even if an Englishman were not the first to plant his country's flag on the North Pole there is no little consolation to be derived from the fact that an Anglo-Saxon established the priority.

There are few nations that are not generalized about, as being superstitious, or untrustworthy, or overpassionate. The nations are overlaid with notions of 'racial' characteristics. Whilst there are distinctions between north and south, and between whites and negros, these are wrapped up in a flag of nationality. How otherwise can the Belgians be deemed to be a 'race'? These are all easy and unexamined generalizations, taken for granted as marking out the wonderful distinction of the English, and only really fierce when it comes to the Germans.

Nationality is one of these general concepts with which people define themselves collectively against others. It can be banal and it can become extreme. It can be exploited in politics or be a matter of cultural curiosity, as in the many English books on France. It can become a manifestation of anger, or a sense of threat. It is nearly always a cause of conflict at one level or another. Even in attempts to break down barriers, as in Europe, there are still clashes between different cultural sovereignties, aspects of national identity to which people relate.[17] There is a distinction between nationalism and national identity, that generalizable sense of cultural hegemony with which people define themselves, for good or ill. Thus there can be wicked or benign nationalisms. Someone living in a 'foreign land' is both more aware of his or her cultural inheritance, and more objective about what it means.

Nationality and religious prejudice

Nationality is just the expression of collective and cultural identity. There are distinctions just as powerful made within nations, like class. There are different types of psychological institutions. One of the most significant of these is religion.

Religious intolerance is one of the fiercest manifestations of prejudice. The belief that there is only one truth and that is one's own is a clear statement about one aspect of the human condition and the way it is defined. At the heart of it is the extrapolation of a personal sense of identity into a whole ontological system. Whilst being the product of cultural circumstances, religious belief turns the very fact around and not only proselytizes but sees the whole world from the point of view of the self. The psychological heart of religious belief is the sense that a higher being has marked out the individual, when in fact the individual has created that particular god.

Modern religions are usually monotheistic and it is these that can be most intolerant. In what are now called primitive times, religions abounded. There were countless gods, as well as other spiritual forces. And all these lived at peace with each other until the advent of monotheism: 'Thou shalt have no other gods but me'. Perhaps this general idea was the beginning of the idea of a nation, bringing all the tribes into one, and making distinctions by defining enemies (and slaughtering them). There have been many periods of religious tolerance as well as intolerance, when people accepted other peoples' beliefs, and sometimes adopted them. Gibbon describes the heyday of the Roman Empire when different people could mix, retain their personal beliefs and accept both the differences and the multifarious combination of gods, each one personal.[18] The preaching of Paul changed that. Gibbon laments the rise of intolerance, and ascribes to the imposition of a set of beliefs, and the inevitable disputes that arose from doctrinal differences, the splitting of the Empire, the fall of Roman civilization and the return to the dark ages.

Differences between religions can cause fierce intolerance, but differences within religions are usually more fierce; this again gives an insight into the nature of prejudice. Distance, like ignorance, is easier to deal with. Nevertheless, from the point of view of humankind's treatment of others, the history of religion makes sad as well as perplexing reading. From Crusade to jihad, the slaughter of others becomes a holy cause. The Inquisition saw itself as doing good in torturing the benighted Indians of South America into the true faith. But there are also instances of tolerances, of different religions able to coexist: Muslim Byzantium, or Charles V of Spain refusing to destroy the Alhambra or the Mosque at Cordoba, and even lamenting the insertion of a new cathedral into it.

It is within religion, however, that the greatest of antipathies arise, between Shia or Sunni Muslims, or Catholics and Protestants. From the Thirty Years War to the present day we have many instances of the use of doctrine as a cultural weapon. Scenes such as the 'Spanish Fury' in destroying Antwerp in the name of a loving god during the Dutch struggle for independence are typical of the sense of collective self-justification which religious belief can afford.[19] There are, therefore, essential contradictions in the way in which prejudice manifests itself. A concern for others in the name of universal love becomes caught up with a fierce determination to proselytize. A disinterested desire to spread the truth becomes intolerance of someone else's interpretation of truth. In its most extreme and emphatic forms religion both defines the complete identity of the self against others and sees those outside the ontological completeness of belief as a form of definition. The very difference of others is a necessary condition of the psychological institution of the collective self.

The attractions of prejudice

Prejudice, at its pathological extreme, is one of the most terrible manifestations of human nature. It is pervasive as well as cruel. Whilst some would argue that it is the expression of self-interest wrapped in cultural forms, it can, like racism, become an end in itself, as well as a political weapon. It is both a natural part of an individual outlook, and capable of being controlled and understood. There is no need for people to be prejudiced. Nevertheless, the self-identity that is a kind of mental self-preservation is shared by all. Distinctions are always made, even if they are not always made on the basis of personal superiority.[20] As the examples of natural chauvinism cited earlier make clear, not all demonstrations of national prejudice are wicked in intention.

Prejudice depends on stereotypes, on the reduction of whole peoples to some kind of generalization. This might be inevitable, as it can constitute a superficial level of understanding, or an attempt to express a more complex insight. The extremes of nationalism are brutal. But there is also a lighter, less serious side to the habits of people in labelling each other. The nature of thought and language is to create simplified associations with words.[21] Everybody, not only those who provide the evidence in this book, has clear images of 'others', of different nations and peoples. They also define differences within nations. This creation of group identities can be dangerous, as in snobbery, but it can also be the stuff of jokes. The question is to whom is the joke funny and to whom is it offensive. Where does one draw the line?

There are triggers for all images, and one of these is national identities. There are prejudices against or for certain groups, particular peoples and different towns. From the sentiment that the people from the north are superior to those in the south, we have the common distinction of geography in many countries.[22] Those in the south of England or the north of Germany are 'superior' to the rest. Those in the south of Italy are deemed so different it is suggested they should be in a separate and inferior state. With the same language and culture such differences are the stuff of jokes. But are they really expressing fear or superiority?

From Shakespeare's depiction of the different 'nations' that make up Great Britain onwards, there have been many assumptions, sometimes positive and sometime negative, about national identities.[23] Who has not heard a joke about the Scotsman, the Englishman and the Irishman?[24] Who has not heard jokes that depend on the picture of national stupidity, as in 'How many Poles does it take to replace a light-bulb?' The stereotypical images of certain countries remain years after the actuality has changed. Sometimes this is deliberate, as in the picture of the capitalist Briton smoking a cigar in a chauffeur-driven Rolls-Royce perpetuated in Soviet propaganda. Sometimes it is innocent, as in the selfsame person wearing a bowler hat and morning suit and wielding an umbrella.[25] The French are associated with a man wearing a beret, riding a bicycle, holding a long loaf and smelling of garlic, as well as having eaten snails. Such images are so much the stuff of national association that they even inform textbooks, television programmes and language courses.[26] When a BBC programme for those wanting to learn French was monitored it was found that their proficiency in the language was barely enhanced but the hatred of France greatly increased.[27]

Even within countries there are clearly defined labels. In Jordan one only has to mention Tafila and people fall about. What about 'Essex girls'?[28] Surveys of different nations reveal hierarchies of national hatred, an accumulation of stereotypes that is supposed to make the complexity of the world comprehensible.[29] There can be benign descriptions of characteristics, as in the depiction by Hindus of a perfect world – of an American income, an English country house, Chinese food and a Japanese wife.[30] Culture shock can be a confrontation with the unfamiliar that is so exotic that it is no threat. It can also be the loss of the familiar.[31]

National stereotypes even become the mainstay of cartoons and advertisements. The news story that Germans are 'hogging' the best places on the beaches by getting up early and placing their towels in their preferred spots kept British newspapers, and advertisers, active for months.[32] A phrase like 'Ve have vays of making you talk' is a mainstay of television comedy programmes. Is this a stereotype that arises from reality? Is it one that has no possible edge to it? Does it have no connection with the past? Does such a phrase have nothing to do with a former Prime Minister's fear of Germany, on which policies were based?[33]

'Even' the 'Krauts' have a sense of humour. The love of order and the respect for rules provides rich comedy in the *Kapitan von Köpenick*. For years the comics Häberle and Pfleiderer drew attention to the absurdities of bureaucracy.[34] Each nation has its own set of stereotypes within which it defines itself, and defines itself against others. Class, accent, region, as well as nation, are all used as defensive distinctions, and the butt of jokes. They can be fuelled out of envy. They can be the armour of self-protection. At the same time they can be the symbol of self-security, of easy superiority over others and a mark of distinction.

From benign stereotypes to pointed prejudice

Underlying all the jokes lies the question of the extent to which the stereotypes of the victims are a matter of nationality, or region or race. In the muddle of stereotypes, a muddle of too many over-simplifications, comes the dangerous association of certain peoples with particular faults. Certain kinds of prejudice – 'I prefer one to the other' – are commonplace. Others, like antipathy towards Gypsies, wherever they are, are dangerous.[35] One of the most extreme, long-lasting, and influential has been attitudes towards the Jews, since this unites prejudice over the whole of the world, and not only within Nazi Germany. The literature of description of what led up to the Holocaust is, rightly, enormous. The literature that tries to explore the reasons for this ultimate of prejudices in action is comparatively thin. When we do have explanations – the mystery of Hitler, the results of the collapse of the Weimar Republic, the deep anti-semitism under the surface in Europe, the fear that there was an alien people, with international connections, rather like Gypsies crossing the normal boundaries of hearth and home – these rarely delve beyond the historical phenomena,[36] as opposed to understanding the individual and group motivations for such prejudice.

The natural and proper response to the Holocaust is 'how could they do it?' How could the people of Goethe and Beethoven behave like that? And the question which follows that is inevitably, as in Goldhagen's *Hitler's Willing Apprentices*, did they *all* know? Is there something about the German people, even if only at that time, that made them mix up race and politics to such a bestial and horrifying degree? The other question is, of course, what is it about people that can let them behave like that?[37] The question in this book, however, is not of the conditions but about the nature of people that can make certain natural tendencies go wrong. It is not only Germans in the early years of the 20th century who associated politics with race. To turn against a section of the community that had proven itself loyal in the 1914–18 war and was a powerful cultural as well as economic influence, meant that some great irrational twist of thought and spirit had to take place.

The secret of what happened psychologically to Germany was the association of political and social relations with the expression of a distinct group of people. Nature and Nurture were closely associated. The assumption that this is the way 'they' are became a political, racist dogma. Whilst that story has been told, the parallel one about how the British began to associate all Germans with Nazis, which illustrates the same period and the same stereotype, has not. The tendency to turn the labelling of nations into genetic rather than cultural stereotypes continues. It explains, even in Europe, let alone beyond it, these extremes of cruelty that make people turn against each other whether the excuse is control, religion or autonomy. Whatever the excuse, hatred and misunderstanding are the fuel.

The present debate over European integration is carried out at a level which is comparatively mild, where instinctive fears and mistrusts are half disguised. All over the world there are examples where there is no debate and no dialogue but outright racism and genocide. We only have to look at the former Yugoslavia to be aware of how deep divisions can go, when antipathies, even if covered by differences of religion, are fundamental. There are examples of a deep-rooted sense of identity as a people, where the political system is closely identified in race, and where ethnicity is all. From Bosnia-Herzegovina to Kosovo we witness the results of such fundamental atavistic attitudes, defying reason or control. Even within what is ostensibly a nation, such as Albania, there are extreme antipathies of separate loyalties and class-based bloodletting.[38]

National characteristics as racial: attitudes in and towards Germany

The fundamental question of nationalism, as of education, is the relationship between the individual's personal make-up and responsibility and the organizational and cultural system in which he or she operates. Nowhere is this debate more significant, lengthy and detailed than in attitudes towards Germany. At the heart of the matter over the past one hundred years is the question whether the German people are fundamentally flawed as a 'race', or whether they have also been the victims of particularly brutal regimes. It is the complexities both of these dichotomies and of the attitudes towards them, on a variety of levels, that are a good example of the ambivalent attitudes towards 'race' and culture. It is not only young children or the immature who display simple labels as tools of understanding. The same sophistication that was a layer of Eichman's thinking is also seen in those reacting against the neurotic rationality of German or Nazi theories of race.

Whilst the material concentrates on that time when the debate was at its height – from Hitler's rise to power to his demise – that should not imply that the problem is in the past. One should only have to say the word 'beach-towel', let alone 'football', to be reminded of the immediacy and popularity of the phenomenon. Whilst the outer manifestations of stereotyping and prejudice might appear amusing, they have more serious undercurrents.[39] Attitudes towards other people reveal as much about those who hold them as about those about whom they are talking.

There has never been a time when the issues of culture, the blending of the individual and the circumstances, have been so deeply, thoroughly and widely debated as in the years of the Second World War. This is not just because all types of feelings of chauvinism and anti-chauvinism were invoked, and not just because the central political issue was that of the purity of 'race' or culture. It is also because the debate was carried out at a number of levels, and embraced all parties, as well as being a constant reminder of how deep the questions are. Nowadays we are accustomed to amusement at the curious manifestations of nationalism by football hooligans, and the way in which these are inflamed and encouraged by the tabloid newspapers. We are also accustomed to the various definitions of what creates a 'culture'; whether the location, the hegemony of such a circumstance is all.[40] But around the period in question all were by attitude or action drawn into that most fundamental of all debates. Nor have the reverberations left us. The question that Aubrey Smith raised at that time – 'Is our enemy the German people or the Nazi party?'[41] – is still a fundamental distinction between person and system. The question is still pressing. But he also raises the more subtle cultural dichotomy. The answer to the question is never simple. For example the Soviet propaganda at the time, unlike that of other nations, drew a distinction between the people and the evils of fascism. It wished to divide one from the other. But the motivation behind this reasonable logic is clear. A Soviet system which denies cultural inheritance, and assumes itself to be beyond nationalism, has to argue that way. What appears at first glance as rational is motivated by political considerations, with disastrous consequences.

The rise and fall of extreme nationalism in Germany, and nationalistic reactions to it, remind us how potent a weapon is the appeal to the 'clan'. The 'chosen people', the 'pure race', 'this blessed isle', are not so much expressions of some deep mighty force as devices used by those in power to obtain strong support.[42] And yet these are not just deliberate manipulations of power. They have to be expressed with conviction, a conviction that binds the sophisticated and educated politician with a mass instinct, whether one refers to Hitler or to Mrs Thatcher.[43] The idea behind the collective will of the nation might be a useful one for those in charge, since it eliminates opposition or diversity, but it is also one that many cling to as a protection against the realization of their own anonymity, or insignificance. A stubborn sense of duty and a wild outpouring of fervour go close in hand.

Nationalism and propaganda

In Germany, long before the advent of Hitler and Fascism, and in England with the sense of the immutable island race given such powerful and sustained expression by Green,[44] the union of people and politics was given palpable expression. Indeed, many have argued that the rise of modern Germany, as an hegemonic State, rather than a collection of estates and principalities, was founded on some inner notion of race. What is certain is that in the political life of Germany, even before the Second World War, the union between the People and the State was supposed to be paramount. Notions of nationality, a 'chosen people', were combined with authoritarianism and charismatic leaders.[45] Even before the First World War, and even in their propaganda to the United States, the assertion of the militarists was that any political act was not just the natural outcome of being attacked by others, but the inevitable consequence of the will of the people.

> The German Army... is a great, living organism, which draws its strength and life-blood from all classes of the whole German folk. The German Army can develop its entire strength only in a war which the folk approve, that is, when a defensive war has been forced upon them.[46]

Whilst this is both a clear attempt to plead innocence and lay blame, it shows how deep-seated is the notion of a nation as a collective will. The whole *Volk* is involved. Nothing can really succeed without the support of every single citizen.

The attractions of belonging, of being part of a favoured group, begin early and can have far-reaching consequences when exploited.

The reaction to the start of the First World War was a similar if less overstated assumption of the importance of the 'People'. Long before Kitchener's 'Your country needs you' came the sense of loyalty to that curious mixture of country and empire – the ambiguous idea of both people and system. Heroic self-sacrifice was based either on the assumptions of tribal loyalty, or on the more questioned duty to a political system, or on the unexamined juxtaposition of both. What is clear is that the organized army, depicted as a living organism, was felt to be the ultimate expression of collective chosen identities. It was depicted not as a political extreme of diplomacy but as a personification of the collective self against the 'enemy'. The army became a version of a gang, even if at a high level of patriotism. The notion of racial characteristics, with Germans instantly detectable by their manner and their behaviour in crude contrast to the English, was part of the psychological institution to which people wanted to belong, even if there were no particular merits in the attribution. Young children's sense of belonging, after all, does not encompass moral or cultural superiorities.[47]

German propaganda linked national prowess and interest with racial characteristics typical of the time. When this was taken up enthusiastically by Hitler, in *Mein Kampf*, it drew a strong and interesting response even in Great Britain. Whilst the British lauded their own characteristics, it was made clear in many popular writings that there was something genetically flawed in the Germans. Stereotypical attitudes towards other countries and the people in them are widespread, but not always turned into the cultural hegemony of hate. The most significant, symbolic and perhaps influential book of unmitigated prejudice was Vansittart's *Black Record*.[48] Sir Robert, as he was when he gave the broadcasts on which the pamphlet was based, or Lord Vansittart as he so quickly became, was the Chief Diplomatic Advisor to His Majesty's Government. His view that a whole people were culpable for the war, women and children included, gives an interesting insight into how deeply racial prejudice informed foreign policy. It should be noted that his own virulent brand of prejudice, long and deeply formed, was not a characteristic of himself alone. In a far more sympathetic and open-minded account of thought patterns in Europe, Philip Gibbs recounts a series of meetings with all kinds of representative individuals and concludes his chapter on Germany with the following reflections:

> And there is something in German mentality, something in this loyalty to Hitler, which is not to be understood by other peoples. The German mind works differently. It is not subject to the same impulses and instincts.
>
> There are mysteries in the German mind we cannot fathom or understand. It is because of these mysteries that other peoples are uneasy and afraid.[49]

Whilst one can understand the reaction to some of the conversations he recounts, that sense that there is something about a collective 'mentality' that works to a shared set of 'impulses and instincts' is strong. It seems to be beyond reason, both by its own inner characteristics and by outside definition.

Genetic labelling

If the idea of national characteristics is so established – the good in any nation are fairly similar, but if each nation has its own way of being wicked – then it is no surprise to find them displayed in so virulent a form by Vansittart. His book famously begins with the image of the Butcher bird. He is crossing the Black Sea on a German ship, having developed his dislike of Germans from an early age, when he notes the following behaviour of birds in the rigging:

> Every now and then it would spring upon one of the smaller, unsuspecting birds, and kill it. It was a shrike or Butcher bird: and it was steadily destroying all its fellows... That Butcher bird on that German ship behaved exactly like Germany behaves. [sic][50]

That note having been struck Vansittart then presents his evidence that every German has the same proclivity as that bird, to attack and kill all other nations, and through that butchery to achieve world domination. From that point of view it is a melancholy comfort to note that he spent the whole day making sure, with his revolver, that he eliminated that menace. What is clear is that there is a consistent typology of the Germans. They are essentially all the same. They are seen as not just products of a political system but the creators of that system. The roles they play in war are depicted as manifestations of personality.

> ... Well-known to those with any knowledge of German Psychology. The three are Envy, Self-pity and Cruelty.[51]

> Germans in the plural are the Brazen Horde.[52]

> Force and fraud, fraud and force: that is the old German gospel.[53]

The phrases that this diplomatic advisor uses are telling. Germans are all 'homicidal maniacs' with the desire to 'destroy us if they could'. Quite apart from the individuals, like Goering who is 'a dope-fiend, a wholesale thief and still more a wholesale murderer',[54] the Germans are generally cited as 'wanting to be barbarians'!

The German nation and the German people are seen as being one and the same. All are equally responsible and Hitler is assumed to be a product of a general characteristic. The virulence, hate, and the assumptions of racial flaws are unbounded, even in a diplomat. This heavy labelling of attributions connects to some of the earliest manifestations of identity in the very young. Trying to make sense of the self in the face of others entails the scrutiny of collective differences. Others, however defined, can easily be turned into a threat, and ultimately an enemy. The complex question, of course, is the extent of collective or individual guilt. Are nations an assembly of individuals who, because of their environment, happen to speak the same language and share the same religion, or is there something more profound about the collective identity? Gollancz's gallant response, gallant because it went against the prevailing opinion, and gallant because he was just as keen to overcome Hitler as anyone else, if not more so, is to question the basis of such virulent typology.[55] If *all* Germans are either 'sadists' or 'docile', what percentage do you ascribe to either? Isn't there a major issue in the domination of the few over the many, or the tacit and collective support of the many for what they all subscribe to? Should we fight racism with racism? The fact that such generalized attributions are contradictory – the idea of 'obedience' cannot, one presumes, be ascribed to all – does not prevent their power. Indeed, it is in the ability of people to accept contradictions that prejudice flourishes. Sibling rivalry is the more powerful because it is based on mutual interest as well as competition. The sense of family, of ontological enclosure, means that the profound sense of belonging is both set against the sense of the other and the more protected for being fragile. The young child wants and resents prejudice; wants it for himself against others, especially the sibling, and resents it when there is any hint that it might be directed against him- or herself.

The general view, that neurotic rationality, that all Germans are evil, was sustained, just as it is sustained in all ethnic conflicts, for many years. The anti-Germanism of the British people was so strong that it was unable to distinguish between anyone tainted by being German and the fact that many of these were rabidly anti-Nazi and Jewish refugees – mostly interned in concentration camps.[56] The reason for the blanket association of belief and race is founded partly on a long and general history of national chauvinism, a shared assumption that being a member of a particular people meant characteristics either good or bad. The promotion of national loyalty – 'Be British' – is one side of the coin. Boys' books of the earlier part of the last century, which constantly reiterate the many singular virtues possessed by the English, are emblematic of this shared consciousness.[57] The other side of the coin is the way in which other people, particularly enemies, are all full of the same characteristics. It is always easier to generalize labels: 'they' can be those with legitimate power or with the possibilities of threat. As long as there is some other to fight against, the collective self is preserved.

Nationalisms compete with each other, just as prayers are offered in the name of the same religion for help in smiting the enemy.

Chosen identities and political will

There is another reason for the peculiarly close associations between the German people and the evil symbolized by Nazism. The propaganda of the party machine, the calls to duty of one 'Volk' together with the superiority of the Aryan 'race', suggests that all the young people are imbued with the same spirit. There are many examples witnessed of young people so hysterically devoted to Hitler that there seems to be some unnatural force at work. As early as 1934 Philip Gibbs notes an example of intense passion. A boy is quoted 'He is our Leader – Der Führer! The whole German nation obeys him. We are willing to die for him. It is our duty, if necessary'.[58] Propaganda is seen to succeed. There are those who see not only the collective hysteria of mass rallies, but individuals unrecognizable in their passion. Irmgard Litten, in her apologia for exceptional Germans, recounts a friend's story.

> ... [they] brought news from my husband. The guards had put out one of his eyes. My boy, who had been asleep, suddenly appeared at the door. 'That should happen to all enemies of the Führer' he shouted in a frenzy. And he stood before me with his face so distorted that all of a sudden I thought 'surely this is not my son'.[59]

Nazi propaganda, including films like *The Triumph of the Will*, makes much of the adulation of Hitler, and his mesmeric hold over the people. The very way in which he, and all the symbols of the fascist state, are presented in books like those handed out to all visitors to the 1936 Olympic Games, are taken as exemplars of all that is dangerous and disturbing. *Darkness over Germany* is an analysis of how the minds of youth are being 'moulded'.[60] The illustrations are the same as in the propaganda books but the captions are different: 'Potter's clay in the making... initiation... enslavement... hysteria.' All this is attributed to Hitler as a kind of medicine man, a man who, like a manic depressive, has at times the aura of indomitable self-belief: 'his absolute belief in what he says at the moment he says it'.[61]

Examples of both mass and individual hysteria abound. The question remains whether this applies, as Vansittart and others even more virulent suggest, peculiarly to Germans. The debate, as in Gollancz's response to Vansittart – *What Buchenwald Really Means* – is encapsulated in a cartoon by Low.[62] A bowler-hatted man looks at the horrors of the concentration camp and says 'The whole German people should be wiped out for this!'. The victims reply 'Don't forget some of us *are* Germans, friend'. It is a minority who continue to insist that one must distinguish between a political system, even a cultural system, and the people who are caught up in it. Not everything is attributable to 'race'. People like George Catlin and Vera Brittain remind their readers of all the examples of decency and mercy shown by the 'enemy'.[63] Thanks to Gollancz there are plenty of reminders both of the opposition to Hitler and of the fact that there were two million Germans incarcerated in concentration camps.[64] But voices such as these were largely ignored in the hatred inspired not only by the war itself but by the discovery of the extent of the horror of concentration camps. The prevailing desire was for revenge:

> There are those who seem to suggest that for the Nazis' control of men's minds and spirits we should substitute a United Nations' control of the minds and spirits of the younger generation in Germany.[65]

There were many extreme examples of the ultimate way to deal with the German problem, from wholesale slaughter to the castration of all males. One could suggest the such genetic labelling is on the edge of the absurd, but that is with the benefit of hindsight. There are many contemporary examples of collective behaviour that exemplify the same unthinking collective attributions of flaws. It is, after all, easier to react to the symbols of difference – to clothes or to colour – than to discriminate between the individuals beneath the surface. Young children are not deliberately taught that there are alien worlds beyond their own house and neighbourhood, that safety is the fact of security against threat. They learn early about the contrast between themselves and others. These others have to be understood in their symbolic boundaries, their collective identities. There are manifest threats in the community, which is close. There are official controls in the wider community of the school. Beyond there are the more generalized awarenesses of the others, the images on a television screen, the subconscious labelling of the collectively different.

This necessary ability to generalize about the others, to make collective attributions, is not just an early means of understanding. It is demonstrated in shared political actions. The atavistic tendency to ascribe racial characteristics to those of a different cultural inheritance is strong. Rationality is easily overcome by instinct that then draws over itself a spurious, neurotic rationality. The example of attitudes within and against Germany shows how complete can be the final manifestation of a personal phenomenon.

Deliberate ignorance and neurotic rationality

In the attitudes stirred to the surface by the Second World War even the most rational were affected by the prevailing racism. This is because this seemed, subconsciously, to be the only way to deal with the puzzle about how people could behave that way. Even those who argue that not all Germans are the same wonder at the extent of the complicity.[66] How much did people merely follow their leaders? Gollancz questions Vansittart's division of Germans into the sadists and the docile.[67] The greater concern is over the docile. Is there guilt in ignorance? And how much did people actually know? This remains an abiding question. It also throws light on the complexities of the human mind, in the ability both to know on one level and be ignorant on another, holding two conflicting beliefs at the same time.[68] The simplest view that does not challenge greater insight is that all must have been aware of what was happening. There are plenty of stories of what happened to the 'good' Germans incarcerated, losing their estates or banished. If these, however, are exonerated, it still points up the fact that concentration camps were known about. What of those who complied?

> In one sense all Germans, except those who have risked everything by actively opposing Nazism, are Hitler's accomplices...
> ... Millions of Germans have willingly allowed their normal political thoughts and human instincts to be put to sleep and have joined what seemed to be the winning side.[69]

One answer to this 'docility' is, of course, the understanding of what it is like to live in a totalitarian state. As Fraenkel points out, at least 95 per cent of Czechs would have been furiously opposed to their Nazi rulers and yet there seemed not a murmur of protest.[70] This does not altogether answer the question about what people knew or chose to ignore. The fascination with the behaviour of all Germans, a fascination which persists, is the question of the 'docile' bulk of the population who continued to function as normal citizens and served in the war effort. One contemporary argument is that at least a majority of people were not actively *for* Hitler, and that a large proportion did *not* know of the awful crimes committed.[71] There were different ways of not knowing. One was genuine ignorance, in rural areas. One was an inability to believe, like Mr Litten's son. And there were those who *wanted* to believe the Nazi propaganda that any rumours of concentration camps were started by Jews and Bolsheviks. But there were also those who did not *want* to know. Surrounded by the Gestapo, careful of what they said, they were also careful of what they thought. In the very young we sometimes forget the pressures on self-control, on guessing what *ought* to be understood, on trying to please. Those guesses that are based on observation, or on what people are perceived to expect, are manoeuvres to please, to put oneself in the right position, to fit in to the epistemologies of others. The need to adapt is stronger than any fear of internal contradiction.

As we learn more about human nature so we discover *deliberate* ignorance and the fact that people believe what they want to, or need to. There are those who say 'For God's sake don't raise any conflict for me – I have chosen Hitler – leave me with my choice.'[72] Even those who did *not* support Hitler at any time managed what is often called an inner emigration.[73] The instinct to obey and not to get into trouble by refusing to oppose a prevailing atmosphere is seen in ordinary everyday life, whether the issues are great or small. Hannah Arendt closely scrutinized how someone as 'banal' as Adolf Eichman could behave as he did.[74]

Prejudice as benevolent or malevolent?

The assumption throughout this was that 'It couldn't happen here'. The argument suggests there is something in the German people, and something different in the British, that make one docile and the other stubborn and independent. It is not so much a different political system that is involved but a whole set of racial characteristics. There are therefore many questions about the extent of different peoples' resistance to the threat of totalitarianism and dictatorship. Given how many examples there are of both at the present time, can one attribute them to the nature of the subjected population? In an account of a student revolt at Munich University even then the question was raised whether anyone would have acted differently if 'the smallest hostile act led you to the concentration camp.'[75] Those seven who did speak out were hanged. But the question is wider. If there is no job without joining the party, do people let their ageing parents or their family starve? The dilemmas confronting a young teacher who refuses to teach the Nazi doctrine on race are clear. Do they emigrate, resign and find alternative employment or go to prison?[76] These choices are all made in an atmosphere where the pupils will anyway detect the slightest lack of conformity and either report the victim to the Gestapo or unceremoniously dump him or her in the river. The question remains both of the extent to which personal gain is through becoming an apparatchik, conforming to the prevailing ethos of the time, and the extent to which a sense of personal threat consciously realized can overcome a deeper, if unexamined, conscience.

Deliberate ignorance is a refuge for those who face a conflict between personal safety and belief. The Germans were collectively accused either of endorsing Hitler's policies towards the Jews or of turning a blind eye to the rumours and the hints. They were accused of knowing what was taking place, and yet not acting on that awareness. The rational argument is whether it was possible to know what Hitler was doing and still do business with him. This deliberate ignorance was the policy of the 'free people of the world'.[77] It is impossible to argue that there were no warning signals, no indications of what was happening. *Mein Kampf* had been published in translation for many years. As one analyst puts it, Hitler clearly states:

> The only way to deal with them [the Jews] is to get rid of them altogether.[78]

The evidence was not just in writing. In some innocent memoirs a priest running the mission to the Jews in Hamburg reveals what he knew before being driven out (he was himself Jewish) in 1938:

> Hitler murdered two million... by most dreadful means: they were tortured to death... gassed, starved, buried alive...
> A Swedish journalist, who happened to witness... cruelties, stated that several nights he could not sleep...[79]

Appeasement was a policy of deliberate ignorance. People like Chamberlain and Lansbury were not just charmed by Hitler: they chose to believe what they wanted to, since such convenience made policy and action simpler. As *Mein Kampf* also made clear, in the acquisition of new territory, Czechoslovakia was a mere stepping-stone.[80] It is not the politics that are crucial, and the outcome of these, but the ability to ignore as well as imbibe signs and evidence. The pressure on the very young *not* to see, and not to understand is as strong as the professed intention of creating wisdom or rationality. In the most sophisticated of adults lies the same tendency psychologically to distort what is clear evidence. It is more comfortable to live with what is known and familiar.

Liberal expressions of racism

The belief that politics is the expression of the people's collective will and indivisible from race also informed the British government's policies in its reaction to the 'German menace'. Any alien from Germany or Austria, even if Jewish, was checked on and often interned, thereby not only wasting a huge resource but earning the hatred of those very people who were innocent.[81] The association of race and politics began early. Opportunities to help opposition from within were all deliberately and shamefully eschewed. The bombing of Dresden is the ultimate symbol of punishing people because they are German. When statesmen planned for Europe after the war they slipped naturally from the concept of Nazism to the guilt of the Germans.

Those who have sinned against the laws of humanity must be punished…
control until the poison has been eliminated from her system.

The thoughts and actions of the German people.[82]

The desire to continue the policy of bombing with further severe punishment is
encapsulated in the Potsdam Declaration, the idea of reducing Germany to a backward agrarian economy rather than an industrial one, ironically echoing Hitler's
policy which led to the desire for more Lebensraum. It was only the realization that
such a policy might have adverse repercussions on others in financial terms that
prevented its implementation.[83] As it was, a policy of indiscriminate racism became
for a time official. Not only were the occupying forces like 'guards at a concentration camp', but racist ethnic cleansing was taking place all over Europe with mass
expulsions of all Germans.[84]

What was expressed towards the Germans echoed Nazi propaganda about other
races. But such doctrines of race were not new. Nor were the questions of 'people
and political will' confined to Germany. The typology of attitudes, so well encapsulated by popular writers from Herbert Strang onwards, has deep roots. The association of the Nazis with nationality and a chosen people ignores the point that
such concepts, including authoritarianism, have pan-European origins.[85] They are
widely shared. Whilst ignored by the 'good', they are taken up in different ways by
the 'bad' of all countries. But they are the same fundamental concepts. The idea of
nationality, the loyalty to a country as well as a people, has a strong, if comparatively recent, past. There are clear philosophical roots to the concept of the
nation-state. When Kant talked about the ideal of pure reason there was no hint of
what Herder would make of it, arguing that the State, as a collective whole, could
equally embody such an idea.[86] From this innocent notion of the State as embodiment of pure virtue it is not difficult to trace the line of thinking, through
Nietsche, to what Hitler, in his garbled but unbridled way, made of it. Nationalism, ethnic or political, has a powerful if recent tradition, as a manifestation of self
and collective identity and prejudice against others.

Symbolic boundaries and neurotic rationality

The majority who subscribe to these collective subconscious instincts are unaware
of the philosophical roots. They do not think but feel the argument through.
When Vansittart talks of the Germans' soul it is a sign of the populist rather than a
considered view. But to draw attention to the connection shows just how

culturally powerful this is. Without invoking the German philosophical tradition he talks of Hitler as having:

> capitalized the German strain of ill-defined mysticism – a blind faith fed on phrases about Germany's mission...[87]

What he actually says is an expression of a belief that can be interpreted in different ways, according to whether the people described are 'us' or 'them'. Whilst he suggests that there is an 'ill-defined mysticism', or, as Gibbs thinks of it, something unfathomable about the Germans, he is in fact unaware of acknowledging the operation of a collective cultural, not racial, expression.

> Impregnate a race with militarism, imbue it with a sense of its own superiority, convince it of its mission to enslave mankind for the good of mankind, persuade it that this end justifies any and every means however filthy; and you produce a race of hooligans which is a curse to the whole world.[88]

Whilst there might appear to be genetic traits in this description and whilst the desire for world domination is a comparatively rare one, the many signs of political chauvinism, having an enemy to overcome, are clear. The definition of the collective self, the party, is all.

Hooliganism as expressed in football is, of course, a pan-European phenomenon. It consists of both finding an excuse for hatred – the opposing team and its supporters – and an increasing sense of collective superiority, however difficult to sustain. Some might argue that it is deliberately fed by the popular media, but the very word 'popular' suggests an audience that is instilled with associations, for example with beach-towels or *Technik*. The fact that there are strong historical roots for such collective attitudes might smack of finding a Cruft's pedigree for a pariah dog, but it is necessary to understand how complex, how cultural, is this phenomenon. By 'cultural' I suggest the understanding of the way in which individuals operate and their motivation, rather than pure reasons, for doing so. Our helplessness is not just due to our genes, but the circumstances and pressures of the environment, just as languages are different not just in semantics and syntax, but in dialect and tone.

The debate about one of the most crucial manifestations of the excesses of the human condition is not over. Indeed, in our time it needs addressing more urgently than ever. One of the most important insights into human potential is how the dignity of the individual can be created and transformed by experience. One of the most depressing is how it can be manipulated. Ethnic cleansing and racism are not necessary or inevitable. They are atavistic. Yet they seem to be accepted as *natural* outpourings of national pride or expression. After the demise of the Potsdam declaration and after the collapse of Soviet Communism it might be supposed that the question of people and system would be centrally addressed. But with the rise of so many national political groupings it seems to be a matter to be dealt with rather than understood. Without understanding such things cannot be dealt with. For they go beyond, and deeper than political decisions in themselves. Taking Germany as an example we might think that the virulent debate about politics and people is over. But chauvinist suspicion remains. Even those books that attempt to explain Germany sympathetically, years after the war, trail their incipient assumptions with them. The Germans are still seen as collectively Nazi. They are affected by 'emotionalism'.[89] And they are still both powerful and nationalistic.[90] There is much discussion of *what* people think of each other, but not enough about *why* they think what they do. Young children of today persist in holding on to the same attitudes. They associate the faults of Germany with the 'Germans', thus perpetuating the attitudes of the past.[91] This is partly because these ideas of the individual in relation to others are rarely examined in a formal way, and certainly not part of the school syllabus.

Are these attitudes so deep-rooted that they will at some time or another, like weeds, emerge from even the most infertile soil? Is it inevitable that people should hate? The answer is, of course, no; but it is equally true that people will bear prejudice. Prejudice does not have to be negative. It can be a signal of detachment, a realization of a particular position, and its limitations. For some, the history of people is the history of their friendships and antipathies; it is a history of major or minor traditions, vertical or horizontal, dependent on place or class. Such discriminations can be positive – as each brings a new or different perspective to bear, enriching the whole – or negative, narrowing the understanding to the easiest perspective to maintain, and defining others as beyond the possibilities of iterative understanding or insight.

It is important to remember the contradictions of human nature. The ability to hold two conflicting beliefs at the same time, to turn arguments around without emotional let alone intellectual logic: these must be understood to be nearer the core of experience than generalized public statements. Similar contradictions surround prejudice and stereotypes: they are both inevitable and unnecessary; they are essential to the proper understanding of the world and they are dangerous. The way people view each other is a mixture of fear and patronage, curiosity and threat. Most of these initial or later exchanges are never analysed in that way. There is too much indifference attached. But emotions of attraction and repulsion are often close together. Views of *other* people can lead to fascination or repulsion. Prejudice is not always against; it can be strongly *for* people, like family. The way in which young children identify themselves rests on the ambiguous distinction between recognizing those who are on their side and those who are against them. For most this is a constantly changing position. They shift their allegiances just as they experiment with understanding. They explore who is to be close and who is to be kept distant. This interplay can be worked out in microcosm or on a horrifyingly large scale.

One would have thought that those with supreme power over others would be secure in that knowledge or that their bullying would be unmitigated by any fear of reprisal for their acts. But the most brutal of dictators, and anyone can supply a long list, are driven by paranoia. Stalin, for example, might have relished his brutality but it was driven by a manic vulnerability. Bullies are driven by fear as much as sadism. The bully and the victim are close.

Preventing the accumulation of too much power in the hands of one man is not just a political will, but a matter of the education of many people. Not all are driven by rabid prejudice. Not all express their cultural tastes in their will to be in command.[92] The development of understanding and tolerance are matters of education. At the individual level, where it all begins and ends, with each individual act of will, there are possibilities for good and bad, the choice to hurt or to support. The underlying experiences that all people undergo, individual as they are, have similar and common characteristics. All have a need for preferences, for discriminations, for social distinctions and for a world simplified into categories. All depend on those kinds of relations in which both have respect for the intellectual integrity of the other, and in which both public and private matters can be shared. All experience the complexities of group interactions, the constant changes of allegiance, the pain of being victimized or ostracized. And all have to learn both the idiosyncrasy of their own personality and the more general effect on others of the role they play.

The possibility of dysfunction is always present. The temptation to hide from challenges is constant. At the same time it is possible to be so immersed in a role or a function that the individual and meaningful self is lost. Both are forms of escape. But it is also possible to conflate the two, to justify the person in the role, to hide from moral challenges in the definitions of the self against others. That is when prejudice becomes not a curious or sporadic influence but the central reason for existence. The example of Germany and the Germans is the most obvious, and the most public. But it shows how deep chauvinistic attitudes can become transformed from personal and parochial instincts into larger, even more dangerous, actions. Most historians and sociologists are interested in these manifestations. Here we want to explore both why this should be so, and what makes people, individuals, act the way we do.

References

1. 'They flee from me that sometime did me seek…' (Wyatt) Shakespeare's great plays have even been described as inventing our idea of what it is to be human. Bloom, H (1999) *Shakespeare: The invention of the human*, Penguin, New York

2. Berghahn, V and Schissler, H eds (1987) *Perceptions of History: An analysis of school textbooks*, Berg, Oxford

3. Plumb, J H (1969) *The Death of the Past*, Macmillan, London

4. Hornby, N (1990) *Fever Pitch*, Fontana, London

5. Pakenham, F (1991) *The Scramble for Africa, 1876–1912*, Weidenfeld & Nicolson, London

6. Kerdourie, I (1968) *The Origins of Fascism*, Methuen, London

7. Kant, I (1868) *Kritik der Reinen Vernünft* Voss, Leipzig

8. Scharma, S (1989) *Citizens: A chronicle of the French Revolution*, Penguin, London

9. Smith, A (1996) The resurgence of nationalism? Myth and memory and the renewal of nations, *British Journal of Sociology*, **47** (4), pp 575–98

10. Billig, M (1995) *Banal Nationalism*, Sage, London

11. The novels of Percy Westerman, Herbert Strang and others made clear discriminations between the 'best' types (Anglo-Saxons) the less favoured (Europeans generally, with Italians not to be trusted and Germans brutal) and the descending orders through South Americans to Africans. Cullingford, C (1996) *Children's Literature and Its Effects,* Cassell, London

12. Green, J R (1874) *A Short History of the English Peoples*, Macmillan, London

13. Carlyle (1845) *The Nigger Question*

14. Hitler, A (1928) *Mein Kampf*

15. Cullingford, C (1996) *Children's Literature and Its Effects*, Chapter 4, Cassell, London

16. Ibid

17. Zetterholm, S (1994) Why is cultural diversity a political problem? A discussion of cultural barriers to political integration, in *National Cultures and European Integration. Exploratory essays of cultural diversity and common policies*, ed S Zetterholm, Berg, Oxford

18. Gibbon, E (1775) *Decline and Fall of the Roman Empire*

19. Motley, J (1884) *The Rise of the Dutch Republic*, Bickers and Son, London

20. Bourdieu, P (1984) *Distinction: A social critique of the judgement of taste*, Routledge and Kegan Paul, London

21. The literature on word associations reveals the automatic connections that the mind makes.

22. Hofstede, G (1991) *Cultures and Organisations: Software of the mind*, McGraw-Hill, London

23. *Henry V*, Act III, Scene II.

24. eg There was an Englishman, a Scotsman and an Irishman who were close friends since for years they worked together putting roofs on buildings. Every day they sat down at lunch-time and ate their sandwiches. One day the Englishman said 'If I get a ham and lettuce sandwich again I'll kill myself'. The Scotsman agreed. 'If I have one more haggis roll I'll throw myself over the edge'. The Irishman said 'And if I get just one more cheese and tomato sandwich I'll do the same'. The next day the Englishman looked at his sandwich. 'Oh no, not again!' He threw himself over the side of the building. The Scotsman looked at his roll and in despair also killed himself. And then the Irishman looked at his sandwich and followed suit.

At the funeral people were puzzled as well as sad. They asked the wives to explain. 'I don't understand it', said the Englishman's wife. 'He never complained about his sandwiches and didn't say a word to me.' 'I don't understand' said the Scotsman's wife. 'Haggis rolls were always his favourite.' 'I don't understand' said the Irishman's wife. 'He always made his own sandwiches.'

25. Cullingford, C and Husemann, H eds (1995) *Anglo-German Attitudes*, Ashgate, Aldershot
26. Ibid, chs 7–8
27. Belson, W (1978) *Television Violence and the Adolescent Boy*, Saxon House, Farnborough
28. What is the difference between an Essex girl and a shopping trolley? A shopping trolley has a mind of its own.
29. eg the antipathies of neighbouring countries, like Turkey and Greece, or Israel and Syria, fear of certain countries like Russia or the United States, or informed indifference, say towards Finland or Moldavia.
30. The same goes on to point out that the world is rarely so perfect and one is as likely to possess a Japanese house, a Chinese income, English food and an American wife.
31. Furnham, A and Stacey, B (1991) *Young People's Understanding of Society*, Routledge, London
32. Husemann, H (1998) *Coping with the Relations: Anglo-German cartoons from the fifties to the nineties*, Secolo, Osnabrück
33. Moyle, L (1995) The Ridley-Chequers affair and the German character, in *Anglo-German Attitudes,* eds C Cullingford and H Husemann, pp 165–80, Ashgate, Aldershot
34. Häberle enters the post office where his friend Pfleiderer serves behind the counter. 'What a great time we had last night' they agreed. 'I think we looked too deeply into the glass...'
After this reminiscence of their old habit of drinking together, Häberle asks for a form. 'Let's see your identity card please' says Pfleiderer. 'But you know who I am; we are best friends.' 'Yes, but that is private. I must know who you are officially...'
35. Toivonen, K and Cullingford, C (1998) Racial prejudice in a liberal democracy: a case study, *Politics, Groups and the Individual,* **7** (1 & 2), pp 45–56
36. Or a sense that a particular people were undermining the historical certainties; Schoenberg undermining music, Einstein undermining Newtonian mechanics, Freud the psychology of the normal and Marx the notions of an ordered society. Goldhagen, D (1996) *Hitler's Willing Executioners*, Little Brown, London
37. Arendt, H (1969) *The Banality of Evil: The trial of Adolf Eichman*, Secker and Warburg, London
Milgram, S (1974) *Obedience to Authority: An experimental view*, Tavistock, London
38. Carver, R (1998) *The Accursed Mountains: Journeys in Albania*, John Murray, London
39. Moyle, L op cit
40. eg Bourdieu, R, op cit
41. Smith, A D (1942) *Guilty Germans?* p 10, Victor Gollanz, London
42. Green, J R, op cit
43. Moyle, L, op cit
44. Green, J R, op cit
45. Braunthal, J (1945) *Need Germany Survive?* p 59, Victor Gollanz, London
46. Sladen, D (1914) *Germany's Great Lie: The official German justification of the War exposed and criticised*, p 86, Hutchinson, London
47. Cullingford, C, op cit

48. Vansittart, R (1941) *Black Record: Germans Past and Present*, Hamish Hamilton, London

49. Gibbs, P (1941) *European Journey*, pp 386–87, Heinemann, London

50. Vansittart, R, op cit, p 1

51. Ibid, p 4

52. Ibid, p 20

53. Ibid, p 30

54. Ibid, p 50

55. Gollancz, V (1942) *Shall Our Children Live or Die? A reply to Lord Vansittart on the German problem*, Victor Gollancz, London

56. Watt, D D (1965) *Britain Looks to Germany: British opinions and policy towards Germany since 1945*, p 31, Oswald Wolff, London

57. Cullingford, C, op cit

58. Gibbs, P, op cit, p 384

59. Litten, I (1945) *All the Germans – Are They Really Guilty?* p 20, Victor Gollancz, London

60. Buller, E A (1943) *Darkness Over Germany*, Longmans Green, London

61. Ibid, p 185

62. Gollancz, V (1945) *What Buchenwald Really Means*, Victor Gollancz, London

63. Catlin, G, Brittain, V and Hodges, S eds (1945) *Above All Nations: An anthology*, Victor Gollancz, London

64. Fraenkel, H (1941) *Help Us Germans Beat the Nazis!* p 13, Victor Gollancz, London

65. Buller, E A, op cit, p vii

66. Zetterholm, S, op cit

67. Gollancz, V (1945), op cit, p 13

68. Cullingford, C (1990) *The Nature of Learning*, Cassell, London

69. Layton, W (1944) *How to Deal With Germany: A plan for European peace*, pp 31–2, News Chronicle Publications, London

70. Fraenkel, H, op cit

71. Litten, I, op cit

72. Buller, E A, op cit, p 182

73. Klemperer, V (1998) *I Shall Bear Witness. Diaries vol. 1*, Weidenfeld and Nicolson, London

74. Arendt, H, op cit

75. Rathbone, E (1945) Preface, in *Seven Were Hanged: An authentic account of the student revolt in Munich University*, W Bayles, Victor Gollancz, London

76. Buller, E A, op cit

77. Gollancz, V, op cit

78. Ensor, R C K (1939) *Herr Hitler's Self-Disclosure in Mein Kampf*, Clarendon Press, Oxford

79. Arnold, F (Rev) (1944) *What About the Jews? Pictures from the gallery of my memories*, p 124, Graham and Heslip, Belfast

80. Ensor, R C K, op cit

81. Judex (1940) *Anderson's Prisoners*, Victor Gollancz, London

82. Layton, W, op cit, p 213

83. Anon (1945) *Europe and Germany: Today and tomorrow*, Victor Gollancz, London
Rimer, A B (1946) *Lunacy in the Reich: The Industrial Counter-Revolution*, Victor Gollancz, London

84. Crossman, R H S (1945) Our job in Germany, in *Europe and Germany*, pp 6–10, Victor Gollancz, London

85. Braunthal, J, op cit
86. Kerdourie, I, op cit
87. Vansittart, R,op cit, p 6
88. Ibid, p 12
89. Mandar, J (1974) *Our German Cousins: Anglo-German relations in the 19th and 20th centuries*, John Murray, London
90. Watson, A (1992) *The Germans: Where are they now?* Thames/Methuen, London
91. Cullingford, C (1995) British children's attitudes to Germany and the Germans, in *Anglo-German Attitudes*, eds C Cullingford and H Husemann, pp 39–56, Ashgate, Aldershot
92. Bourdieu, P, op cit

2

Sources of information

The formation of structures of thinking

This chapter describes the empirical evidence on which the book is based, but it also explores the sources from which the evidence derives. The minds of young people are full of masses of data which they are continually attempting to sort out, to organize and categorize. Information comes in raw forms from many directions, and does not appear labelled with explanations. It is up to the personal and sometimes idiosyncratic efforts of the young to put some sense and structure on the information. 'Labelling' is a personal construct.

The data in the book comes from semi-structured interviews, in which children talked freely and openly about their attitudes, opinions and ideas. There are still those who remain suspicious of the validity of what people say. This in itself is an interesting psychological fact, but part of the reason for this refusal to listen carefully is the old research tradition which still hankers after the 'hardest', most quantifiable of facts, and part of it is a suspicion that children either cannot have informed opinions or are attempting to present to adults what they think they wish to hear as if all adults were teachers. The art of listening to people, or, more significantly, hearing what they say, has many political as well as educational ramifications, which would be worth a chapter in itself. At this point it should be sufficient to say why and how one can be sure that what children say is valid and reliable. The real cultural hegemony of the individual is not a choice between social or sociological theories or constructs, even if informed by them, but something more fluid and more fluent. To explore the way in which the personal sense of identity coalesces with shared and perceived psychological institutions depends on the interview; personal reflection takes the opportunity to make itself manifest.

There are many examples of different types of interview, from the formal, almost questionnaire lists of pre-formulated answers as in polls, to the question so open ended that it almost doesn't exist.[1] There are also a number of ethical questions that surround the notion of informed consent. To what extent is it necessary for the interviewee to know what research question is being pursued? To what extent should they subsequently re-examine and improve on what they have said freely and spontaneously? There are, however, some essential rules that should govern the conduct of all interviews, in order to allow the evidence to emerge without self-consciousness or attempts to please.

That interviews should be conducted with confidentiality and anonymity is paramount. It is also important that the interviewee is convinced this is the case. Information passed on to someone in power is not only breaking essential ethical practice, but the suspicion that this might happen contaminates the data. This can cause difficulties if the interviewer is in a position of authority, or has access to authority, or is known to the interviewee. It can cause difficulties if there are things learnt, as in a confessional, that have possible repercussions on other people's lives. The interviews, as in confessionals, must be confidential, and circumstances where there could be other uses of the information gathered should be avoided.

The crucial point is that the interviewee should be free to talk openly, and not to a particular agenda. At the heart of this confidentiality is respect for the individual, taking what they say seriously. Validity depends on interviews being carried out in such a spirit of openness that there are no suspicions about possible responses. Clearly one must be attentive to the dangers of the guessing game. Children, after all, spend most of their time in school trying to work out what the right answer is, not so much what they *think* but what will please the teacher. For them all questions are 'closed'.[2] They are accustomed to constant testing where there are only some right answers, since these tests rely on the regurgitation of facts.

Given certain conditions children will want to please, or to shock. This is why group interviews can be misleading, with personal and social agendas spoiling the free expression of true and unguarded opinions. But children will also want to talk. It is a pleasure to extend the general chatter that they have with each other to talking to someone who is essentially there to listen. There is no particular reason for them to dissemble if they do not guess what kind of information is of interest. In that respect they can be very different from adults. Putting aside questions of psychoanalysis or counselling on the one hand, and political opinion polls on the other, there are at least two significantly different traditions of interviews with adults. One tends to delve into memories of the past, creating the archives that store accumulated experiences.[3] In these, people are under no pressure to feel guarded or to make a good impression. They are talking about the world as they see it, and about their own reactions to experience. Should there be any doubt that such responses are honest? We might feel that there are misinterpretations, but that strengthens the very argument for true expressions of personal opinion. Even the misrepresentations are conceptually revealing. As in the guarded expressions that reveal subtle prejudice, and as in the ambiguities and contradictions of what some people say, there are revealing insights.

The other tradition of interviews with adults is the more public and formal kind where teachers or head teachers, for example, are being asked about their own practice. Sometimes it is obvious that they are presenting a case which justifies what they are doing.[4] They wish to present themselves in the best light. Whilst it is possible to go beneath the surfaces of self-justification and persuade teachers to talk freely about their personal beliefs, one can detect in some cases a tendency to create a story that is apt for a particular audience, rather than a story that is the opening up of the mind. People can perform as if they were in a formal interview for a job. Even in these circumstances it is possible to analyse what is *really* the case rather than that presented. Self-justification can be exposed in such a way that it comes across as self-deception when compared to actual practice.[5] One could argue that even self-deception is an authentic point of view, but it is normally only present when there are questions of professionalization and practice. The contrast between detecting the reality of thoughts in those trying to disguise them and understanding the actualities of thoughts and feelings in those attempting to express them, could not be greater.

When adults or children are asked about matters that are personal or neutral, rather than professional or academic, the freedom and openness of talk are far greater. The desire to communicate leads to the kind of revelations that are clear indicators of the authentic. What emerges is unselfconscious as well as reflective, natural as well as analytic. The interview is then carried out not only in confidentiality, but with all the attention of the interviewee, who does not even need to know the particular subject of enquiry. It might become obvious that it is narrower than a general life-history, but interviews begin with an open agenda, unthreatening and undefined. It is the interviewee who brings up the subject matter and creates the definitions. Even professional adults talk the more freely if they compare memories of the past, which is neutral, with experiences of the present. One does not need a deliberate 'placebo', a pretence that one is after information on one subject when one is in fact interested in another. Several open questions will normally elicit enough clues to be able to pursue a particular subject in depth. The opportunities to ask why and to delve further in the subject are always there. This is the structure in semi-structured interviews: all cover the same topics but in no formal order.

It is important that all the definitions, the vocabulary and the general terms used come from the interviewees. The job of the interviewer is to say as little as possible whilst lubricating the conversational wheels. There is an art in some people's ability to ask questions that enables individuals in all kinds of circumstances, from dinner parties to train journeys, to talk at great length about themselves without asking any questions in return. Semi-structured interviews are a formal and justified version of such self-referential and absorbing self-interest, which is widely shared. Just as some have learnt the art of 'keeping the conversational ball rolling', so the interviewer provides the example of the good listener, curious, genuinely interested, and never shocked. 'Why?', 'How?', 'Tell me more' are examples of the markers that indicate encouragement to the tendency to want to express ideas which is shared by all.

Interviews as (conscious) revelation

These interviews are called semi-structured because there is a structure but not an obvious one. The essential goal is to make sure that all the interviewees cover the same topics. This is to avoid the charge that a statement that summarizes a point of view is dependent only on a minority of the sample. It does not matter in what *order* the questions are raised, for this will inevitably vary, but it does matter that there is some steer so that the topics are covered in depth. The interviewees will put what they want to say in their own terms: the interviews do not proceed formally from subject to subject, but follow up those ideas that are pertinent.

The main bulk of the research reported here, and the quotations which are representative of all, is based on 160 lengthy semi-structured interviews with children aged from 6 to 11. Questions of sampling, and the motivations for sampling and the reliability of sampling, are always interesting as well as arcane. The most delicate questions of sampling arise if the evidence suggests some kind of representation, if the research seeks to pinpoint differences between one group and another. Examples of this are the aspirations of different minority ethnic groups, or the differences between socio-economic backgrounds. But sampling is also a matter of ensuring validity.

The children in the main survey represent a variety of backgrounds and circumstances. They come from inner city areas, from suburbs and from the countryside. They represent private as well as state education. They include minority ethnic groups. And there are an equal number of boys and girls. This is defensive sampling, making sure that there can be no accusations of bias or selectivity. If there were clear differences in opinions and attitudes between different parts of the sample, gender differences or divisions between these from contrasting economic circumstances, then they would emerge. Care is taken to ensure that if a point of view is taken as representative, then the statement can be justified in quantitative terms. A long and complex process of analysis was undertaken on this basis, but the results demonstrated a degree of consistency and homogeneity of outlook that rendered statistics unhelpful.

The transcripts of the interviews, all taken from the tape recordings, were analysed and re-analysed. At one level there were the usual levels of content analysis, the detection of themes, like attitudes towards different countries. But the real interest in analysis is the concepts that are expressed, the indication in terms and phrases of certain styles of thinking. How something is said is of interest as well as what is said. It is for this reason that such trouble is taken not only to reflect on the transcripts but to relate them to other works, to other readings and to other similar research that also informs the ideas expressed here. Any analysis of the human mind includes multiple levels of thinking, contradictions and ambiguities.[6] The mind consists not only of single statements and crude prejudices but of complex associations. The greatest excitement in analysis is seeing these complex patterns of thought.

The irony is that the nearer one gets to the true picture of the mind (messy, ironic, critical, associative, laden with images, stereotypes and reactions) the more the data appears 'soft'. Hard evidence is often associated with crude or simple facts. It is always possible to find correlations that can be proven by isolating distinct variables. For instance, we can find out if there is a tendency in left-handed people to prefer fried to roast potatoes. But is it worth it? To try to delve into the mind is to have to acknowledge and accept a certain messy complexity. Despite this there are clear and simple findings that are consistent and widespread.

Between the complexity of the individual and the distinct variable lies the shared cultural consciousness that is both complex and simple. That people express open prejudice, towards the Gypsies for instance, is clear.[7] But *why* such prejudice develops is more complicated. Attitudes towards other countries, far richer or poorer, are consistent, but the relationship of those to the personal sense of status and meaning is more difficult.

In the interviews we are trying to detect both shared cultural attitudes and personal and individual interpretations. At the same time we are made aware of the many sources of influence that help create the individual and the groups. One of the underlying conceptual revelations of the interviews is the way in which sources of information are inadvertently revealed. If one attempted to trace the source, like a stimulus, and its effects on the mind, we would find it impossible, and there are many examples of failure.[8] But if we listen to what people say we begin to detect the way in which they receive and analyse information. People are vulnerable to influence.[9] Usually they are unaware of it. But overheard remarks, anecdotes, sudden glimpses of revelation, often inadvertent, deeply influence subsequent opinions and actions. What is difficult to know, out of the mass of information received every day, is what is particularly influential. It is impossible to find out by testing an a-priori hypothesis. We can only find out in hindsight, in exploring the structures of opinion within the human mind, and the selections it has so clearly made.

The plethora of inadvertent information

In a world of facts, of tests and news, of information technology and communication, it is easy to forget the other influences on the way people form their minds, in all the disorder of emotional associations. The culture of oracy, in its relation to the feelings of the individual, is still with us. Knowledge is still situational rather than abstract.[10] Gossip, as well as the overheard remark, gives a sense of collective as well as individual order.[11] Emotional reactions are provoked by a whole series of images and news items, even when they are supposedly free of any such associations.[12] And young children have the capacity to understand, in their own way, complex social interactions so they can analyse the meaning of the raw data presented to them in magazines and on television as well as on the Internet.[13] They are also capable of a mature historical sense, even if this is rarely made use of.[14] One of the interesting findings about children's knowledge and understanding of the world is the way in which such little effort is made to enable them to structure their understandings. The issues that dominate childhood are those of meaning; of life and death; of truth and falsehood, or right and wrong; and of individual and collective self-justification: the points of view. And yet these are just the topics that are rarely mentioned in the formal social systems in which they are engaged.[15] Instead they have to find their own way of social understanding.

There is a strong tradition of research in psychology, based on a scientific model, that tries to connect a particular stimulus with a correlating response. Despite the arguments about the complexity of the human mind and the almost infinite information it receives even in one day, let alone one week, attempts to single out particular effects of individual sources of information have persisted. It is as if the fascination with possible statistical variables and the drive towards some kind of deductive logic had overcome all sense of realism. To trace a source of information starting from the source and following it through is impossible. It is not only impossible in a pragmatic sense, for such a study would involve not only a vast timescale but millions of people, but it is not sensible. It is only the human mind that can be aware of those influences that are significant. There are always deep traces of important events in the forming of the mind, as psychoanalysis reminds us, but these can only be discovered through the mechanisms, the perceptions and the decisions of the mind itself. The individual, whether on the psychiatrist's couch or talking freely, is the only true judge of how he or she has learnt to think in certain ways and how he or she has come to the opinions held.

How, then, do we explore sources of information in such a complex experience of daily life? The answer lies in the patterning of common experience, in the choices between different variables that emerge naturally from the reflections made by individuals when they show a collective sense of unity. In all these interviews there were traces of the sources of information, not elicited through narrow questions but arising naturally in the context of the interview. There might be a generalization made: 'How do you know?' The response to a question might be 'it's like this' immediately followed up by 'I know it is so because'. Both in a formal and acknowledged sense, and in a more subliminal one, it is clear how and why children acquire the information that helps them make sense of the world. They do not merely acquire information that helps form their idiosyncratic attitudes to the world; they are aware at a multiplicity of levels of how they have acquired such information. It is not a simple matter of accepting opinions, for each is an individually formed, personally identified approach to the question, whether carefully worked out or 'off the cuff'. We should not underestimate the human mind's capacity, indeed propensity, for having a point of view of its own. The information in this book derives from children's free associations in their own mind about how they have learnt what they have. And yet, as in the rest of the data, the children were not assuming that they were being asked to trace influences; nor did they suppose that the whole point of the interview was about themselves, their teachers, their parents, their friends or their view of the world or about secondary sources of information.

Children's responses about what they know and the sources of information arises naturally from their responses to other questions. These are the questions embedded in the empirical: 'What do you think of?', 'Do you know about?' The resulting consistency in the results is again significant. It might seem clever to prove that certain children will tend to say one thing and other children will do something else – based on class or ethnicity or gender – but the real task is to gain an insight into the human mind. The empirical facts are more significant than any manipulation of the data. What children express and reveal is a particular vision of the world as seen from the individual, the 'egocentric' point of view. Each answer is unique but each one accumulates into an understanding which is collective: a consistent pattern of experience.

Whilst each individual has a unique perspective, each is faced with elements that are in common with others. There are very few people who do not know about cars, or have not travelled in cars, and there are fewer still who have not seen television. And yet these are two major features of life that are unique to the times we live in. All children are involved in the normal (and distinctive) features of modern life. They all know at first hand about traffic and pollution, about space, both cramped and open, about the immediate environment and the world outside. And they all have adults around them, peers and other sources of information through which they learn about the world. Their sense of discrimination, of patterns, is as powerful as their sense of their own enclosed spaces, the place they happen to live, the car they are in as they travel somewhere else, observing different scenes.

The global village of information

One of the dominating sources of information – probably the most potent, as will be demonstrated – is television. This comes across clearly because when children are asked how they know something the usual refrain is 'I've seen it on the telly'. There was a time when people assumed that the 'gospel' was whatever was printed. But now, for different reasons, it is television that is assumed to be the authority – not because it gives the last word, or even the first, but because it gives pictures. Here are seen to be the images of reality. Even if there is a marked suspicion of television by commentators, the pictures stay in the mind. 'As seen on TV' is *not* the same as real life, but the imagery has a potency that words alone cannot rival.

When children are simply asked how they know that what they are saying is the case – whether about the 'first' or the 'developing' world – or when they are asked to cite any information that is on the news, whatever is happening, they revert to the cry that it's 'as seen on TV'. The television is cited again and again as not only the most important source of information but, in most cases, the unique one. It is the genuine window on the world. 'How do you know' meets the inevitable response:

I just see it on television.   (girl, 6)

'Cos I seen it on the news.   (boy, 7)

Because I have to watch the news on Thursday, because my favourite programme is called *Blue Peter* and that's after the news. So I have to watch the news on Thursdays and find out things.   (girl, 6)

I see it on the news.   (boy, 8)

From an early age children are aware of the news and what it entails. Having experienced and observed their own microcosms of society in the home and the neighbourhood, and having understood the volatility of human interactions,[16] they are at the same time aware that such events take place elsewhere. There is a whole world beyond. There is little sense of the small enclosed village of their own, of containment, of their own experience. Instead, one of the early truths that they have to accept is the vast multifariousness and sheer tragic energy of the world as a whole, of events or things going wrong, of people and countries, good and bad, of disasters that are accidental and disasters deliberately fostered by people.

Children might not wish to see the news, but whether they like it or not, it remains the most significant source of information for their understanding of the world as a whole. The pattern of scheduling makes this both an inevitable and a resented fact. Children return from school and immediately re-enter the world of background entertainment. The television is on. There is not necessarily anyone to play with. Tea is not ready. Their own favourite programme will shortly be available. Children's programmes are scheduled to coincide with their homecoming. If there is nothing else happening, the news will be watched, whether they want to see it or not. And this is how children learn about the world. It is not through careful introductions and explanations that children learn about their circumstances. There are few people who either protect them from worldwide events or try to make them understood. Instead of analysis, children acquire their information from what is overheard or 'overseen'. Suddenly there are the appearances of the world outside: The News. This is supposed to give an insight into the reality of life. Their parents take it seriously. The tone is not light. The ideas presented are the facts: this is how the world is. And what do children see on the news?

> Well I watch television after school... news; dead people everywhere, massive guns everywhere and these guys with guns.   (boy, 9)

> You can't really tell 'cos just on the television you see all the smashed up houses and it's quite hard to see what they are.   (girl, 8)

> I've seen wars going on and things. And, er, I've seen, starving people and other things.   (boy, 8)

> When I hear on the television there's been a fire or something – somebody's died – that makes me sad.   (girl, 8)

Parents might take the news seriously but they rarely explain it or feel they have time to, since the next picture or the next item follows at once.[17] Images, especially negative images, abound. It is clear that there are dreadful things happening, that the world beyond is not a happy or a peaceful place.

Television as a source of influence

Television is the major, if not unique, source of news and insight into the world as a whole. Children do not seek out the news any more than they go in search of a newspaper to discover what has happened. Nor do they cajole their parents to explain all that is happening in the world. The news is of no immediate interest to them. It hits them the harder for being accommodated with difficulty into their longed-for shared understanding. What does the news consist of? Essentially it is the challenge of what is different; a reminder of the flimsiness of a personal 'locus' or personal sense of epistemological security. Anything fit to be on the news has to be based on inconsistency or disorder, an aberration from ordinary or normal life. It has to be a sensation. Sensations are dislocating. What children overhear and oversee is the primary dislocation of life: death, suffering and anguish.

> I've seen the wreckage of Bangladesh and, er the cyclone. The starvation
> in...
> (boy, 7)

> Well, there's this advert about really sick and poor children and they have
> sort of like their eyes are all funny and their faces are just sort of weird and
> they've got rashes and stuff on their hands. (girl, 8)

> They come on the news. They showed one last night and there was this
> tiny baby with just a nappy that didn't fit him. It was floppy because he was
> so thin. (boy, 8)

The television is a pervasive, consistent and uncontrolled source of information. Whilst it is in the background and unexplained it nevertheless remains powerful. It presents violent images and stark realities. It has a constant theme: people quarrel and hate each other, kill each other; people starve to death; people suffer; there are wars; there are natural disasters; there are many kinds of suffering. It could be argued that for an insight into human strife the radio is the better medium. Each morning on Radio 4 comes the quarrel of the day – one person's point of view against another. But children do not listen to Radio 4. Their news is acquired largely from television. And it is acquired not in the form of argument or discussion, but by osmosis. Here are the pictures, the images of reality. The way that children talk about their understandings make it clear that they are most dependent on images. They cite whatever they have 'seen', what has been conveyed to them in its raw form. And in the images come details, like particular images of an individual baby or an individual face. It is the children who have to make some generalizable sense out of what they see. It is not done for them. This means that the news at one level can remain unexplained.

> I remember seeing something about them on the news but I can't remem-
> ber what it was. This was about the only thing I've heard about it but I
> can't remember what is was. (girl, 9)

One result of inattentive viewing, when the pictures are not framed by explanation, is that stereotypes become very powerful pictures of particular kinds of people. It is the repeated images that gradually become clichés embedded in the mind. The type of programme, whether serious or light in tone, whether pure entertainment or documentary, is not as important as the visual message. It is the picture and its association that remains embedded in the mind.

> Our customs and stuff. French people have just got onions all round them
> and stuff. So they might like onions as well.   (girl, 9)

The ways in which children learn from television naturally depend on the closeness of attention that they pay to it. They are capable of very impressive feats of memory, if they have decided beforehand to recall all they have seen. But this is not the way that television is habitually watched. The reader only needs to try to recall what was seen last night, or even this morning, to realize that in a welter of material only some things – mostly recognized rather than recalled – can be brought to mind.[18] There has to be an organizing principle that reduces a mass of information to reasonable proportions. This principle is one of recognition rather than ratiocination. It is one of repeated imagery rather than argument. There are, therefore, certain moments of programmes that stay in the mind very clearly.

> It's got lots of fruit and stuff. And I would chop the bananas down. And
> then they put them in boxes and then, then a big lorry comes along from
> the forest and then and then you thrown them in the, and then you put the
> boxes on the lorry. And it takes them away back to all their homes.
>   (boy, 6)

This picture of the Caribbean as seen on *Blue Peter* is supposed by the boy to be about Australia. The essential fact is erroneous. But the picture remains vivid. The point on the programme – to educate about a particular country – might have been lost, but the image is not.

> Well, I've seen like, I've seen a country, well it's not actually a country
> programme, it's just the country and some people they get from the water
> loads and loads and loads of fish, and the telly's just talking about that.
>   (girl, 8)

Children are distinctly aware of television as a source of information. That is where they say they have learnt things. What they have learnt might not be clearly defined. Indeed, one sees all kinds of confusion, for the pictures rather than the verbal descriptions or explanations dominate. There might be confusion about events or where they take place but nevertheless what is just seen as television has a strong imprint on the mind.

> Like I remember when they were talking in this restaurant and they just…
> they were talking about this bank or something. It was over-erupting or
> something. Going on about this bank… people, like, didn't, like, they took
> all the money out because some kind of person were – or is it falling down.
> I think it was falling down. And everybody was trying to get their money
> out of it. And all the money managers were trying to stop them and every-
> thing because you could easily built it up again. But they were all quickly
> trying to get their money but people were trying to stop them I think… I
> think it was in China.   (girl, 6)

It is, of course, impossible to trace every effect on the memory of all the information that children have received. There is no doubt that compared to their fore-
bears they have had an incalculably greater amount of visual presentation of their
own and other people's worlds. They will not only have heard about all the calami-
ties of the world; they will have had them starkly presented.

Television is, in its vivid imagery, a potential source of fear and anxiety.
Children are clearly aware of this and, as previous research has shown, they will all
have had at least one experience of being frightened by what they have seen.[19] The
wonder is that they are not *more* frightened, nor more palpably taken aback by the
news. Do they think, when they see a starving baby, 'that could be me'? Or do they
become as immune as their parents, given the diurnal dose of tragedy? After a time
one can only suppose that, like their elders, they become inoculated against grief
and personal sympathy. Nevertheless there are images that haunt them, especially
in their first approaches to television:

> They show it on old films and I saw an old film, and I was scared stiff when
> I saw it. It was when I was about four or five. I saw it on the telly and I was
> late to bed for one reason. I don't know why, and I saw it, and I went down
> to get a pillow in case I got too frightened and I saw the beginning and I
> just went. My head went straight into the pillow.   (boy, 8)

There is an argument that a certain amount of fear is a matter of pleasure, but this
memory is typical. The fear was genuine and palpable. There might have been a
fascination with the images but that did not minimize being frightened by them.

The visual imagery of the world

All children will have seen horrifying images in one programme or another and
they have all had to cope with them. There are all kinds of ways of dealing with
what should have given them nightmares.

I like being me because whenever I watch horror films I'm always allowed to stay up and watch them because I'm never frightened of them and I never have bad dreams. Since I was four I haven't been frightened of horror films or anything. My sister's quite scared of them.   (girl, 8)[20]

I see other countries – sometimes I watch programmes about other countries with animals in them. I usually only watch it because it has animals in it. I watched a horsy programme and it was all about horses. And all these countries where horses lived.   (girl, 7)

Even those programmes looked at without any intention of learning stimulate very impressive memories. It does not follow that what is presented is imbibed, but certain images are. Children watch a great deal of television. They see whatever is on after school – and this includes programmes they would not choose to see like the news. They tend to watch in the mornings, at weekends and also often quite late into the night. This chapter is not about the amount children view but about what they learn and where they learn it. Nevertheless there is a connection between the two because the more that is watched the less easy it is to recall any particular events.

The stereotypes that are the way of ordering information become the more strong. There have to be means of making sense of a plethora of information. Children, like their elders, feel that they ought to deny how much time they spend watching television (whilst in fact revealing how much they do). It is as if they subconsciously accept that as a medium of information, television is both vivid and unpenetrating. Images, without meaning, abound. Little is actually explained so that even the news is a form of entertainment.

Ask a child what time he or she goes to bed and the answer will be dutiful. Ask someone how much they watch and there is a tendency to say 'little'. Ask *what* they have watched and it begins to sound like the complete listings of the *Radio Times* or *TV Times*. But children are more honest than adults, despite the development of this characteristic and have less propensity to deny what they actually do.

Well, I watch television after school. Like everyday I watch the *Neighbours* and Children's ITV or BBC. *Home and Away*. And on the weekend I watch films and I watch *Voyage to the Bottom of the Sea* and *The Lone Ranger*. And sometimes, like when I stay up really late, like eleven, I watch films then.
                                                                             (boy, 9)

The amount watched and the pleasure that is derived from the experience do not go hand in hand. Television is often seen more as a distraction than a pleasure.

I never do nothing when I go home. I just watch telly. I don't like watching telly. Because we've got nothing to do in our house.   (girl, 8)

It is in such a context, an almost dismissive sense that television is not to be taken too seriously, and that it is primarily a source of distraction or entertainment, that children imbibe the facts of the world. Thus the information that is presented to them is in the framework of a wide background of much discarded material. Television is an extremely important source of information but it is not taken as a particularly significant one. Whilst there is a sense that it is so because 'I've seen it on TV' this does not give television the authority of a teacher. It is *known* to demand a different type of viewing, one that is not explicitly full of information:

> *Neighbours*. It doesn't really tell you nothing. It's just a programme.
>
> (girl, 8)

Television is entertainment for its own sake, and taken as such rather than as a source of learning. Those who watch it are conscious of the fact of watching, programme coming after programme, with few pauses.

> On TV, they looked sort of browny black. 'Cos when you see it in really life, you see them black. But when you see them on TV they sort of look a bit – 'cos our TV's very very old. If it was about one day old you'd probably think it was real black. But our TV is very old it only shows you browny white really.
>
> (boy, 6)

There is often a juxtaposition of the world as seen on television and immediate and personal reality.

> I have seen French people on the television wearing berets. [Did you see them do so when actually in France?] Not really.
>   Most of them [the Gambia] don't wear any clothes... on television.
>
> (girl, 7)

The world is therefore seen to be filtered through television. At one level the images, unexplained, abound and are both pervasive and repeated. At another they are not taken that seriously as they are part of a medium of entertainment. Meanings have to be imposed. This is at the heart of stereotyping, the patterning of experience into a series of categories, from simple alternatives, 'either/or' or 'rich and poor' or even 'good and bad' to the more circumstantial 'us and them'.

Television might represent it but it clearly is not real life in itself. Children acquire an equivocal attitude to television. Most of what is seen is fantasy – nothing more nor less than entertainment. Every now and then a documentary combines reality with this entertainment. Television depends for its impact on its visual qualities. There is a juxtaposition between sound and sight. It is the words (not listened to with great attention) that carry the arguments and explanations. It is the pictures that carry the impact.

The impression that children give is that television is a medium which, in terms of information, is almost 'overseen' just as so much important information is overheard. Children's insights into the world are made by their perceptions, by their strenuous attempts to make sense of a great deal of miscellaneous material. Children do not acquire from others a coherent point of view. Principles and prejudice might be laid before them and they will certainly pick up some of the practices and attitudes of their parents. They have to create a coherent sense of the world of their own from a mixture of pieces of information. Children try to do the best they can, with what they overhear and 'oversee'. The images appear and reappear on the television. Out of these juxtapositions children have to make a sensible structure of the divided world: of prejudices and antipathies, of implied bonds and assumed securities as well as abstract meanings.

Individual identity exposed and collected

Television dominates as a source of information about the world at large. It is the one background source that does not need to be sought out. What it presents is almost 'inadvertent information'. The television is on. It can be ignored or watched, or responded to in a mixture of viewing styles. In comparison, other public sources of information work in a different way. To find out the news from newspapers, for example, takes a conscious decision. Newspapers and magazines are very rarely mentioned as sources of information.

> Sometimes it shows some in the newspapers and things like that. Well mostly from the TV. And people talking about it.   (boy, 8)

> We used to get the evening paper but we used to get the *Daily Mail* but we don't any more.   (girl, 9)

Newspapers are rarely mentioned by children. Information so portrayed and explained, even in the tabloids, does not seem to impinge on them. It is not sought out. And yet their world-view depends on what they see and, as they demonstrate, they do have a distinct view of the world. For those who *want* to know, there are distinct sources of information, like books.

> I read encyclopaedias about them. And books about the countries, programmes and the news.   (boy, 9)

> I've got a book about the world at home. And it tells you all about Germany and Spain and all the countries like that.   (girl, 6)

The citation of sources other than television are, however, rare. Children are aware of this. They know that their wider world-view is formed in the ostensible privacy and security of the home. Enclosed in the supposed security of the family they are confronted, without explanation, with the lives of other people, people like themselves, crying, wounded, dismembered. To the raw young mind these are not alien. Television is not the place consciously to seek information. Indeed, it is not seen as a source of information at all. For information you read books or talk to people. And yet children know they watch a great deal of television and they are aware of where their information comes from. Of course, it is difficult for anyone to trace sources of information; how, after all, were we formed? And yet what stands out in the children's responses is the dominating way that *images* emerge. They might not know where the influence comes from:

> Well, I've seen them on television and on the news and on the radio. On my sister's homework, she does about different countries.   (girl, 8)

But we can detect, in the way in which they cite what they know, how important is the way in which television works. Children 'oversee' television, like looking over a shoulder at what someone else is viewing or reading. But they also hear information, taking it in without seeking it out. Other people are an important source of opinion and fact, one mixed with the other. Television might be an ostensibly secondary source but is in fact a primary one. It is as pervasive a background as parents. Children like to cite where they acquired information.

> My dad told me and it said on telly.   (boy, 6)

> Well, just 'cos people have told me and, er, my mum's told me and well I just learn all the rest.   (boy, 8)

Whilst they assert what they *know*, they assume their opinions are based on authority. The facts stand out clearly. Children also know that the facts demand an opinion.

Private insights and the public domain

In the various sources of information from talking to parents to watching television it is interesting to note that what should be the most significant source of all –

school – is rarely mentioned. This has a lot to do with the fact that the subjects raised in the interviews, namely children's attitudes to themselves and the actual world, to their own environment and circumstances and to other countries, are just the subjects that schools do not deal with. The national curriculum is prescribed and covers many themes and consists of many levels, many of which are to be tested. But it contains little in the way of values or attempts to understand a democratic society, despite some attempts to add 'citizenship' to the curriculum.[21] There are many skills involved in the curriculum, but hardly a mention of its purpose, or of understanding. The one overlap between the curriculum in school and children's views is geography – their knowledge of what other countries are like. This is the one time that the experience of school is involved. And yet for every mention of knowledge acquired in school there are many that cite nature programmes on television as the main source. Again, it is the pictures that stay in the mind, and when children describe in any detail the experience of people in foreign countries their awareness is more likely to come from nature programmes or documentaries than from school.

Occasions when a topic of salience concerning news in the wider world is mentioned in school, either in the class or in an assembly, are, in the children's minds, exceptional. They are unusual events or unusual enthusiasms that arise beyond the ordinary things.

> We seen it on television. We had our Assembly about Africa. We've been doing our topic about countries last year, just saying that some countries are poor and other countries are not. And we were just saying what had happened to the countries and everything. (girl, 8)

One can argue that children should be made aware of issues at school, for when they imbibe information from television it is surrounded by emotional associations rather than neutral explanations. But when one thinks of the time alone spent on mathematics and writing, there is little room for discussion. Topics about other countries do emerge occasionally and exceptionally.

> When I was in Miss K's, right, she told me. This house, right, it don't have an upstairs. It only got a downstairs. The teacher talks about countries. (boy, 6)

School is an unimportant source of information compared with the masses of evidence about the world that is paraded on television. School seems to have only a small role to play in helping children form their opinions about themselves in relation to others. Opinions are traced to a variety of sources:

> Sometimes I watch things about travel programmes. But that's only when I've got nothing else to do. I've heard some things on TV and we went there once for a day. I pick them up from the telly and the man who comes and, um, our project on Russia and the *Discovering Our World* book.
>
> (girl, 9)

No one can trace where these opinions come from. The sheer wealth of detail of the rest of the world, while watched from positions of embedded, if false, security, is such that it must be put into order and given some kind of subliminal meaning.

It is not easy to prove any connection between one particular stimulus out of many and a particular response. The only way is through tracing influences through memory, where the most salient experiences are clearly marked. Children can cite particular programmes which made them frightened. They also are aware of where they have learnt what they know. It is more difficult to pin down where opinions are acquired. The phrase 'seen it on telly' when applied, for instance, to the images of Africa, demonstrates a stronger response and attitude than neutral storage of information. The views of the world, of the rich and the poor, the happy and unhappy, are taken from many sources. These sources include friends and relatives, people sharing their thoughts and their personal experiences. Children are aware of why they know, or think, certain things.

> Because my next-door neighbour went to France and they sent us a post-card. And we saw what it was like.
>
> (boy, 6)

The personal assembly of fact

Each insight is all the more real and more influential when it is connected with people children know. Friends and relatives or the experience of *au pairs* help join the other significant sources of information.

> It was on *Newsround* and *Blue Peter*. When I go to my grandma's in Bir-mingham, she's got pictures that people took in the war of her husband, my grandad, and other army people.
>
> (girl, 8)

> Sometimes on the news. And sometimes on the radio. And sometimes when, um, Granny's sending a letter, she tells me a few things.
>
> (boy, 8)

Attitudes to the world are formed partly through the images presented through the media and partly through discussions – more often with peers than with parents.

There are occasions when personal anecdote intrudes. Positive images or negative images are acquired, often by chance.

> I've never been [to the United States]. It's just, my friends have told me about it and I thought, well, I'd just love to go there. And, er, I've seen films and pictures from my cousins and stuff.
> Because my art teacher she used to live there and she just got out of the plane and she was dripping wet and she was just sweaty.
> On the news. It was on the news lots of times and Chris, he's in form two now, he went to Germany.   (boy, 8)

Anecdotes, overheard remarks and images all have their part to play in the formation of attitudes. The individual child needs to construct his or her own individual vision of the world. There are few signs of formality, in the sense of being given structured points of view. Only very occasionally do children mention receiving a 'message' alongside information:

> Well, our church, we're doing about 'Tear fund' about other countries and in the evening when I come sometimes they have videos about the poor people. Because last Sunday mum and dad were talking about it and sharing pictures about what it would be like to be there.   (girl, 6)

Here we can see definite opinions being formed – and parents taking a central part. This kind of parental influence, acknowledged as such, is rare. As previous research has shown, the television news is rarely described or commented upon.

> Parents talk only to their friends, but when my brother's not around and we're not around.   (boy, 8)

> I don't know because they always want us out of the room when they talk about it.   (girl, 9)

> If anything exciting happens… they talk about it but otherwise they don't.
>   (girl, 9)

Just as certain subjects are excluded from school, so children feel psychologically left out of serious conversation. There appears to be a mythology that children are not ready to comprehend the world, or that they should be protected from the very information that is constantly visible on television. Children see the images but are left to make up their own mind about them. There are many different experiences and facts that they can only acquire through television. The very poor in other countries and the very rich are presented to them essentially through television.

Like see people on telly and they're rich and that. And an advert about rich
blend coffee. Only in adverts. On telly.   (girl, 8)

Nevertheless, out of this heterogeneous range of material children form distinct
views of the world.

Most of the information that children acquire they acquire by chance in the
sense that they happen to pull certain bits out of the accumulations of presenta-
tions before them, both factual and fictional. Children are sophisticated in their
viewing. They have to discriminate.[22] They must select and interpret. But from the
point of view of the producers and the presenters the idea of an audience is a far
narrower one. There is an assumption, natural if self-deceiving, that the ideas and
information that are delivered will be received intelligently, open-heartedly and
completely. There is a fundamental difference between those who try to communicate a point of view, and those who respond. The focus of attention and the con-
centrations are different. With television, the inadvertent is paramount. One
programme follows another. It is inevitable that most will be, must be, forgotten.
Only the occasional images remain, subliminal to an extent in the mind of the
recipient.

News, information and propaganda

The juxtaposition of the designs of the communicators and the response of the
audience is an important one. If producers have a viewpoint they want to convey,
propagandists of different types will be the more adamant that they can manipulate
the reactions of audiences. In certain conditions, where the personal and social
concerns overlap with the deliberate message of the State, such propaganda, as in
Nazi Germany, can make an impact. There are those who believe that schools can
make a similar impression, even if they eschew the idea of propaganda as such.
'Values', 'citizenship': such are the words that signal these designs. But even these
concerns are peripheral to the central propaganda of knowledge rather than
thought, of skills rather than abilities that inform the centralized curriculum.

The underlying instinct to manipulate the mind, for good or ill, is always near
to the heart of any education system. Should not all teachers try to influence? Does
this come about naturally and hidden or not at all? The rhetorical question is not
that this is too big a subject but that there are certain conclusions that are significant in the light of the ways that children learn both to stereotype and to be prejudiced. What teachers present and what pupils learn are fundamentally different.
The only question is the extent of the overlap, which is more subtle and complex
than any single theory can suggest. What we can detect is the way in which,

whatever the designs of teachers or the systems of which they are part, children make some kind of structural sense of what is received. They place themselves at the heart of a world-view.

Designs on the ways in which pupils are supposed to look at the world and at the nations that inhabit it are manifested in a number of different ways. The sources of influence seen in the novels of the earlier part of the 20th century and earlier are reinforced by the school textbooks that were commonly used. Whilst obvious stereotyping and chauvinism are no longer the informing characteristic of 'politically correct' textbooks, the image, the tone and the attitude towards other countries are clear.[23] The way in which these images are responded to is far less clear. The ideas that children have of other countries might not be the same as the deliberate message conveyed. This implies that they retain their own point of view, but it does not stop the designs of those who wish to influence them.

The development of the European ideal, as in other cross-national visions, has demonstrated some of the strands of thought in attempting to correct stereotypes and prejudice.[24] Parties of healthy young people are to be sent to learn a foreign language, imbibing the culture that surrounds it. Football supporters follow their team and absorb the atmosphere of other nations. The great hope is that experience, first-hand, and primary information will far outweigh the mass of secondary data that people receive. In fact, primary data is as selectively dealt with as any other, even when there is far less of it.[25]

The need and the tendency to form judgements, to juxtapose the self against others will be there, in some degree or another, whatever the sources of information. There will be designs on the forming of the mind-set. Each person forms his or her own mind. Cultural influences abound. But they are subtle. And they can only be understood by understanding the ways in which individuals create their own position.

References

1. Spradley, J (1979) *The Ethnographic Interview*, Holt, Rinehart and Winston, New York
2. Barnes, D (1965) *Language and Learning in Secondary Schools*, Penguin, London
3. cf the Essex University archives of recorded material of interviews from different communities.
4. eg Brighouse, T and Moon, C eds (1990) *Managing the National Curriculum*, Longman, Harlow
5. Sharp, R and Green, A (1975) *Education and Social Control*, Routledge and Kegan Paul, London
King, R (1978) *All Things Bright and Beautiful? A sociological study of infants' classrooms*, Wiley, Chichester
6. Cullingford, C (1990) *The Nature of Learning*, Cassell, London

7. Toivonen, K and Cullingford, C (1998) Racial prejudice in a liberal democracy: a case study, *Politics, Groups and the Individual*, **7** (1 & 2), pp 45–56

8. Milgram, S and Shotland, R (1973) *Television and Anti-Social Behaviour: Field experiments*, Academic Press, New York

9. Bourdieu, P (1977) *Outline of a Theory of Practice*, Cambridge University Press, Cambridge

10. Ong, W (1982) *Orality and Literacy: The technologizing of the word*, Methuen, London

11. Sabini, J and Silver, M (1982) *Moralities in Everyday Life*, Oxford University Press, Oxford

12. Hayes, D and Casey, D (1992) Young children and television: the retention of emotional reactions, *Child Development*, **63** (6), pp 1423–36

13. Cullingford, C (1999) *The Human Experience: The early years*, Ashgate, Aldershot

14. King, R (1989) *The Best of Primary Education?* Falmer, London

15. Finn, G (1990) Children and controversial issues: some myths and misinterpretations identified and challenged from a cognitive-developmental perspective, *Cambridge Journal of Education*, **20** (1), pp 5–27

16. Dunn, J (1988) *The Beginnings of Social Understanding*, Basil Blackwell, Oxford

17. It is worth noting that if there are pauses, even small ones, far more of what is seen is retained. Sturm, H (1991) *Ferusehdiktate: Die Veränderung von Gedanken und Gefüklen*, Bertelsmann, Gütersloh

18. Cullingford, C (1984) *Children and Television*, Gower, Aldershot

19. Ibid

20. The moral censorship reflects that of adults. Whilst they themselves are sophisticated enough to be able to watch anything they choose, they do not think their younger siblings should be exposed to the same material; indeed they should be protected from it.

21. eg Crick, B (1998) *Education for Citizenship and the Teaching of Democracy in Schools*, HMSO, London

22. Buckingham, D (1996) *Moving Images: Understanding children's emotional responses to television*, Manchester University Press

Robinson, M (1997) *Children Reading Print and Television*, Falmer, London

23. Berghahn, V and Schissler, H eds (1987) *Perceptions of History: An analysis of school text books*, Berg, Oxford

24. Cullingford, C (1998) National and personal identity: the formation of prejudice, *Politics Groups and the Individual*, **7** (1 & 2), pp 1–24

25. Cullingford, C (1995) Children's attitudes to holidays overseas, *Tourism Management*, **16** (2), pp 121–27

3

Early discriminations: the forming of group identities and the self

Close observations of the immediate

The powerful capacity of the mind of an infant is only slowly being acknowledged. The more we explore the phenomenon of critical if inarticulate scrutiny the more we discover the early ability of the human being to discriminate, to make judgements, and to make order of all the information that is observed and experienced. There are many studies of cognition and the intellectual and social abilities of young children.[1] All we need to do here is to underline the significance of these abilities.

The process of learning is based on making distinctions and making judgements. Learning is not a matter of absorbing information, but of making sense of it. The ability to categorize, to group different things into particular typologies is crucial.[2] In a world of buzzing visual and aural confusion young children pick out what is meaningful and concentrate just on that. Their very earliest experiences of learning are based on drawing distinctions. If we take language as an example we realize that every word is a kind of generalization, that 'chair' refers not just to a unique object that might be the immediate centre of attention, but to a whole host of others, all of different shapes and sizes. One concept is picked out and accorded a meaning that denotes exclusion as well as inclusion. The generalized concept 'chair' refers not just to a vast array of different shapes and colours but excludes other concepts such as stool, sofa or bench.

Learning comes from understanding the difference between what is meaningful and what can be ignored. The power not to pay attention to certain things, which clues to ignore, is as important as absorbing information. Discrimination, making distinctions, preferring one object or sound to another, are all the heart of the learning process. Prejudice, in this sense, even if it is benevolent prejudice, is at the heart of learning.

The understanding of the world as seen develops through the need to classify, to group objects, to recognize the familiar and separate it from what is new or different. This curiosity about the visual world is demonstrated by the interest shown in the unfamiliar, and in complicated stimuli. Young children spend time deliberately exploring complex pictures, and become bored with a lack of visual excitement.[3] They demonstrate their understanding by showing that they can count by the age of a few weeks, and take pleasure in a trick when one of three objects is seen to be taken away at one moment but is still there the next.[4] The ability of young children to see the world objectively and make sense of it has to be understood if we are to understand how they later form their set world-views.

Objects and visual stimuli, like language, are given mental images and meanings. The way in which children build up their understandings depends on associations.[5] They have to make sense of their experience in their own ways. That the early years are important is generally acknowledged but their influence on all subsequent attitudes and understandings is not fully explored.[6] We tend to think of learning as discrete, as the acquisition of language and fact, but it is in fact as much social as representational. Language is, after all, a dialogue, not just a classification system.

The learning of language depends on differentiating what is meaningful from the meaningless, since only certain sounds, phonemes, carry meaning. In Chinese, for instance, there is no distinction between 'l' and 'r'; to the native speaker they sound the same, as do 'b' and 'p' in Bengali. In English these differences are crucial. Each person has his or her own personal dialect, yet can still be understood by others. We know from a generalized sound what to take from it that carries meaning and automatically discard from our attention anything that does not add to the conveying of information.

Young children prefer certain languages and sounds to others.[7] They learn to pay attention to certain sounds and after a time almost automatically ignore background noise, like the sounds that might be surrounding you as you read this, like that of the wind, or a fly, or a computer, or traffic. Attention is shifted to matters that carry meaning, despite auditory interference.[8] It is only what is attended to that is remembered.[9] This again demonstrates that learning is an active engagement with information, so that meaningful sounds can be heard in conditions in which nonsense syllables are not.[10] This innate capacity to understand meaning, to make sense of experience, applies clearly to language but also to the observation of other people's behaviour.

When young children make their own first utterances they are not just 'babbling' meaninglessly but practising those sounds that are particularly directed towards them, by their parents. They then apply the rules that they have discovered to other new experiences. When they classify, for example, they might make mistakes, like overextending or underextending meaning.[11] A word like 'car' might apply at first as well to a bus or lorry. Or it might refer to one particular toy. But these are intelligent mistakes, just as grammatical mistakes – 'he hitted me' – are also based on the application of rules.

Social relationships under scrutiny

We know much more about children's capacity to discriminate about objects than about people because it is easier to research. We can demonstrate the ability of the infant to know that a particular toy exists even when it is not visible. The operative knowledge that a particular object can be viewed from all kinds of angles can be clearly demonstrated.[12] But as the re-examination of the experiments of Piaget reveal, children look as much for social clues, and observe people as closely as objects, as they do more abstract challenges.[13] The complexity of visual information, presented in defining terms such as 'tall', 'high', 'broad', 'wide', 'thin' and 'slim', also draws attention to the distinction between individual people, their facial expressions and tone of voice, but the quite different and deliberately simplified learning strategies are still applied to the clues that underlie formal learning.

The acquisition of knowledge and the capacity for learning have generally been demonstrated through the experience of auditory and visual stimuli. Language development has naturally attracted the most attention, but less concern has been paid to social understanding. And yet the ability to strike up relationships, to understand other people and one's self is perhaps the most significant of all kinds of learning. One of the best examples of the capacity of young children to discriminate and understand is their ability to understand distinctions between truth and falsehood.[14] This is perhaps the most sophisticated of all social learning. It implies a realization not only of points of view, but of false representation. Attempts to trace back the ability to understand the distinction cannot fathom the earliest point it occurs in a child's life. This is for want of proof, or finding a test that could demonstrate it. By the age of three children are able to articulate their understanding. They show how acutely and intelligently other people's actions and words are observed.

These observations of other people's behaviour are not neutral. Children are learning by interaction. Other people's actions have a direct bearing on how they understand themselves in relationship to the world. Prejudice, the preference for some over others, the suspicion of motives and actions, is acquired far earlier than its application to a particular group. Social learning includes reciprocal interaction. Responses are not just a matter of reacting to stimuli but acting on experiences and being able to reflect upon them.[15] The ability to understand their own actions in moral terms, between private and public good, is acquired early.[16] The ability to sympathize emotionally with others is demonstrated by babies.[17] The understanding of the physical world is developed in a factual, steady way. The understanding of the social world is far more arbitrary, and dependent on the particular cultural and personal factors that are brought to bear.[18] The way in which young people think about themselves and their relationships with others is formed very early on.[19] If we trace the beginnings of the insecurities that lead to prejudice, to exclusion and the inability to relate to others we always end up in examining the home.[20]

The influence of early relationships and experiences on subsequent achievements and experiences is a vast subject. That these personal relationships influence motivations, attitudes and success almost goes without saying. In particular they depend on close emotional and intellectual relationships with other people, whether they are personal friends or those in authority. All we can do at this stage is to trace some of the emblematic moments that demonstrate the sense of discrimination and rivalry, of personal identity as defined against others. Just as the learning of the use of language is the perception of another person's point of view against one's own, so is the learning of social positioning.[21] Children do not automatically have a relationship with their parents. The idea of 'blood' relationships, of genetic factors, is meaningless.[22] It is the actual interpersonal understanding that is crucial. However strong the emotional bond might be, it is the intellectual understanding, the awareness of what is shared and what is not, which counts. This embraces not just an emotional interaction but the ability to share a view about someone or something else.

Babies show an interest in faces, which comes about because of their understanding of other people's inner feelings.[23] They see the expressions that contain meaning and react to them accordingly. And they therefore seek positive reactions. Two-year-olds already demonstrate considerable intuition about other people's minds.[24] They are able to distinguish between behaviours that are ordinary and expected and those that are uncommon and peculiar.[25] They are also able to understand vicariously how other people feel.[26] All of this implies that they are very aware of groups, of those who respond well to them and those who don't. They seek positive attention. They wish to share ideas. All these needs are either met or denied; usually children experience a mixture of both.

The home as community

One of the earliest manifestations of rivalry and of prejudice, of the desire for warm intellectual relationships and for compatible others, is the tension between siblings in the home. The home is a microcosm of society. It demonstrates friendship and familiarity. It reveals the possibilities of disinterested concern for others, for self-sacrifice and love. It offers the warmth of the embrace, of protection within the confines of a space. But it can also reveal the opposite, of quarrels and disagreements, of jealousy and rivalry. The very first 'gangs' can be formed in the home. The family can be a unit defined against others. But it is within the family itself that the earliest indications of suspicion, envy, jealousy, superiority, and all the other manifestations of prejudice arise. Like any society a family depends on rules or accepted norms of behaviour. It provides hierarchies, structures and roles to play.

Families can be stressful as well as havens of peace and security. Tensions between parents, between parents and children, and between children themselves abound. Much is made, since the work of Adler, of the psychological effects of sibling rivalry. But little work has been carried out about how children relate to each other within the home. The studies of friendship have generally concentrated not on home life but on school.[27] Yet there is ample opportunity for the exploration and testing of relationships within the home setting: indeed, far more. This has generally been eschewed. Instead of studies of human relationships within the home there has been a tendency to use twins to explore matters of environmental against personality influences on behaviour and social success. Rather than explore relationships the fascination has been with genetics, with nature and nurture in the broadest sense.

It is clear that children's scrutiny of their home life includes extensive experience of their siblings. This experience, more than that of single children who have their own subsequent problems, can be particularly revealing. The moment there is a sibling, complex pressures are set up between them and with their parents. The larger the number in a family the more obvious are the complexities of relationships.

> Guess how much brothers, boys, I've got? Six. Two are gone. One's been
> at my mum's. One's with foster parents – that's Chris. And David is with
> my mum's mum.   (boy, 8)

Nearly all the children have experience of older or younger siblings with whom they have important relationships, sometimes positive and sometimes negative. They vie for the attention of their parents, they observe differences of treatment, and they are conscious of the times when the younger child appears to be given the benefit of the doubt or more attention. They also play together, argue, often sleep in the same room, share toys and activities and discuss their feelings together or ignore each other. What is certain is that siblings are a significant part of children's experience, and a particularly formative part in so far as the children have strong emotional ties. These are permanent relationships, not, as in the case of friends,

exploratory or short-term ones. There can be sustained enmities and temperamental differences, and the learning of avoidance techniques and longer-term
antipathies than those of peer groups. This makes them the more intense. The
results of the effects of siblings on each other can be long-term, especially in terms
of self-esteem.[28]

Prejudice and envy

One of the most fragile aspects of the relationships between siblings is how they
see themselves and each other in relation to their parents. One of the strongest
feelings expressed is that of jealousy, a jealousy that causes insecurity. Often it is
the jealousy towards a younger sister or brother, the sense of having a secure position usurped. This is often the first sense of a threat to a relationship, when the
intense need for personal reciprocity is diverted, and attention paid elsewhere.
There are those who never learn to share. One such example explores all the different aspects of jealousy: the difference in treatment and the perceived preference, the insecurity and the desire to be younger again, the feelings of unfairness
and alienation:

> At home I get all the blame all the time really. My sister just gets to play
> with her dolls. Sometimes she gets cuddles and hugs from my mum and
> dad and I don't usually get them. I think it's because I've had my turn of
> having cuggles [sic] and hugs when I was a bit, well, younger. And maybe
> mummy and daddy think that I'm a bit too old to have cuggles and kisses
> and hugs. But I like having a nice cuddle sometimes. 'Cos it makes…
> sometimes when I have a cuddle it makes me feel loved and cared for.
> Which I am, even though I sometimes think I'm not… Sometimes it's just
> that, well, mum and dad are just saying to me 'Go upstairs and play and
> don't come down'. Like, I never get a chance to go downstairs and see my
> dad when I come home from school. My mum says 'go upstairs and play'.
> But then my sister sneakily comes down and then I see she's just going
> down to talk to them, but then she ends up staying down and not me.
> Mum and dad say 'you should remember things and set a good example
> for your sister. She's four years younger than you.' And sometimes I don't
> like getting told off that much. But sometimes I think I deserve it. So I
> don't always feel sorry for myself. Sometimes I do but not all the time. I'm
> gonna have one child because if you have two, then they might start argu-
> ing like me and Sarah do.   (girl, 8)

As will be apparent, a lot of the tensions and jealousies that are expressed are about *younger* siblings. They seem to cause all kinds of difficulties, and appear in the eyes of their older siblings to have gained particular privileges by their status as being younger and more innocent. This isn't invariably so. Sometimes the older brother 'sneaks' in to the parent's affections:

> And sometimes he climbs in mum and dad's bed when I don't want him
> to and I want to.   (boy, 6)

But this older brother is acknowledged as being kind, nevertheless. The everyday experience is of vying for attention, of forming an intimate and safe, even protective group. The earliest groups are, after all, of relationships with one person. They consist of friendships, and for some, their own general group identities remain exclusively with one other person, sometimes permanently, and sometimes one at a time. The individual defines him- or herself not just in the relationship but against those who are outside it.

The desire to have close attention and be responded to is very strong. The fact that other siblings are seen to receive kind treatment only makes the child's desire for their own security in affection the stronger. But they also seek attention from each other. They do not need to be in a kind of rivalry. They perceive the friendship that they receive from a sister, or brother. And they also feel emotionally distraught on behalf of their siblings:

> It makes me sad when like my brother gets beaten up or something.
>   (boy, 8)

> When my sister falls over: when she falls out with someone. She's seven.
>   (girl, 8)

Friendship will always be a part of the relationship between siblings, but that includes all aspects of friendship, with argument and rivalry as well as emotional bonds. One of the perceived usefulnesses of siblings is their very presence: people to be with. Children do not like to be without friends.

> Well, I ain't got much friends over there. In our Close there's no girls up
> there.   (girl, 8)

> I haven't really got any next-door neighbours or any friends.   (girl, 7)

Company is important, especially if children can choose when to see people rather than having their presence thrust upon them. Children need to find friends from wherever they can, even if the relationships are changeable and volatile.

I like my two dogs. And Edward's next door to me, so I can play with him any time I want. Sometimes Edward's my enemy and sometimes Edward's my friend. And other times Jason's my friend and he's my enemy. Jason is another boy. (boy, 6)

Arguing the sense of identity

Such volatile relationships are also apparent in children's attitudes to siblings. Together with rivalry and jealousy they go through a lot of quarrelling. The relationships they have are not easy and fighting is a common occurrence. The change from friendship to enmity, a kind of testing ground for understandings, is crucial. It is the application of intellectual discrimination, of re-definition of the self as an identity. The distinction between being with or against someone is the means of discovering common ground, those shared interests that others can be associated with. At home, just as happens later at school, the volatility of relationships is expressed in physical terms, including an element of bullying.

My brother punches me. He's fourteen. I sometimes beat him up. And he sometimes beats me up. Giving me chin kisses. He always just gives me chin kisses. He gets his chin and he scrapes it along my cheek.

(boy, 8)

I'm a bad person as well in a way because I fight with my sister sometimes.

(girl, 7)

I have lots of fights with my brother. My brother says I'm a bit silly. I think I might be a bit. Just generally being stupid. (boy, 8)

It is often, but not always, the boys who express their quarrels more physically, as if they relish fighting. As in the case of bullying, they have their own way of manifesting their strength, whereas girls tend to use different types of weapons:

My sister keeps calling me names. She say's 'Oh, you can't do that. You're too small.' And then she calls me names sometimes. (girl, 8)

She's always teasing me and punching me. She's six. (boy, 8)

Quarrels abound. One of the most pervasive perceptions that children have of their relationships is quarrelling; not just crying for their parent's attention but locked in fierce argument.

> When my brother fights me it makes me sad. When he says that was his
> and it's mine. He gets bothered with me. (boy, 8)

Children who relate behaviour from which they suffer refer to older and younger
brothers and sisters. There is no clear pattern of older ones bullying younger ones,
or of younger siblings gaining more attention from parents. These relationships
depend far more on the personalities of the individuals: what is in common is the
pervasive extent of quarrels and arguments for all kinds of reasons. The children
often refer to small incidents, almost trivial excuses for a quarrel. It is as if quarrels
were latent, always possible and often likely.

> If my brother and sister were all taking the micky out of me I'd kick 'em in
> the nose. That's all. (boy, 8)

> I don't like my brother waking me up. He comes in and pushes me.
> (girl, 7)

When children discuss the quarrels they have within the family they do not simply
place the blame on everyone else. At this stage their sense of their own limitations
is as strong as their sense of grievance. They know they can do wrong and that they
do not always do good. They have a sophisticated sense of private and public
morality.[29] They do not form the impression of an antipathy against the world – a
definition of self purely through prejudice. Instead, the litany they give of arguments and actions includes their own faults and mistakes as well as those of others.

> I tear out my sister's earring. (boy, 11)

> When my brother is home he torments me when I'm tired. (girl, 10)

> I push my sister about. (girl, 10)

> Sometimes my little sister starts fighting me, so I push her off and I get
> into trouble. (boy, 11)

Quarrels are a central part of children's experience and it is difficult to isolate particular reasons for their occurrence. The sheer proximity of other people is one
factor. Arguments over things that both would like to possess – toys and affection –
are another. But it is as if arguments are experiments in behaviour, like kicking
someone just to see what will happen. The testing of truth and falsehood, the
explorations of feeling are all subconscious attempts to understand the framework
of oral social behaviour. It is a process of learning about the self and how to deal
with complex relationships. The volatility comes about because there are no fixed

terms of reference in the sense of acting out a role, or following norms of behaviour. It is because of this volatility that children are so honest about the equivocal nature of their own behaviour. Their sense of relativity is strong and it is a basis for their later understanding. The very same brothers and sisters whom they find fun to play with are the ones it is a particular pleasure to annoy.

> If my brother doesn't wanna play with me, with his own stuff because we've got Micros and that, well, he just says 'Oh I can't play', because he doesn't want to go upstairs because he's left his upstairs.
> I don't let my brother play with them and, um, well, sometimes, well like when he's getting dressed I say 'I'm gonna beat you'.
> I like to beat my brother out and take down his and make snowballs that are kind of really round and then smash his wall down if I could.
>
> (boy, 8)

Friends and enemies

Quarrelling sometimes seems like an extension of play, another way of being together, where competition is part of the pattern of friendship. This is not to suggest that fighting and argument is not taken seriously. Children might take this aspect of their lives as inevitable, but they do not take it for granted. It has a strong emotional impact, like bullying.

> I've got a brother and sister who I quite get annoyed with. 'Cos they're annoying. They do things that annoy me and sometimes they boast a bit. When I'm annoyed with my brother and sister I get all grumpy inside. When my brother gets annoyed, when I get annoyed with my brother and I get all grumpy. I don't like the way it makes me feel.   (boy, 8)

Quarrelling and fighting are manifestations of underlying tensions. They cannot be isolated from the daily arguments and jealousies, the perception of unfairness and discrimination. There may be many moments in home life that are pleasurable. Indeed, the overall pattern may seem one of undiluted and equable pleasure, especially in hindsight. But children express great awareness of the difficulties of home life as well as its potential security. Their very desire for security suggests this. The tensions between them and their parents are many. The children were not asked, after all, to talk about quarrels. They were asked about their brothers and sisters and parents. They were not quizzed about difficulties. They were simply asked about their life at home. It is the children who defined the difficulties. Some of these are everyday ones: the complaining about 'sweeping up the floors and tidying up the bedroom' when 'my brother's lazy' or 'having to get out of bed when I don't want to' or the general feeling of exclusion.

> I want to be on my own. I don't want to have any brothers and sisters. My brothers won't let me play with them.   (girl, 8)

Life is not depicted as unmitigated contentment. One of the pervading phrases at school and at home is 'It's not fair!'. Differential treatment is perceived as supporting this feeling.

> Sometimes it's not fair. My sister has ice cream and I can't.   (boy, 6)

> She gets cuddles… and I don't usually get them.   (same girl, 8)

It is as if having siblings automatically leads to conflicts and difficulties. As a result the desire to be 'on my own' and *not* have brothers and sisters is shared by a number of children. This is a sign of a desire to retreat from having to deal with social complexities. Most children cannot or do not hide from them. There are some, however, like those brought up in laissez-faire families where parents do not really care about them, where the retreat from relationships has long-term consequences. These are the ones to feel estrangement and hostility to others. The difficulties of relationships are perceived by many as greater than the advantages. There can be particular reasons for this.

> I don't let my brothers go in my room and stuff. I don't think it would be a very good idea if I did.   (girl, 8)

> He normally doesn't play with me when he's ill. 'Cos he feels like being on his own. 'Cos he doesn't feel like being crowded when he's ill.
>
> (boy, 6)

The confines of the family

'Not being crowded': children express a strong desire not to be harassed by others, to be free of outside constraints, but also free to approach others when they wish. The perfect world is one in which they make choices. They are afraid of being lonely, but want to be alone. A number of children express the need for company because 'I don't like being by myself' (boy, 9), and they look for distractions:

> I would like to do lots of different things when I'm alone so I won't get
> bored.
>
> (girl, 10)

> I am alone when my mum goes to get my brother and I watch TV most of
> the time.
>
> (boy, 10)

The difficulty for children is to avoid loneliness at the same time as avoiding the
tensions that come with living with brothers and sisters. One of the prime reasons
for their arguments centres not on sharing affection or toys but on sharing space.
Children quarrel over space, or the lack of it.

> My brother keeps on at me. And also, when we had a bunk bed it was just
> trouble. 'Cos like, he was up the top and I was down the bottom and once
> he fell out when I had a gap in bed. Because we were playing like making
> going like tents in our beds and well, he fell out of his bed and fell right
> down onto the floor because he was on the top bunk.   (boy, 8)

Such close proximity leads to the clearly remembered game, but it also led to
everyday arguments. The problem with living in a confined space is the opportunities it gives for friction. Children are aware of the tensions of home life, particularly with their siblings. Living so close together does not help.

The values of place

Space is both real and symbolic. As in the imagined communities of nationalism,
whereby people adhere to a sense of identity that connects them to countless
anonymous others, space becomes a series of definitions against some outside
world. A space is where people belong: a boundary that defines a personal possession, like a room, a sense of self clearly separated from the shared neighbourhoods where conflicts can arise. Within the home there are rivalries over space.
Outside the home the question is the extent to which there is some kind of hegemonic control over a defined sense of place which is known and safe.[30] The place
to which one belongs marks out that sense of personal and shared identity that is
the extension of the categorization of groups. Whilst schools in themselves both
define and dislocate the sense of shared space, a sense of personal possession is
already well established. Boundaries of indoors and out, safe and dangerous
places, places where threatening people live and those in which you are at home
are all strongly pressed on the consciousness of children.

Children have their favourite places, at home and in school.[31] They are quick to recognize the location of things, and use landmarks of familiarity.[32] Their sense of location, finding lost objects for example, is established early.[33] Thus the social rivalry for attention is also a rivalry for personal space. The social self-definition against others has its own strong symbolic form, symbolic of a sense of belonging and possession. The same children who feel abandoned or lonely for want of the presence of a parent also cling either to moveable objects, like a blanket, or to a particular location in which they feel safe. It is the sense of 'us' against 'them' defined not in terms of personal volatility but in the sense of a physical and emotional boundary. It is significant that very young children understand the difficult concept of maps as early as they learn about truth and falsehood.[34]

This interest in places is not just academic. Personal space has symbolic value. The understanding of an immediate locality, of familiar landmarks, is a very important connection between the everyday emotional reality of relationships and the sense of personal identity in a vast world.[35] This is why the concept of a 'habitus' has such potency.[36] It is not just a place, but an emotional construct that confronts the external world. It is the personal space in a social organization and also the symbol of society within the individual. Discrimination, that desire for personal hegemony that is not just isolation but a sense of a collective support, is central to the definitions of the self.

The social science of 'proxemics' deals with the ways in which people relate to each other physically. It explores the interaction between people, how close they get to each other, how much they touch and how distant they wish to be. It explores the behaviour of friends and of anonymous people behaving in particular ways in crowds. The study of the way masses of people behave has been long established, from observing spectators at football matches to the propaganda purposes of mass rallies. At the same time the psychological study of 'inner space' – individuality symbolically addressed in terms of physical closeness or distance – has gained currency in understanding the way in which people feel about, and can be observed to express, their identity in relation to others.

'Proxemics', like so many fields of observation, has, however, rarely been applied to children, although the subject could be deemed to be especially important in the way that children relate to each other in groups within the classroom and in games on the playground. With their need to adapt themselves to group behaviour, and to the demands of controlling many people in confined spaces, children learn rapidly about the dynamics of physical relationships. They are aware of how much space means to them, not just in terms of symbolic value but in actual physical consequences. One does not need to observe their behaviour with each other to notice how space, or lack of it, can be a point of confrontation. Can some children resist poking others when standing wedged in a queue? How much physical aggression manifested on the playground is due to overcrowding?

The dream of unconfined spaces

When children reflect on their feelings about the circumstances they live in, and their environment, it is soon apparent that having enough space to manoeuvre in is important for them. They talk about space within the home and outside it; they associate space with freedom. One of the points of argument they have with siblings is the tensions that can arise from having to share a room. There is no child who actually relishes sharing a bedroom. The idea might be attractive as a novelty – as when a friend comes to stay – but their everyday experience of it is negative. One of the domestic problems most often mentioned is the necessity of sharing:

... but I have to share a room with my sister.   (girl, 8)

I think I'd like to live in a house instead of a flat. 'Cos then you get your own room. I have to share a room with my sister.   (boy, 8)

At my granny's I have to sleep with my brothers. One is just a very low bed and one with me. I like having a room of my own.   (girl, 8)

All of the children who have to share a bedroom say how much they dislike it, for all kinds of reasons.

I have to share a room with my sister. She's always talking in bed and when she makes a mess I have to clear it up. I would change my big sister. I want her to be older.   (girl, 8)

I have to share a room with my sister. Sometimes we argue. Sometimes we're nice to each other, but sometimes we get annoyed about sleeping in the same bedroom.   (girl, 7)

For all the children who do not have it, having a room of one's own is one of the most strongly felt desires. It is as if they imagine that they would then avoid the arguments with brothers and sisters, that they would then have some kind of personal command over their own actions and tastes. Again and again they repeat the same refrain: 'I would like to have a room of my own'.

Children fantasize about what they would like, and this invariably includes plenty of room. But the core is their own bedroom, however small, as long as it is exclusive:

If there was a big house – if we changed to go in a big house, probably I'd have a bedroom of my own. And my brother would probably be moved...
                (girl, 7)

I'd be able to write more things and I'd be able to have my room as I want. And I'd be able to have a bed of my own because it's kind of like attached to my sister's bed.   (girl, 7)

They've… got lots of rooms. I'd be able to have a bedroom of my own.
                                                                                        (boy, 8)

It is not only those children who long to have their own rooms who feel crowded or cramped, who appreciate the luxury of having plenty of space. The possession of their own bedroom is mentioned as a salient point in the benefits of their own home:

It's a nice big house and it's got loads of space. I've got my own bedroom and everything.   (boy, 8)

And inside it's really big. And I've got a big bedroom to myself. Peace and quiet. 'Cos when I read – I do a lot of reading, not so much TV – I don't like people talking 'cos it distracts me.   (boy, 8)

Of course having their own room *can* mean personal responsibility for keeping it tidy, but this is a minor problem compared with the untidiness caused by others, when each wants to blame the other. At least personal possession makes the responsibility clear.

Children's concept of space is not exclusively defined against notions of their own bedroom, or against the avoidance of too close proximity to others. It is also a symbolic value, of freedom to make choices, of not being psychologically pressed or confused. They like room to manoeuvre; they also admire those who express such freedom. Their envious sense of what it is to be well off centres on the ability to have room – in which to live, to play and travel. They all express a desire for big, detached houses:

In the street where I live there's big houses. There's a big house and there's a few other big houses in my road. It's very nice. And I like big houses. And I've got a very big house.   (girl, 6)

Large houses have clear advantages; they provide individual bedrooms and space for playing. But they are liked almost for their own sake; part of the admiration for the United States is the perception that houses are bigger there. Praise for a foreign country includes the citing of 'lovely, big houses'. Children are driven to admire large houses because they contrast with the feelings of being cramped. The size of houses and the amount of space needed to avoid people getting on each other's nerves is clearly a subject of planning as well as argument:

We're changing house in three weeks. We're going to an old house because we're not having enough room in our other house. (girl, 6)

Cramped space means enforced sharing and possible argument, an association children make on contemplating the images of the poor in underdeveloped countries. Large houses symbolize having enough space to play in, undisturbed:

My brother's friend's house, well, it's a big house and it's really good fun. It's good for playing lots of different games 'cos it's very big. I'd like a house because we just live in a flat. 'Cos you get more space to play in. (boy, 8)

I like to live in houses which are in the country, like nice big houses. (girl, 8)

The children who admire large houses are not just those confined in council flats. It is a shared, collective perception that, of all things, a large house with plenty of bedrooms and a big garden is to be desired. The very rich might have great mansions; for that, too, becomes the measurement of wealth. But all would like adequate space, in order to do what they want to do. Being poor means living in a small house. They would like space to move in, partly to be able to make, or to avoid, noise.

Psychological and real space

Large houses make good neighbours. They provide enough space to enable children to do what they want to without disturbing others and without being disturbed. Large houses also mean large gardens, and gardens are specifically valued as places where children can play:

'Cos you've got a big garden. 'Cos my dad's gonna make us a big patio and he's gonna, if he could, he's gonna build a big pond in the garden. (boy, 6)

And my friend's garden was huge. It's easily bigger than this room. And my friend's mum didn't like mowing the garden because the grass used to go pssshh. (girl, 7)

Space is, after all, practical as well as psychological. For the kinds of games they wish to play, children desire gardens. Sometimes it is because they also provide facilities like climbing frames and swings. But it is eventually the space that matters and the extra dimension given to a house – aesthetically as well.

> They've got nice gardens and they're quite big and they've got nice flowers and that. And there's lots of trees to climb and you have lots of fun there.
>
> (boy, 7)

> I like it 'cos I've got a big garden. And dad's dug a pond out and me and my dad made this massive climbing frame as big as the room. (boy, 8)

> I'm happy where I am at the moment because it has a nice big garden.
>
> (girl, 11)

Children are seen to observe all kinds of circumstances. They compare their own to other people's, objectively. Whilst they must accept their own lot and look at it pragmatically, there are certain things that they would like to have. They appreciate space when they have it, and long for it when they don't:

> Considering to other houses we haven't got a very big, big house. Our kitchen's smaller that other people's. Some people have a big garden and we've only got a bit of a garden.
> They might be able to have a really big garden and [be] happier. I would be able to get my own house. A big garden and a big house.
>
> (girl, 7)

Those children who lack gardens are aware of it. They cite the cramped space for all the activities that they like to undertake. And it is not only boys who are worried by lack of space for physical activities:

> It's just that I haven't got a very big back garden. Sometimes I like grass and sometimes I like gravel to skate around on. Some of them have got big gardens and big houses. They do have a big house. Probably as big as my mum's sister's house. And she's got quite a big house. It's got a front garden and a back garden. And they've got... (girl, 7)

Gardens are symbolic of space. They are the sign of a good house. The strength of feeling for them rests partly on their utility. They are places for play. When children do not have gardens they appreciate playgrounds. But gardens are also symbolic of freedom, of the space to manoeuvre, of having choices, being able to roam and *not* being told where to stand, when to move, and how long to sit still. The perception of the countryside as desirable, in contrast to the town, is not just a suburban ideal created by planners, but has deep psychological roots. Gardens, and the countryside, symbolize freedom from unwanted instruction or attention, from being forced into particular actions. Outside, the freedom of imagination has even greater play.

If the open spaces of the country are not available there are still those places that can be provided for children. One of the sources of pleasure that children mention are those provided by the local social services:

> I want to play in the playgrounds because they've got this thing where you have to go through all these hoops without touching the hoops.
>
> (boy, 7)

> I liked it that we lived right next to a playground.　　　　　　　(girl, 7)

> There's lots of playgrounds and places to play and there's loads of things to do 'cos there's not just, there's lots of trees to climb and sort of things, like, that you can do.　　　　　　　(boy, 7)

Playgrounds are an artificial environment, providing urban children with games. Playgrounds also provide space: they are usually set in larger parks, and for every child who appreciates playgrounds as a facility, there are many who like parks, the open spaces in or near towns reminding them of the open spaces of the countryside. When the effects of poverty, in terms of the communities of socio-economically deprived, are described, the lack of enough space, freedom to manoeuvre, the ability to be by oneself, is rarely explored. Lack of room has psychological as well as physical consequences. It is a matter of real significance to children. The sense of being unconfined, of being able to have choice, to discriminate between attractive spaces and unattractive ones, makes a strong impact on children's thinking. They associate particular places with particular threats, like a bus shelter full of drunks, or the bicycle sheds where certain bullies congregate. But they also see the symbolic need not to be cramped, or confined. They do not want physical confrontation any more than psychological confrontation.

Space, therefore, has obvious practical value. It allows children room to play with their friends and to have physical exercise. It is also valued almost for its own sake. The one commodity for which children long is space, inside and outside their homes. They make judgements based on space. They see their own inner and exclusive space as liberating them from the confinements of arguments, the proximity of quarrels. Space is one factor that separates the contented from the discontented.

Space remains both real and symbolic. The contented can cross boundaries, and enter into and appreciate other environments. The insecure find difficulty not just in travelling but in making an imaginative journey into other people's forms of thinking. It is possible to go from place to place in a group and learn nothing about the culture of the locality. It is also possible to have such a completely imagined world that the people beyond the narrow confines of one's own are defined as alien, as 'foreign demons' and in some subtle way subhuman. All these atavistic instincts are the result of the peculiar conditions of the home, the first locus of identity.

We have, then, three themes for understanding the development of prejudice. The first is the potential of observation, the ability, from an age when no one can explain it, to understand the points of view of others, and the untrustworthiness of those points of view. The second is the fact of relationships, the need for personal attention, for intellectual and not just emotional warmth. The family therefore is not only a source of the demonstration of human limitation, but a place of potential conflict, of rivalry and jealousy, of the desire to create a possibility of personal distinctiveness against others. The third strand is the translation of emotional hegemony into an environmental location; it is the outward manifestation of the instinct of space. Young children create their own understandings of the world in which they live. They have to make sense of the clues that come to them.[37] From an early age this either enables them to embrace the possibilities of difference, of separate identities, or makes them narrow and defensive, against others rather than for them.

References

1. Pinker, S (1997) *How the Mind Works*, Allen Lane, London
Donaldson, M (1978) *Children's Minds*, Croom Helm, London
Donaldson, M (1993) *Human Minds: An exploration*, Penguin, London
Cullingford, C (1999) *The Human Experience: The early years*, Ashgate, Aldershot
Dunn, J (1987) *The Beginnings of Social Understanding*, Oxford, Basil Blackwell, 1987.
2. Bruner, J (1974) *Beyond the Information Given: Studies in the psychology of knowing*, George Allen & Unwin, London
Bruner, J (1996) *The Culture of Education*, Harvard University Press, Cambridge MA.
3. Krull, R and Husson, W (1979) Children's attention: the case of TV viewing, in *Children Communicating: Media and development of thought, speech and understanding*, ed E Wartella, Sage, Beverley Hills
4. Wynn, K (1992) Addition and subtraction in human infants, *Nature*, **358**, pp 749–50
5. Parvio, A (1969) Mental imagery in associative learning and memory, *Psychological Review*, **76**, pp 241–63
6. Cullingford, C, op cit
7. Mehler, J *et al* (1988) Precursor to language acquisition in young infants, *Cognition*, **29**, pp 143–78
8. Norman, D (1969) Memory while shadowing, *Quarterly Journal of Experimental Psychology*, **21**, pp 85–93

9. Davis, J and Smith, M (1972) *Memory for unattended input, Journal of Experimental Psychology*, **96**, pp 380–88

10. Bruner, J (1996), op cit

11. Clark, E. (1972) On the child's acquisition of antonyms in two semantic fields, *Journal of Verbal Learning and Verbal Behaviour*, **11**, pp 750–58

12. Bates, E (1979) *The Emergence of Symbols: Cognition and communication in infancy*, Academic Press, New York

13. Donaldson, M (1993), op cit

14. Flavell, J *et al* (1992) Young children's understanding of different types of belief, *Child Development*, **63** (4), pp 960–77

15. Turiel, E (1983) *The Development of Social Knowledge, Morality and Convention*, Cambridge University Press, Cambridge

16. Webb, C (1998) *Young Children's Views of Social Behaviour*, University of Huddersfield, Huddersfield

17. Dunn, J, op cit

18. Furnham, A and Stacey, B (1991) *Young People's Understanding of Society*, Routledge, London

19. Cullingford, C, op cit

20. Cullingford, C (1999) *The Causes of Exclusion: Home, school and the development of young criminals*, Kogan Page, London

21. Macnamara, J (1982) *Names for Things: A study of human learning*, MIT Press, Cambridge, MA

22. Solomon, G *et al* (1996) Like father, like son: young children's understanding of how and why offspring resemble their parents, *Child Development*, **67** (1), pp 151–71

23. Cox, M (1991) *The Child's Point of View*, Harvester Wheatsheaf, London

24. Wellman, H (1990) *The Child's Theory of Mind*, MIT Press, Cambridge MA.

25. Jones, E and Davies, K (1965) From acts to dispositions: the attribution process and person perception, in *Advances in Experimental Social Psychology*, ed L Berkowitz, Academic Press, New York

26. Eisenberg, N *et al* (1995) The role of emotionality and regulation in children's social functioning: a longitudinal study, *Child Development*, **66** (5), pp 1360–84

27. Davies, B (1982) *Life in the Classroom and Playground*, Routledge and Kegan Paul, London

28. Coopersmith, S (1967) *The Antecedents of Self Esteem*, Freeman, San Francisco

29. Webb, C, op cit

30. Hart, R (1979) *Children's Experience of Place*, Irvington, New York

31. Cullingford, C (1991) *The Inner World of the School*, Cassell, London

32. DeLoache, J and Brown, A (1983) Very young children's memory for the location of objects in a large scale environment, *Child Development*, **54** (4), pp 888–97

33. Plumert, J, Ewert, K and Spear, S (1995) The early development of children's communication about nested spatial relations, *Child Development*, **66** (4), pp 959–69

34. Matthews, M (1992) *Making Sense of Place: Children's understanding of large scale environments*, Harvester Wheatsheaf, Hemel Hempstead

35. Spencer, C, Blades, M and Morsley, K (1989) *The Child in the Physical Environment*, John Wiley, Chichester

36. Bourdieu, P (1999) *The Weight of the World*, Polity Press, Cambridge

37. Bruner, J (1996) op cit

4

The divided world: perceptions of inequality

Societies, relationships and organizations

The experience of home could be likened to a tribal organization in miniature. There is a hierarchy and a jockeying for position. There is a sense both of personal ontological worth and a feeling of jealousy, of rivalry for attention, and of unfairness. Sometimes that all-embracing understanding of a collective sharing of values and importance can break down, not just at certain moments, which is the experience of everyone, but more permanently.[1] The experience of being in a group, in a social collective, defined against these 'others' who are outside, is strong. Just as there are categories of the physical and social world, so there are definitions of belonging and exclusion.

The archetypal organization of human beings remains, in one sense, the family. All the discriminations and the rivalries as well as the acceptances of authority are there. All studies of the ways in which organizations work, both large and small, find tensions between the mechanistic ways in which they operate – power, control, rules and duties – and the more complex fluid reality of ethos, of personal behaviours, of rivalries and particular cooperations. Managers, like politicians, would like to think that they can set up structures that will by themselves create the conditions for better performance. This might happen by chance but the reality of any organization is more chaotic. It depends on emotional and intellectual conditions that influence or undermine performance.

We need to remind ourselves of this fact, so extensively researched, since there is a tendency to see organizations as powerful means of persuasion, as if a manager were able, at a stroke, to cause fundamental change.[2] This assumption includes the demonstration of political will, as if one politician, one 'leader', were by him- or herself to manipulate the receiving minds of the followers. Nationalism and the sense of nationality can be culturally traced to a particular starting point, but there is a moment when the confines of the family are embedded in a larger sphere, where there are other families, and more anonymous encounters. But whilst small groups are physically observed, the fact of the existence of too many other people to know personally is one that also intrudes early. In early peoples such awareness of other people will have been passed on orally. Today, the intrusion of the outside world through the media is immediate and visual, lively and multifarious. The tribe will have known that there were aliens, others in the wider world. They bartered and they traded and set up systems to organize themselves so that they understood each other. They appreciated the differences of what others could organize. But apart from physical contact there was no daily sense of the intrusion of others. The understanding of the value of trade, both personal and commercial, was a gradual one. Young people had time to appreciate the different boundaries between groups.

The understanding of differences between those belonging to one's own family or group and those who are outside gives rise to the distinction between the private and the public. This has become the more marked as systems of mass communications have grown. It is argued that until the end of the middle ages there were no clear differences between public and private behaviour and morality.[3] It is only through the organized intervention of the modern state, with its police, moral or otherwise, that strong boundaries have been created. But we could argue that through mass communication systems this is no longer the case. The whole world intrudes on the consciousness of the young. Different people and national identities are constantly presented to them. This suggests a basic shift of emphasis in the way the social world can be understood. In the past there has been a strong sense of society as a hierarchy. As within the family, there is a particular individual who rules. Each person knows his or her place. As in most religions there is a sense of order, of command of leaders and authority over others. It might be one spiritual family but there is also obedience to shared beliefs. In the past the cohesion of society has depended largely on this hierarchical sense of order, and through the acceptance of different levels of power and influence, a sense of stability. Nowadays all are confronted by a mass of contradictory beliefs and behaviours.

Before the global communication system the sense of structure, even when disrupted, could be interpreted as a natural sense of belonging. The consciousness of the young today is essentially different. They see and know about others and their separate and complete systems. The whole world, in its variety of races and languages, is displayed before them. The sense that there is a natural hierarchy of order which surrounds them is replaced by the awareness that many different people have their own peculiar sense of order and meaning. Definitions of the self within the family are complex; but definition of the self against many others marks a shift of emphasis, from a simple reflective and atavistic sense of 'us' and 'them', to a greater confusion of 'thems'. There is more choice. There are so many other versions of the outside world.

The feeling for hierarchical organizations is challenged by relativism, by the sense of a variety of differences and distinctions.[4] There is an intrusion of other families, of different and conflicting beliefs. This might mean that there are clashes and a more defined sense of collective being, but it also gives an insight that others have their own peculiar and individual points of view. The understanding of the differences in attitudes to the truth is reinforced by the awareness of constant, global international arguments that take whole peoples into their domain.

Children's understanding of politics, of general social institutions, is not carefully fostered despite the confusion of information. It is acquired piecemeal through their perception of what is happening. Long before they can articulate the particular forms of social organization displayed in the political and legal systems, they experience their effect. They understand some of the complexities of political ideology before they command the language to describe them.[5] Long before they know the name of a temporary president or prime minister they are aware of their power, their limitations and their influence.[6] Politics, as in the politics of groups, of parties and of rivalries is of no real interest.[7] But children are aware of the power of those who have influence, and feel excluded from decision making.[8]

The social judgements of children depend upon their making sense of the mass of collective data that is set before them. The personal belonging to a family is set against the obvious fact that others belong elsewhere, not just as incomers, intruding occasionally into their personal space, but as genuine outsiders who are as proud of where they are from as anyone else. The social world is more and more diverse and relative, and each person forms his or her own coherent system of understanding the discriminations inherent in it.[9] Whilst the knowledge of the physical world is comparatively objective, the awareness of the social world is altogether more arbitrary, dependent not just on the chances of information received, but on the uses to which this information is put.[10]

The experience of children is therefore full of paradoxes. Children are at once the centre of attention but ignored. They have access to virtually all the information that is presented to adults, but little is explained. There are few concerted efforts made to involve children in the wider aspects of their own lives.[11] Children are asked to trust impersonal and abstract systems of organization, not, as in the past, with a belief that they are sacrosanct but with an awareness that they are the outward manifestations of arbitrary power, according to the chance of who is in a particular position at a particular time.[12] The same complexity of negotiation within family life is revealed in the workings of public dispute.[13] What we therefore see is children's attempts to make sense of a social world, beyond the confines of their family, a social world full of contrasts as well as paradoxes.

Fairness: personal and global

In children's own experiences one of the most important concerns for them is the concept of fairness. In the home the desire for personal attention is such that any sign of unequal response, of inconsistency, is resented. Why should some siblings gain advantage over others? Such a concern for smooth and equitable social relationships is naturally the more significant in school. Here the very organization depends both on different groups and on control. Fairness of treatment is a particular issue. There are other, deeper, concerns with fairness. These are not just to do with behaviour but ability. The fact that some children are able to do work faster and more easily and with more success than others, the fact that effort is not automatically linked to achievement, is something that can come as a shock when, by the age of eight, it is made apparent.[14]

Unfairness is also seen in the world outside. There are those who are successful and who achieve fame. There are pop stars and celebrated footballers, people of talent and good fortune. The contrasts could not be greater. These are not confined to the fortunate few. They are symbolic of the more everyday and widespread sense of disparity amongst all people. Some have larger houses and larger gardens. They have more money. Whilst this is rarely explained to children (perhaps it is, in a moral sense, inexplicable) it is closely observed by them.

The most obvious contrast in the observed world is between those who have and those who have not. There are many levels of international comparisons between the rich and the poor, and many examples in the more immediate environment. Beyond children's rivalry for emotional capital in the home lies a sense of comparison of their state against that of others. There is also a sense of contrast in the environment. There are those observed to be rich. These might be seen through the media but they are also observed at close quarters. Those who are poor, by contrast, have a more immediate impact on the experience of real life. They are rarely part of mass entertainment. But the contrast remains clear. Whilst there might have been a vertical hierarchy of power, control and wealth, into which everyone is slotted, there is for young people also an earlier and simpler contrast between the wealthy and the poor. Just as they understand the relativity of their own position in the family so they understand the many gradations of wealth, but they are most conscious of the differences. They are aware of the extremes, since these are imbued with symbolic value. Envy is the stuff of television entertainment: the desire to be wealthier, to win. On the other hand are stark warnings, often inadvertently through the news, of what to avoid. There are people, and conditions, to be rejected.

At this stage it is not a question of 'us' versus 'them'. This is the world as it is, taken in and analysed, consumed as information and ordered in a particular way. Such knowledge is acquired early: the basic political facts are absorbed a long time before they can be articulated.[15] The basic values that lead to tolerance and understanding or to antipathy and rejection are developed, without theory or expression, early on.[16] The first instincts that young people express are towards a sense of fairness: that the contrasts, in global and personal experience, are wrong. The contrasts are there, but the first reactions to them are not to endorse them, but to be concerned at them. Personal identity, the positioning of oneself *against* others, is still a private and almost secret function, without public expression. But it is informed by what is seen and experienced. The actuality of essential differences, of juxtapositions of power and possessions, is clear; but the choice is then whether these are matters of order and hierarchy, or whether they are unfair or a threat. The deeper question is where the individual fits in with such a world of contrasts. Before the distinctions that arise in school – in dress, ability and popularity – larger distinctions manifest themselves in the larger world. Television films contrast lives of squalor with the power of money, of abject poverty with extremes of self-indulgence. This is almost a neutral, an accepted fact for most young people, but the potential for an angry sense of injustice is there. Some can turn that into missionary instincts. Others take it more personally. The cry of 'unfairness' can have a deep pathological edge.

The 'rich' are presented to children, sometimes in the demonstration of some generosity, a member of the family, or an acquaintance, revealing the power of money to give pleasure, but more often the rich are some abstract and distant role made famous and public. Children's reaction to the notion of riches, that they mean social distinctions, leads to their sense that there is something emotionally flawed about such largesse in the hands of some people. That there are richer people than others, that there are huge gaps in the distribution of wealth, is clear, but children object not so much to the riches as to the emotional labels attached to them, to the sense of snobbery and superiority.[17] Whilst there is a jealousy of the rich, and a wish to be likewise, the essential moral position – prejudice – is against them.

> Some people are rich and some aren't. Well, I like watching these films about Robin Hood and that because they say 'rob from the rich to feed the poor'. And I think that the rich should give money to the poor to help them live and that. 'Cos they've got a lot of money and the poor people haven't. (boy, 8)

The ideal state of general human interaction is envisaged as equality, and fair distribution of wealth. Children express the view that there should not be too many contrasts, that there is a deep unfairness in the fact that some are so much richer than others. The sense of essential unfairness, of injustice, and that there are some who are deprived, is strong. Prejudice arises from personal threat and a desire to feel a sense of personal and collective authority. Contrasts in people's status and power is just one of these distinctions that can atrophy into a feeling of threat and envy. At one level children accept the fact of unfairness. This is how it is. But it always has the potential for anger, for envy and for a stronger sense of personal assertion, for the respect they think they deserve.

The rich are seen as spoilt. This is no simple matter of envy. There is more than a touch of resentment. There is a sense of personal alienation from the rich as if they were a kind of enemy, an identifiable group who through their own selfishness or greed choose not to help others. The chance of their position – for they are a group, a category – is associated with their desire for possessions. The idea of the 'entity' of being rich is therefore closely linked to a perceived moral failing as well as good fortune. The rich are typically observed as greedy.

> Rich, yeah, but I'm being greedy, you're being greedy if you want to be rich. I do want to be rich but I don't want to be greedy… I don't think they really care.
>
> (girl, 8)

The moment that others have responsibility on which they do not act, they become targets of a certain moral obloquy: they do not 'care'. So the rich, impervious, generalized, not associated with any particular social or racial group, are like an alien species. They are separate and different. But they are also clearly different from the way in which young people see their own relative selves. The rich are symbols of the divisions of the world, and are a constant reminder of the contrasts of circumstance.

The rich as symbolic and as real

Most people's experience of the rich is occasional and distant. They are a symbol of a divided world, of those who are privileged against those who are not. They are perceived as different, perhaps part of a hierarchy. Their wealth is a matter of chance, of random distribution. But it is also a symbol of distinctions, of control over power and possessions and of the potential of envy. Feelings about the *poor*, however, are far more distinct and personal. These are not people who are a matter of fame and information on the television or in newspapers. The poor are always with us. They are seen and they are experienced. They also help create a sense of social distinction.

In forming their views of the social framework of the world children are aware of the mixture of personal experience and secondary information. The outcome of their interpretations of the social world depend to a significant extent on the relationship between the two. Personal experience can be generalized into a broader reflection on the world if it is reinforced by the news, by documentaries and by conversations. On the other hand it is possible that children presume that what they know theoretically about the world does not apply to them. There are facts that are clear and understood – but these could apply to other people, or other countries. This constant shifting in the balance between experience and knowledge, between personal engagement and theoretical understanding, applies to a variety of subjects. As children make a map of their inner worlds they need to see it in relation to other people. The question is the extent to which they are able to relate their own individual needs to the needs of others. There is a desire to generalize from their knowledge, to be able to understand not just their immediate family and friends but how others behave and how others feel.

Whilst there is a constant interplay between different kinds of experience, the understanding that children acquire is full of emotional effects. Contrasts in styles of living cannot always be seen neutrally. Children's acquisition of social knowledge is a complex interaction between different levels of information, emotional and moral as well as cerebral. The world is seen as full of binary opposites – good and bad, rich and poor – whilst the children see themselves, and strive to be, somewhere in the middle.[18] Of course, being aware of their own circumstances, and those of their friends, they understand that the people who fit into the extremes are rare. Children after all never think of themselves as very good or very bad, and observe few of their friends as being so, especially very good. But they do realize that it is the extreme cases that form their framework of the world; the extremes, the opposites, clarify how they fit into the world.

Developing feelings towards the poor

Children's fear of being poor derives not so much from their own personal experience but what they observe. Whilst some of the children in this sample would be classified on any socio-economic scale as being poor, they do not see themselves in this way. Those whose parents earn considerably less than the average wage, and those with unwaged single parents still do not classify themselves as poor. They describe the circumstances of poverty clearly: the cramped conditions, for example, of which they are so aware. But they do not actually recognize themselves as poor. This is not because they hide it, even from themselves. It is because they genuinely see two different sides of the world that contrast with themselves. They see the very poor – which they define as having *no* house rather than a small one – and they recognize the difference between their actual conditions and the conditions in which they would *like* to live, as in the countryside. So they see the inadequacies of their own lives, and wish for better; but they also accept them. They recognize the contrasts between other people, but do not label themselves. This is as true of rich children as poor. They do not label themselves as wealthy – for they see there are others more wealthy than themselves.

No one wants to be poor, and no one sees themselves as poor even whilst they develop their understanding of what poverty means. Their view of the poor has something to do with a lack of social amenities, like a nice house or a car, and something to do with a lack of basic necessities, like food. But essentially the poor are seen as the homeless, the lost, the down-and-outs.

One of the reasons for interpreting the poor as being an extreme is because of the awareness by all children that such people exist, that there is a social system that allows contrasts. The very poor are also a constant feature of the information that children receive from television. There they are depicted in documentaries, in feature films and in the news. And the poor are universal.

> Some got money and some ain't. I don't like them eating beetles... I seen them on telly. Brown and black. I seen them on telly. Because they're poor. Because they ain't got no money. 'Cos I hear it on *Newsround*.
>
> (girl, 6)

One of the clearest images of the very poor comes from Africa. No one can forget the images of the starving. If *that* is poverty then they cannot say that they themselves are poor. For compared to the developed world the images of Africa with depictions of ragged clothes and deserts are consistently extreme.

> People with no homes, just rags on their clothes, fetching things from their homes. And their house is a bit, not very nice. Fetching things, like water from wells and rags for clothes.   (girl, 8)

> On the news I think there's, there's these people that don't have any clothing and they don't have food to eat. They're brown skinned and they don't walk properly. They don't have much food.   (girl, 8)

That is the image of Africa, as clear as an advertisement. There are diseases that strike them down. We will find that the idea of poverty, whilst reinforced by television images of other countries, lies much closer to home. The same girl who talks about the news depicting people without clothing goes on to say:

> Like they play instruments and they can get more money.   (girl, 8)

She immediately sees a link with the events pictured on television and the observations made on so many local street corners. The images of the developing countries contrast in many ways with the children's own world, but there are also some natural connections, so that poverty is confined not only to the sufferings of distant people but is applied to the equally visible people who inhabit city centres. Children are constantly confronted by all sides of the world, in its abject states as well as in its entertainment and self-celebration.

> You can see lots of people in the background trying to shelter from the sandstorms behind the pillars of shops and things like that.   (boy, 8)

'People in the background' make an impact on the consciousness of children. They are the unknown. Their personal sufferings are nevertheless understood.

Children accept poverty, up to a point, as something inevitable. This is certainly true of their views about Africa. There is little mention of the possibility of change there; and, as we will see, little real hope of change in their more immediate environment. But the developing world is clearly in a static state:

> They're poor. 'Cos they haven't got enough money. 'Cos the people who have babies didn't have much money 'cos they spent it. And they got poorer and poorer 'cos they didn't have any money and eventually they haven't got any money at all. Most of them don't wear any clothes.
>
> (girl, 7)

Visual images are important and influential. Poverty is when people look ragged. Poverty is also linked in children's minds with age.

> Sad people, unhappy. 'Cos they haven't got enough things. The old people. They can't get about as much as us. They're old. Most of them are old and they have torn clothes and sad faces. Wearing rags. They'd be freezing cold.   (girl, 8)

> I see people who are very old, that don't get much. And they haven't got homes so they have to live in cardboard boxes.   (girl, 7)

The imagery of the developing world includes as many dying babies as old people. Nevertheless the association between age and poverty persists; partly because of the children's interpretation of their personal experience in which the down-and-outs look old (and ragged).

Personal observation and the generalized 'others'

Personal experience plays a major part in children's assessment of poverty. They see the extreme edges of society in city streets: the homeless and the hungry. That is what defines the poor to them. There might be link images from television and from other parts of the world, but what really makes the question of poverty palpable and definable for children is the fact that they have *seen* it. Having seen poverty they also wish to define why it exists. They seek explanations for the fact that there seem to be so many beggars in the streets; their witnessing of the fact and their attempts to reason out an explanation go together. Whilst we show how children express their personal confrontation with poverty, it is important to remember that their visual descriptions are often followed by attempts to explain or justify poverty.

We will first take children's personal encounters. Through these they define poverty, not as an abstract definition but as a palpable experience. The visual image – of the homeless in cardboard boxes – is what is most telling, especially if it is seen in real life. Whilst we have noted the power of television imagery to give a general impression, children need to form their attitudes on personal events. One reinforces the other.

> We went into Mexico and people, because they didn't have any homes and shops, people were very poor.
> (girl, 6)

The 'other': personal experience goes deeper than a general impression or association. This is demonstrated by the way in which children talk for greater length about their own experience and fill their talk with attempts to explain. They do not just label, or repeat the most obvious images. They try to define the experience as well as relate it. They acknowledge the emotional effect as well as the fact.

> Someone on the streets in one of those sleeping bags. I thought about someone down the road… homeless. Down my road… I know the people on the street are poor but some, lots of people are poor.
> (girl, 8)

> People who carry their houses in carrier bags. There's just cardboard boxes. Just down the road from my house. It's an old lady. She normally walks past. And she wears plastic bags on her feet for shoes. Because she's hardly got any money.
> (boy, 8)

> Out in the street, maybe, with no money, lying in a shelter or something like that. Outside the library there's this old lady and she's been there since I first started the library. She's been there since I was about three. And

she's always hobbling round there with a trolley full of rags and clothes
and things.   (girl, 8)

The single experience of the old lady or the old man can be recalled in all its detail;
the clothes worn and the odd habits as well as the dirt. When children try to con-
jure up the idea of poverty they bring a particular individual to mind as symbolic of
the type.

I've seen men, a man and a lady with a dog around Waitrose and there's
this man called Swifty and he was a tramp. He lived in this house and it
was all messy and the people had to clean it up every so often.   (boy, 8)

I see people who are very old, that don't get much. And they haven't got
homes so they have to live in cardboard boxes. I saw one today. She was,
she had a stick. Although her eyes were open, really, her eyes were closed
because it's a bit hard to explain 'cos her eyes were open but she's blind.
                                                                       (girl, 7)

The question remains why there should be some who are down and out. 'Lots of
people are poor'. These images must have some explanation. One such experience
becomes symbolic of the others and is reinforced by images presented in films.
The recall of a particular incident does not mean that it is an isolated event, for
children realize that the poor are numerous. The fact that they have witnessed
them gives an extra edge to their knowledge. They can *prove* that they know about
the problem. But it also demonstrates how powerful is the personal experience.

There's people on the streets. When I went to London with my mum and
my mum's boyfriend and my brother we went past some of these shops
that had shut down and there were people kicking cardboard boxes and
people walking around.
    Ragged houses with smashed windows and people sleeping in card-
board boxes. In London. A lot. They're sitting on like dustbins asking for
money.   (boy, 8)

These are groups of the excluded. Children have to learn how to deal with the
emotional impact of those who display the results of unfairness or injustice. Even
if single episodes are an important factor in the formulation of children's views –
just as stressful events are – children are perfectly aware that these are not isolated
or exceptional phenomena. They expect to find similar sights all over the country,
just as they expect to see their picture of Africa confirmed by a visit. The difference
is that a visit to any large town in Great Britain *will* confirm their view of poverty.

There's people who've left home and they have no food or anything. In the streets. Everywhere in Britain. Everywhere really. They've got loads of bags. They look in dustbins. They wear baggy clothes. And they're dirty.

(girl, 8)

They had really dirty clothes. One of them had a trolley. No form of transport except their trolley and things like that.

(boy, 8)

This, then, is the image of the poor. They are the extremely poor, not just those who have to be careful with money, or live in council houses. Poverty to these children means not just poorer than themselves but the very poor. To be without money means to be down and out, to be homeless. It is as if in all the many differences between people it is the extremes that matter. The only response to this is some kind of personal exclusion of the emotions of pity or equity. How otherwise do they continue their daily rounds? These extremes underlie all other contrasts, and the complicated differences between people. For some the world is then simplified into a personal anger of 'me' against the others. Most children accept the relativities; they do not take it particularly personally. They might be comparatively poor or rich but they do not define themselves as such. But there can be a time when inequality can mean personal and simplified resentment, a realization of contrast turned into prejudice.

Giving reasons for social exclusion

What explanation do children give about the reasons for such contrasts? They clearly look on the poor with some measure of shock. They would hate to live like that. They need to come out with some explanation. When they do so they reveal how they see the poor as an inevitability: the poor are always with us. They also see the very poor as being as they are because of some personal crisis. We are not offered general political or sociological comment. The children do not have any broad social theory to explain the homeless. The reasons for poverty are personal, like being 'kicked out of home'. This suggests that while children do not feel poor themselves – nor are they in comparison with those they cite – they do have a sense that given some bad luck something of the same sort could happen to them. Sometimes the fact of homelessness and begging is seen to be the fault of the individual. Sometimes it is misfortune, a product of where the people happen to be. And sometimes it is a matter of choice, as depicted in a personal way.

It's like poor people might need help and some people 'cos they're poor, they just can't get round and that. People like grow up and go out of their home 'cos they don't want their mum and dad to look after them any more and they become poor and then they just lie on the streets with a blanket or two. Because they don't want to live with their mum and dad.

(boy, 8)

There are after all many stories of children leaving home, of running away, stories of alienation or exclusion that reverberate in all children's lives. One of the messages that children hear on the news is of young people leaving home to go to London, trying to acquire work and failing to do so. Poverty then seems like a personal choice. Other children, however, see homelessness as the result of people being 'kicked out'.

I think if someone throws them out of the house and then they just walk along the streets. They, their clothes just gets ripped. That's all. Oh yeah, me and my brother saw this homeless boy, so we gave him six pounds and fifty-five pee. So he just went off. He wasn't begging. He just had this 'homeless'. In the tunnel, London.   (boy, 8)

Mostly on the streets of London. 'Cos that's the main place. Because they're young people and they have, they go out and they think that the streets, they think that they're gonna get a big job, just pop out. But they find they don't. So they cannot make the money and also some people fall out with their mums and dads and go and try to find and look for a job and don't, so they have nowhere to live.   (boy, 8)

Such observations have a personal edge. The feelings of rejection and insecurity are understood. The transfer of money is no longer a theoretical stance. The reasons for such a condition relate to the children's attempts to understand in terms of their own lives. For all the association of the poor with the old, the attempts to understand homelessness in particular lead children to concentrate on the young, especially those who go to London. That is understandable. A choice is made, whether by the individual or their parents. It is a social phenomenon that does not need complex explanations. The connection between a general sense of unfairness and a personal choice is a potentially dangerous one. Pity might become annoyance, seeing the condition of poverty as self-inflicted, a matter of fault rather than chance. Trying to understand poverty does not demand particularly subtle analysis.

If you wanna pay your rent because if you can't if you haven't enough money to pay the rent and you really want something and you haven't got it and you haven't got enough money and you can't get it, that would be kind of poor.   (girl, 8)

The fact still remains that there are groups of people like that, in that condition. They have to be accepted. They could also be resented. Children's understanding of the exact meaning or value of money might be poor, but they do understand the difference between having enough money and not having enough. They might talk of their father being rich since 'I got like fifty pounds' (boy, 8), but they understand the idea of being poor, of not having enough money for the basic necessities. And they see the results.

> Someone on the streets in one of these sleeping bags... because they haven't got anywhere to stay. Because someone chucked them out or they just haven't got any money, so they can't afford a house. (girl, 8)

> She might have been robbed or she just didn't have, she spent all her money and not putting any in the bank. People who can't afford to buy food and can't afford to buy a house or anything. (boy, 8)

There are many definitions of what it means to be poor – not buying a house is at a very different level from not buying food. But this indicates something about the symbolic value of money and of the association of poverty with homelessness. Not being able to buy things is the emotional side of poverty. Whilst children do not think of themselves as poor in relation to others, they do understand the meaning of this kind of deprivation. What children see is the extension of this lack, its extreme form.

> Maybe she's got no money and she can't really pay for a home, so they won't give her one. And maybe she grew up in an orphanage or something.
>   Some poor people actually have a home and food but they can't really afford very much money. But some poor people are poor because they've got nowhere to live or they've got no food or people to turn to and tell them what they feel like or something. (girl, 8)

It is very hard to be able to define why some people have no money. Personal choice seems to enter into it as if there were something to do with the character – 'Do you sincerely want to be rich?', 'Do you really want to be saved?' – or it could just be the downward spiral, that continuation of personality and events that marks out the individual's life.

> He can't find a job anywhere 'cos people don't normally give jobs to people that can't have good clothes.
>   They start off rich, they leave, they forget about getting a job, and they can't get a job, then, and they can't get it. It's probably their fault. It's more their fault than anyone else's and it might be their fault. (boy, 8)

Conditions and personal choice

Children do not see people as helpless victims any more than they see themselves like that. They have too much a sense of their own autonomy – the inevitability of being themselves. And yet they accept that some people end up without anything, with no possessions let alone a job. At the same time the children stress the inexorability of the process. Once without a job, once a drop-out, once poor, it is assumed that people will stay like that. As in the case of the inevitability and changelessness of the state of Africa, as perceived by children, so they do not expect there is any real chance of changing conditions, of upward mobility as well as downward. The world is seen as a static state. The explanations for poverty are therefore the more simple. This is how things are.

> There's people who've left home and they have no food or anything.
> (girl, 8)

> If you don't have money then you can't buy things. You can't buy your food so you can't survive.
> (boy, 8)

The idea of leaving home reminds us of the way in which children, however poor or even critical, associate their home with some kind of base. They might not all feel utterly safe or secure against burglars, but it is better than being out in the street. Home is the centre, the almost laconically accepted centre, of their world.

In a short distance from the children's centre of the world are the very poor. Their presence pervades the children's consciousness. They look on them with a certain bewilderment and distaste. They evince sympathy but also a sense of distance. These people have 'left home' and are short of money; that is how it is. When it comes to explanations for this the children think of personal reasons without any hint of analysis of social conditions. The condition is part of the personality. There are signs of a more subtle distancing of people into groups. Beyond the stark contrasts lie personal responsibility as well as personal chance. This mixture of acceptance of the case and sympathy leads children to think in terms of charity. Money can be raised in all kinds of ways.

> I had all these He-Man figures and in the end the whole collection and there's over a hundred things to get and I didn't want them and my mum thought I was really kind. I gave them all to this sick home. The children have got no mothers but that's not really poor, but sort of, you know, they haven't got very much.
> (boy, 9)

There is a streak of sadness and pity that lies behind children's close observation of the poor. They would *like* to give money. Whilst they see them as part of the social condition, they are still seen not as a result of socio-economic circumstances but of more personal fate and choice.

> Really sad, things like people sometimes say 'there's a twenty pound note'. And I feel quite happy when I give the money for really poor things.
>
> (boy, 8)

> I feel quite sad 'cos I feel quite rich and they feel that I'm the king or something and they're like slaves and things. I wouldn't like to sleep in a cardboard box and get cold on freezing cold nights. (boy, 8)

> I just wish I could do something for all those poor people in Africa and in this country, really. But there was this lady who used to live in our house and she, well... it's to help poor people and they don't even know she's dead yet. So they send letters to her asking for money to give to the poor. They didn't even know she's dead so we got a letter one day and we opened it and it said blah blah blah and then it said 'We are now serving some poor people in Monte Carlo' and there are hardly any poor people in Monte Carlo really. (girl, 8)

There is an acceptance that the poor need charity, and an implication that this is done not by the State but by private agencies. It is a response that shows the balance of sympathy with acceptance of the facts. There is, after all, clearly in children's minds the contrast between themselves and the very poor. They would not like to be like them. All the children who live in towns or have visited towns can remember signs of extreme poverty, reinforced by the pictures that are sometimes shown on television, or advertisements by charitable agencies. They also hear of social problems both here and abroad through their church or school. Whilst these events are not in themselves of the same significance as observation, they do reinforce knowledge and feelings of charity. It is as if there were a permanent and fixed imbalance in the world that is a structural unfairness.

The experience of contrast lies between pictures of whole nations, or continents, and between people within the same country. They are two quite different sets of groups. They are categories of a clear kind, and easily turned into a sense of fear, threat or superiority over people in different conditions. They reinforce each other, and underlie the distinctions between people.

The poor are defined by children as the homeless, the tramps and the beggars. Ordinary everyday poverty is not seen by them to have the same significance when compared to the extremes, the images of penury here and abroad. It is people living on the street who are seen to be poor, with the occasional exception:

There's people, I won't say they're poor but they don't have bags of money…

I suppose some of the teachers. They don't get very well paid, with all their sixty-year-old minis. Like Mrs –. She's got a Ford that's about a hundred years old.   (boy, 8)

Of course the hierarchies of distinction include that most observed group of official people, the teachers. They are acknowledged as being at once in a position of power, of authority over the pupils, and also despised for earning so little. Teachers' places within hierarchies of authority are also clearly observed. They might be in charge of a class, but they are observed to be ruled by the head teachers, who are in turn ruled by governors. And all are seen to be terrified of inspectors. Thus the realities as well as the symbols of power are closely scrutinized.[19]

Money and the structure of society

Money is one symbol of power. It is not always clear to children how it operates but that it makes a difference to people and causes clear demarcations is important. In one sense the contrasts between rich and poor are almost a neutral, impersonal factor. They are not a matter of personal prejudice. They are simply the way the world operates. Children accept differences. They have moral views about these differences. They want to be neither too poor nor too rich. They therefore create for themselves a desire to be neutral, to be secure without prejudice. They seem to hold on to a moral centrality of open acceptance in the face of all the information given to them. But this very neutrality can be overcome by prejudice as they get older, and as they experience more personally the consequences of inequality. Children might seem to start with an open mind. The education system might ostensibly be designed to foster social understanding. But for many prejudice feeds on the reality of social distinctions.[20]

One of the problems with understanding the bases of nationalism, clearly an artificial construct according to particular cultural norms and propagandas, is the sense of the inevitable, of some atavistic force that directs attention in a particular way. Similarly, racism appears to be constructed upon a narrow definition of obvious difference.[21] But these are constructs; they are built upon a far more general attitude towards difference. They are lubricated by the distinctions between those who have power and those who do not. They are formed by the far more neutral understandings of the way in which the social world operates. The social world has, of course, several levels of communication. There are verbal interactions at a variety of levels, but there is also the transaction of money.

Money, with its power and inequitable distribution, seems a passive or neutral factor. But it is also a potent means of displaying differences. It is an emblem.

The poor are particularly and appropriately sensitive about money.[22] Some would argue that it is only they who need to be, although it could also be concluded that those who care about money the most are rewarded for their acquisitiveness. Children understand the importance of possessions, of knowledge as well as power, of holding on to identities as well as the manifestations of a group. They might not understand the way in which the economic outcomes of such distinctions operate but they do know the consequences. About money itself they can be very vague. But they are not vague about its symbolic values. Money, as a form of socio-economic transaction – a bartering between people, a social interchange that transcends personality and family – is a symbol of generalized communication. There are many levels to the understanding of money. It is freely available. It also acquires things and is of central and palpable importance. [23]

Children experience the power of money and the differences it can make long before they fully understand how it operates.[24] Money is a very emotional subject long before it becomes an economic one. We have to remind ourselves that many a social prejudice or stereotype is based not just upon power, or threat or weakness, but a possession. Money is a symbol of distinction. It makes lines of demarcation within as well as between societies.

Children have two strong motivating forces that form the background to their attitudes to money. The first is their fear of poverty. The second is their suspicion of the rich. Their attitude to money is also ambivalent. They know they need it, but do not know how much they need. They see themselves as inhabiting the same role as they play with their peers: going to neither extreme, having neither two little nor too much, being neither too slow or too clever, popular but not a show-off. There is a sense in which they wish to avoid extremes, poverty for obvious reasons but also riches, as if that were somehow a mark of false superiority. The irony is that they do not understand very clearly how money works, and what values mean, but they do like what money does.

The conception of money and possession reflects the children's sense of the two extremes, or the vast contrasts between the very rich and the poor. They see symbols of this on the television as well as in the street, in other countries as well as their own.

> Well, the white, the rich ones live in nice houses and poor ones live in mud houses. Because the poor ones the white are pushing, the white people don't like the black people. They think they are different to them, knock their houses down and kill them. I've seen on the news, I've seen the white people killing the black people and I've seen what happened there. The poor, they wear old raggy clothes. The rich, nice clothes.
>
> (boy, 7)

Contrasts are as simple as black and white or the rich man in his castle, the poor man at his gate. Possessions, like houses and clothes, are symbols of these contrasts. Seen in those terms there is bound to be more sympathy for the downtrodden than for the oppressors. Children would hate to be poor themselves but they feel sorry for the poor. They often say that if they themselves were rich they would give their money to the poor. They feel that this is so strong a duty that the rich would then no longer be the same, as if the rich were rich because they are uncharitable. This is one reason why the very rich are despised, and closely associated with snobbery.

> They'd probably be posh. Because I think of posh people as rather snazzy people and I don't like being rather snazzy.   (boy, 8)

> You have to be good and you help people. You make money and get money and then send it to the people that are poor. I don't like, I don't get all the money and keep it and say 'Oh, I'm gonna give it to the poor' and then I keep it for myself.   (girl, 7)

Real charity would mean giving enough away not to remain rich. It indicates both a perception of the moral side of money and its uses and a misunderstanding about its function. The assumption that children make is that the supply of money is limited – that it would not take much for the rich to dispose of their income. The concepts of assets and interests does not seem to be applied.

Money, envy and antipathy

Children wish to have enough to acquire what they need. They assume that if they had more they would be under a moral obligation to be charitable, to help towards the equality of circumstance, to overcome the contrasts. As long as they have enough to spend on food and clothes they feel that their essential needs are catered for. They might not like the place they live but they take it for granted. They do not speculate about ownership or mortgages. They see the differences between large houses and small, but however modest or substantial their own house they never see it as a symbol of riches or deprivation. Like parents, the house is just 'there'.

What children *do* appreciate, however, is the power of money to buy things. It is the possessions that count, rather than the more abstract notion of money and exchange. Buying things is the clear function of money. If you have enough you can buy whatever you want:

> You can buy nice things like China. China has got quite nice things, like all sorts of china pieces like dishes, bowls, glass bells and things, for children. And I bought these earrings and this nice bow.   (girl, 6)

> Well I've got some nice toys and we've got everything that you would like. Everything you need.   (boy, 8)

On the other hand the lack of money leads to a need to control greed, if not desire.

> If you don't have much money and you wanted to get something and then you got it and then you want something more, you couldn't get it, but if you were rich, you could just get it.   (girl, 8)

> So I can spend things and stuff, and when I go past shops and think Oh! I really like that but I can't buy it.   (girl, 8)

Generally children feel they have enough, but they are still tempted by possessions. They might not think of themselves as desiring much more but all are tempted by the possibility of buying things. The majority of children express acceptance with their lot. They do not indicate a sense of envy or insecurity, and do not indicate that this might lead them into a positive hatred for the inequalities of society. But the evidence is there. They have ammunition if a personal sense of grievance takes a social, general form.

Given the amount of advertising of desirable toys on television, and given the peer pressures of fashion, it is not surprising that children should have an interest in material possessions. Indeed, they associate some of the 'good' places in the world with riches. The United States is the haven of possessions.[25]

Personal and fashionable possessions are significant but even when associated with the countries they come from they can symbolize too much riches. Germany, for instance, is characterized thus:

> They don't like cheap things. They like valuable things so they have watches that are gold and they like that sort of thing.   (girl, 6)

This is one of the triumphs of advertising: a deliberate stereotyping by association of a country with technical quality. Possessions as a symbol of riches can come in a variety of forms, in houses and in cars and swimming pools. The most pervasive form of possessions, however, lies in giving and receiving presents.

> The best thing I have done is save up for ages to buy my mum a Christmas present.   (girl, 11)

I've just got the present that I really liked. And before, my mum and dad said they couldn't get it because they didn't have enough money and then my nanny, 'cos she didn't buy me a present she gave some money towards it and then they had enough to buy it and I really liked it.   (boy, 8)

Whenever I ask for a present I really want I usually get it. And also at Christmas. I have about four bags, giant bags filled with presents.
(boy, 8)

The meanings of financial systems

What money is capable of doing, buying things that are necessary or desirable, is clear. What remains far more hazy for the children is the way that money works and how much a particular amount of money means. They see the symbols of wealth; they know what a gold watch, for example, stands for. But they are unable to place a value on it. Children know about the everyday fact of pocket money and what they can do with it, but they are unable to clarify what would be a good income. Whilst they realize the importance of accumulating enough money to buy a house, they have little idea of how much a house costs. They have, in fact a very limited grasp of the capitalist system, of market forces and the meaning of amounts of money. They are aware of the *power* of money but cannot put this awareness into numerical terms.

The currency is sort of higher. It's 124 yen or something for like one pound. I wonder how they got up that high in the first place. I just think it's weird how they got up there in the first place. Their currency went up there just like that.   (boy, 9)

Just as children are knowledgeable about different languages they have an awareness of different currencies. They know about the power of money but not exactly what this means.

'Cos they got dollars and I like dollars. 'Cos they're different than pounds. You see, I wanna see a dollar.   (boy, 8)

When it comes to significant amounts of money children are very vague. About small amounts, like pocket money, they are far more precise. But riches is a fluid concept and they quickly accept that they do not know.

And then he got there in two weeks and he won loads and loads of money.
(girl, 7)

And for the massive businessman, he'd want buckets full. But you only need about ten pounds a week to live if you have a simple diet, eat only what you need. You don't need much to live on. (boy, 8)

Not only are their concepts about large amounts of money fairly vague, but the children also show almost a distaste for knowing too much about 'filthy lucre'. When large amounts of money are mentioned it becomes associated with extravagance. They confess they do not know much about it.

It is important to have some though. To buy clothes and things with. And houses and things like that. I don't know much about money.

(boy, 8)

I want to have, er, not a lot of money but enough money. I don't find much interest in money. Because it just winds me up really. I get confused and I count it and I count it again and then I lose some and go down to the shop and buy something and I found out I haven't got enough money, and I have to put it back and I'm quite upset that I can't buy it. So I don't really find much interest in it. (boy, 8)

This expresses anything but a lack of interest. The lack of money is painful. The lack of knowledge of the precise details of money does not mean that the need for money is not acknowledged. Children do not find the idea of earning money difficult, nor that money is necessary in order to buy things; they see the very poor enough to remind them of the fact. But they do not know what constitutes an average income, as if no one had ever explained the way in which the economic system works. They remain at the edges, seeing on the one hand the big symbols of money, but only being allowed to handle the small amounts. On the one hand they try to guess what a large amount would consist of.

Well, you have to have money to have a business. The business gives you money. The money gives you things to eat and keeps you alive. Average would be £200. About a month, or £300, £200, £300. And that would probably keep you alive.

If you have to hire a house and then you have to earn money to give to the people to let you hire the house 'cos to make up the time that you've hired it. And if you're poor and you don't have a house in the end and you've just got to live in the street. And probably finish off the food which is in your house and then you just have to live in the streets. (boy, 7)

It is about small amounts of money that children are taught. Pocket money seems to be part of an initiation ritual, a glimpse into the world of financial transactions.

There is a significant gap between some of the conceptions that underlie money – the necessity for it and the means to buy things – and the lack of precise knowledge of how money works. The small amounts, like coins, are understood and have no doubt been explained, but not, it seems, the economic system. And yet the basic principles – the difference that money makes and the contrast between rich and poor – are deeply embedded in children's minds. Money is seen to be a safety net. It needs to be there in case of emergencies or else they will be on the street.

> Obviously you've got to build up your money to pay the rent and things like that. And I think as I got more money then I wouldn't buy loads of things and then save it up and buy a big house and then stay at that for the rest of my life. Unless something drastic happened.   (boy, 8)

> So that I would be, well, not poor but so I can stash some money somewhere if ever I need it for emergencies and I would be short of money really. You need money to pay the gas bills so you can still have your light or electricity or something. If there's no electricity and you have no money you could not have fires because you would not have the money to make fires or you would not have the money to buy the coal to light the fires.
>   (girl, 8)

Children mention the obvious needs, like food and clothing and shelter. They are also very aware of the threat of homelessness. The need to pay the bills and keep up with the rent is paramount. The connection between possessions – material goods – and the *necessity* of having enough money is made by the concern with housing. Money buys shelter.

> If you don't have money you can't live and you wouldn't be able to work, you wouldn't be able to have a house 'cos you wouldn't be able to earn the rent and stuff like that.   (girl, 8)

> I don't think I'd have the money to live in a house. I just think I'll be living in a flat.   (girl, 8)

Put in these terms – what would happen if they didn't have money – children readily understand the system. But they have far less grasp of how the system works – how capital is accumulated or borrowed. They also do not know how much particular amounts mean. There is, however, one exception to this. One of the children interviewed knows exactly what things are worth – this boy knows what his shoes cost, what a good pair of shoes would cost, what he would do with the money. This is the boy who is shaping up to be a future criminal.

Notions of capitalism, like democratic politics, or the legal system, can be very complicated. Some understand the way in which the constitution works far better than others, but all are equally affected. Children learn to make sense of their experience. They know that their own involvement, at home with their possessions, or at school in the hierarchies of power, is of a particular kind. But the larger society impinges on them and they try to make sense of it.

This results in some studied simplifications. Children have to categorize, to see the major distinctions, the essential ways in which society operates. They note the contrasts, and the possibilities of exclusion. These differences are at once close to them and generalized. Whilst they find their own position in what they observe quite complex and quite relative, the possibilities of being set *against* other groups, either through envy or distaste, are already before them. Prejudice against sections of society can go either way, into an envy of those who are more successful or better off, or more adaptable, or a sense of discomfort or even loathing of those who are so poor that they could be dangerous.

References

1. Cullingford, C (1999) *The Causes of Exclusion: Home, school and the development of young criminals*, Kogan Page, London
2. Cohen, M and Marsh, J (1974) *Leadership and Ambiguity*, McGraw-Hill, New York
3. Elias, N (1982) *The Civilising Process*, Blackwell, Oxford
4. See the books on scientific realism and chaos theory.
5. Melton, G (1993) Young children's political rights, *Childright*, **93**, pp 17–19
6. Cullingford, C (1992) *Children and Society*, Cassell, London
7. Bulman, J et al (1992) *Careers and Identities*, Open University Press, Milton Keynes
8. Cullingford, C (1973), op cit
9. Turiel, E (1983) *The Development of Social Knowledge*, Cambridge University Press, Cambridge
10. Furnham, A and Stacey, B (1991) *Young People's Understanding of Society*, Routledge, London
11. Qvortrup, J (1995) Childhood in Europe: a new field of social research, in *Growing up in Europe: Contemporary horizons in childhood and youth studies*, eds Chisholm, L et al, de Gruyter, Berlin
12. Chisholm, L (1995) in Chisholm, L et al, op cit, pp 21–34
13. Büchner, P (1995) in Chisholm, L et al, op cit, pp 43–60
14. Cullingford, C (1999) *The Human Experience: The early years*, Chapter 6, Ashgate, Aldershot
15. Melton, G, op cit
16. Whitmarsh, G (1974) The politics of political education, *Journal of Curriculum Studies*, **6** (1), pp 133–42

17. Simmonds, C and Wade, W (1985) Young peoples' least ideals in five countries, *Educational Review*, **37** (3), pp 289–98

18. Cullingford, C (1999) *The Human Experience*, op cit

19. eg Cullingford, C (1991) *The Inner World of the School*, Cassell, London, for children's analysis of power, and *An Inspector Calls: The effects of Ofsted on schools* (1999) London, Kogan Page, for observations of teachers' experience of inspection.

20. Toivonen, K and Cullingford, C (1998) Racial prejudice in a liberal democracy: a case study, *Politics, Groups and the Individual*, **7** (1 & 2), pp 45–56

21. As in the experience of National Socialism.

22. Billig, M (1995) *Banal Nationalism*, Sage, London
Garner, P, Jones, D, and Miner, J (1994) Social competence among low-income preschoolers: emotion, socialisation practices and social cognitive correlates, *Child Development*, **65** (2), pp 622–37

23. Firth, H (1980) *The World of Grown Ups*, Elsevier, New York

24. Holroyd, S (1990) Children's development in socio-economic ideas: some psychological perspectives, in *Economic and Industrial Awareness in the Primary School*, ed A Ross, NELP

25. See Chapter 6

5

The sense of self in the environment

Personal and social landscapes

Whether depicted on the television news or other programmes, or experienced personally, the environment is not just a background for personal feelings and understandings. It is something that demands constant engagement. It is not an imaginary landscape but a place of personal exploration. The environment, like cultural geography, is a matter of relationships, with and between people. Whilst there are symbolic spaces and whilst buildings and neighbourhoods have their effects, they are given meaning by the way in which each individual makes sense of them in his or her own way. The need to discriminate continues. The relationship between personal position, understanding and a map of the outside world is central. Any relationship is more than an iterative communication with one other; it is a shared insight into something else. 'Place' or 'environment' is not an abstract concept but the ground of social development.

Children's sense of themselves is always formed by, as well as juxtaposed to, the social world that they observe. They see the personal meaning and the status of others, of the rich and the poor, and of the hierarchies of power. Nowhere is this more apparent than in schools. These combine two of the most significant aspects of experience and understanding. One is the formal social system of rules, obedience to authority, discipline and order. The other is the undercurrent of complex and sometimes violent relationships. The rules that support the hierarchy are needed because of the volatility beneath the surface.[1]

The sharp and precise gaze that children bring to the social institutions they experience is one that can be likened to an hierarchical map: an instinct that everyone has his or her place. They see not just in terms of a mental map, but of a fluid movement of people in relation to each other. They observe power, however subtle. They see people who both try to hide their effects on others in politeness, and who wield it at what are deemed appropriate times with a cutting edge that is sharp and hurtful. Most of the time this power is directed at the weakest in the hierarchy of the institution, the pupils, but it is also a struggle between the teachers, those in authority. Just as some teachers are seen to be weaker than others in their relation to pupils, so their relationships with each other are observed. This is not a matter of status, but an observation of how, in adults in institutions, groups are formed, and latent opinions revealed. There are groups who are 'in' power and those who are 'out' of it.[2] The environment is observed, actively engaged in, and made systematic. There are places (and people) to avoid, and places of safety and security.[3] The relationship between a child and the environment as it is observed is a form of cultural conditioning.[4] Certain places are associated with fear, like dark or derelict places, symbols of oppression; and others are reinforced and associated with parental fears, of traffic or the dangers of falling or drowning.[5] There are different ranges of exploration of the world, from the habitual, the everyday and that seen presented in domestic comfort on television, to the occasional and far distant, experienced as on a holiday.[6] All these experiences are a continuation of direct experience, visual and kinetic, and the indirect, of the absorption of ideas, attitudes and stereotypes, through interpersonal or mass communication.[7]

Sensitivity to the environment, and the meaning of the environment in the larger sense, is well established in children by an early age.[8] Their understanding of 'green' issues, of matters of sustainability and pollution, demonstrates an ability to understand political issues. The same awareness of different points of view between individuals is applied to groups of people, or nations, expressing disagreement about major global issues. Children understand the fact that these are *shared* points of view. This makes the idea of the relativity of an idea more powerful. People express an act or an intention from the shared position they come from. Whilst this can be from an authoritative position, say from a teacher, it can also be from a group, such as a gang of bullies. The neutral awareness of different points of view becomes translated both into statements of collective self-interest and into the sense of good causes and immoral actions. Children feel strongly about many of these issues. They might not find them deeply explored in school, as being too controversial, but they are not only aware of the issues but have clearly stated opinions, especially about those on which it is easy to take sides.[9]

The school curriculum might not pay much more than lip-service to personal and social education or to the meaning of citizenship, but schools themselves are powerful if unselfconscious purveyors of social meanings. This is not only a matter of the organizing of large crowds of people into groups, and moving them from place to place, nor a matter of power and command, but a sense of place, of some parts of the school being associated with particular events and attitudes. As well as personal experiences there is the need to give general symbolic values to particular places, so that a cultural map in which types of people are associated is created. The typologies of riches and power, of bully and victim, are translated into distinct, less personal places. Children perceive school as much more controlling than the home: whilst offering activities and being the main social centre, school remains a place of constraint, with less freedom of movement.[10]

Schools also demonstrate the transmission of values through the environment. Pupils observe when there is clear neglect, or if there are attempts to care for the spaces both within and outside the buildings.[11] Physical factors are linked to social and cultural factors, so that there is a sense of meaningful boundaries and places.[12] Just as observers of effective schools note down the number of thriving potted plants as an indication of intellectual health (a correlation, not a cause), so children perceive the ethos of the place from its manifestations.[13]

The social symbolism of the school

Attending school gives children their first opportunity to observe a social system in action and to become part of it. They will have already experienced a variety of relationships with other children and with adults, and have imbibed some notion of social hierarchies. By the time they attend school, they are aware of social stereo-typing, like the association of doctors with men, and nurses with women, so that their observation will have been primed for the first visit. But school demonstrates two important social phenomena for the first time. Children observe both the need for rules and order, and the dependence on a hierarchy.[14] It is clear that they are aware of the latter: not only of the relationships between adults and children, but between adults of differing importance. They know not only about the status of the dinner lady against that of the teacher, but also of that of the teacher against the head teacher. Furthermore, children rapidly become aware that even the head teacher is not an autonomous power but is answerable to other shadowy figures, like governors.

Children see school as a formal system, with each person given certain, and different, responsibilities. They also recognize the importance of the rules that make the whole system work. They are, indeed, adamant that without clear rules that all obey, the school's internal system would break down. They subsequently apply this observation to society as a whole.[15] It could be argued that their strongly conservative sense of the need for law and order, for the social control of otherwise unruly people, derives from their experience of school. This sense of rigid hierarchy certainly lends itself to the demarcation of society into groups: those formally in control and power, and the anti-establishment culture that is hidden but potentially far more powerful. Normally the two sides maintain a balance, an equilibrium of sorts. Sometimes the formal system can submerge all opposition. Sometimes the counterculture of the majority can prevail.[16]

The school is a formal social system. There are rules and expectations, a clear agenda and an attempt to make all pupils and staff share a common purpose and a common morality. There are hidden and implied rules as well as those clearly stated. There is a great deal of emphasis placed on groups and the behaviour of groups, whether these are small, for the purpose of working together, or large, as in assemblies. The system of schooling is clearly laid out, like an incipient pattern of groups and hierarchies of power.

The formal and hidden agendas of the school

There is another important and alternative system that children experience in parallel with that of the school. This is the system of relationships: the forming of friendships and enmities, the social discovery of pupils in relation to each other. This system is the most important for many children, for it includes the pressure and influence of peers. The social system of children dominates all the areas outside the formal curriculum. It operates in the playground and at break times. It continues, under cover, in the work of classrooms. It spills over into life away from school. Many of the real tensions and difficulties, as well as the pleasures of school, arise from this system of relationships.

The formal and informal social systems associated with school overlap. This can be undermining. It is possible to trace the development of truants to the way in which one system – formal schooling – is rendered powerless in the face of the other – the pressure of peers and the forming of gangs.[17] The ways in which children test the formal system in their relationship with teachers shows how powerful and influential is the alternative one and how aware all children are of their own culture as well as that of the school.[18] The widespread occurrence of bullying and teasing is all part of the hidden informal life of a school, although it does not need such obvious symptoms to detect children shying away from the real demands of school.

For children the network of relationships outside as well as within the classroom is an extremely important part of school, and for some the most important. When they describe the experience of school, they concentrate on the social factors: the emotional effects of relationships made the more complex by the competitiveness of which they are all aware. There are, in fact, two overlapping themes that keep emerging from their descriptions of school life: intense relationships, including bullying, and self-conscious awareness of their own work performance in relation to that of others.

There is a constant juxtaposition in the experience of school of the demands of the classroom and the pressures of relationships. When children explore their experience they are far more concerned with the latter than the former, even when they talk about the curriculum. The children cited here were not invited to comment at any length on the curriculum or on teaching styles, so that the evidence that emerges is interesting in its bias away from the formal experience of school: writing, fulfilling the demands of the teacher and working together. There is a commonly observed phenomenon when children are asked, perhaps by their parents, what they did in school. The answer is often 'nothing' or 'don't know'. It is as if the world of schooling was separate or shut off, or just too boring to talk about. In these interviews there was no unwillingness to talk. What children felt to be most important and what they wished to relate was the emotional experience of school rather than the formal curriculum. What is learnt at school, often cited as the hidden curriculum, is the powerful impact of social relationships and inter-personal power.

The open and closed curriculum

This does not mean that children do not talk about the curriculum at all. Sitting in classrooms undergoing arithmetic is a part of their experience. They do talk freely about it, but what emerges is a sense of the arbitrariness of the curriculum. When they talk about particular subjects they are chiefly aware of whether they are good or bad at them, and whether they are better or worse than others. When they talk more neutrally about the academic experience the focus of attention is more on topics.

> We were talking about different countries and the most countries we were talking about were Germany and India. But this year we're talking about chocolate.
> (boy, 8)

> We did something about the Celts. And we're doing about France.
> (girl, 8)

There are different levels to children's experience. On the one hand they are 'doing' certain subjects. Mentioning them seems to be enough. On the other hand they are experiencing the pressures of doing well or badly. Most parents will receive a first level answer to what they did in school: 'We did cooking'. It could be an unwillingness to cross the boundaries into a different world but, given the chance to talk, what emerges is neither shyness of communication nor a desire to please but a genuine sense of bewilderment. Inadvertently, the subject matter of school is revealed as having no underlying meaning. When the pupil goes home and cannot articulate what they have learnt it is because they have not been told the meaning or purpose of the experience they are undergoing. They are 'doing' things, being kept busy. They are given facts on which to add to their mental structuring of the world and their unique place in it, but they are not supported in deriving meaning from these facts. Prejudice is often linked to ignorance. Pupils here do not lack knowledge. Information abounds. But it does not seem to relate to them, as if they are encouraged to use their own prejudices to make sense of what they learn. Prejudice can be fed by selected knowledge.

The laconic depiction of the experience of school is of 'doing' something. Certain teachers introduce topics:

> But in Mr N. when you get to his class you will talk about Germany. Because they do Science and about countries... (girl, 6)

> We're doing a topic on America. (boy, 8)

> At the moment we're doing about South America. There's 22 countries in it. (girl, 8)

Subjects are 'covered' and there is little further detail or analysis of the experience of 'doing the topic'; that analysis appears in a different context and is rarely related to a particular subject as such. Sometimes a particular experience is picked out.

> When I was in Mrs C's class we all dressed up like and we did dancing and we had funny sort of clothes on. (girl, 9)

Sometimes a teacher is remembered for a particular enthusiasm.

> At my old school in the last class when I had just become eight my teacher was very interested in Green things. And I remember a couple of girls in my class; they set up this jumble type thing and they just gave the money they'd take to Miss C...
> And also we did projects on like extinct animals. I keep all my exercise books I take home. I've got a massive basket full at home. And I've still got the project book and I've drawn pictures of dodos and seals and everything. (boy, 9)

Such a marked enthusiasm for certain projects is significant in its rarity. The occasions on which children talk with relish about the subjects they have covered and what they have learnt are few and far between. They are far more likely to point out the *longeurs*. This is only partly to do with the 'don't know' syndrome. It has far more to do with the other experiences of school that are more significant to them. The curriculum is what they are there for. What they learn is somewhat different.

Teachers are observed as the authors of much pain and pleasure, if not nearly as much as fellow pupils. The teachers are the ones who initiate the proceedings, who choose the topics and set the learning tasks. They are the arbiters of who is rewarded and who is punished. Above all, they are the people who set up the formal systems, who carry out the assessment. They are the ones who create groups of learning. All the tasks that children undertake are in response to a teacher's orders.

> I don't like writing when the teacher tells us.   (boy, 9)

> When we are on the computer and you've got to do it in a certain amount of time.   (boy, 8)

The rewards that teachers give can be an important motivating factor. But they are also a discriminatory act, choosing some individuals or groups over others.

> This term I've got the teacher's special award in assembly and quite a few gold stars and quite a few team points.
>   It means they've done good work and they've behaved. Some of the things Mrs B our headmistress said about me when I got the class award was that I was helpful. I brought, I produced good work and I did good work and I never gave up doing the good working system.   (boy, 7)

Children recognize that they are within a system, and most of them accept that fact and adhere to it. It is the very fact that the school is such a formal system that some children react against, clinging to their alternative systems of peer relationships and peer approval. Very few children have the opportunity to realize that there are other school systems, and other ways of going about education, including other teaching styles. When pupils do observe something different they can also be enabled to see more clearly some of the better characteristics of their own system, as well as different standards.

> The teachers kind of help you and in Italy they always say 'work it out by yourself'. Because I've been to my cousin's school to see how it was. But I didn't like it. I spent an hour there, just seeing all the words. And they were kind of like too old-fashioned books and everything.   (girl, 8)

> I'd like to be quite clever. Plus they [Japanese] make you work at it until you get it perfect. I like that.   (boy, 9)

I'm not a fast learner and everything I learn, sometimes it goes out of my head. If I went to that school [abroad] it would've probably been all right.

(boy, 8)

Those who have had the experience of something different can see the possible alternatives and therefore adapt better to what is actually given them. The more focused the information, the more that can be made of it. It is in the confines of experience, the realization of its limitations, and the clash between that and undreamed-of alternatives that conflict arises. The children are always aware of different standards. They are made aware of this partly by the expectations of teachers and partly because they know that they are in competition with each other. By the age of eight the children are aware that hard work and academic success are not closely related.[19] They observe that some of their peers seem to be more naturally gifted. More significantly, they reassess themselves and their own achievement, or lack of it. It is at this time that they can feel alienated from the systematic expectations of teachers and their peers: failure in school work begins to become a real problem. They are put into a group. They are labelled. They realize that society as a whole has ranks and hierarchies and that these apply to them. Their sense of vulnerability because of their lack of success also exposes them at the same time to blame by their teachers and teasing by their peers.

Schools are then associated with groups. On a private level are personal sympathies and approvals, or enmities and cruel labels. These are the more powerful because they involve both the formal side of school and the informal. Particular teachers are suddenly identified as being 'friends', as listeners and personal carers. Others remain distant. For every friend who is a supporter there is a potential threat, a person who would rejoice in seeing someone else hurt. Each chooses friends. Discrimination is central.

The exclusive systems of school

One immediate result of not doing well at school is being made to do more work. Everything takes longer, and this is partly due to the 'do it again' syndrome which children associate with teachers. The system as a whole isolates and punishes.

Everyone might have done it too quickly and made it not very neat and if I spent a long time doing it it might come out neater than the others. My teacher might make me practice instead of getting on with my other work.

(boy, 8)

Every child wants to do well at school, but nearly all of them feel under a significant strain. They do not think they are very clever. They feel they have to keep up, or, sometimes, catch up with the others. They see others doing much better work than they do, much faster. The strain of their awareness of this constantly shows:

> I feel I haven't learnt much. They've got stuff right and I've got them wrong and feel that I've not learnt much and I haven't been paying attention. No one's good at anything. They just try and try but sometimes they strain themselves just to do it.   (girl, 8)

> I'm getting really frustrated with my work. I'm very slow at doing things.
>   (boy, 8)

> If they've got difficulties and they get more right than you, I feel ashamed. Like they sort of like haven't got much, many brains. 'Cos they say if you don't finish it you've got to stay in and do it. And if the person that's not as good as you does it before you, you feel sort of not very good.   (girl, 8)

Groups, streams and 'classes' become deeply imbued. The pupils are aware of categories, of differences, of a social order which makes distinctions between collective success and failure. The pressure of competition, of keeping up with their own expectations as well as that of the teachers, is very strong. This makes children very aware of their own limitations. They all feel that they become a minority, even isolated as individuals, and this makes them compare themselves against others.

> When I mean I'm not very good at writing I mean I'm not very good at spelling. 'Cos I try to do words and I get a few right but not as much as I get wrong. I mean I get more wrong than I do right. I'm worse than some of them and better than others.   (boy, 8)

> When I do something wrong I have to write it out again and again. Sometimes it's a bit hard 'cos sometimes I don't know how to say something. And it's a bit hard to write it down for me. Sometimes I want to be able to finish it off. If I don't finish it people think that I don't know much things about them.   (girl, 8)

> I look at other people and they've done it much better. Sometimes I think it's because people suddenly write really fast and I start writing really quickly.   (boy, 8)

'Other people' belong to a different category. They are quicker or neater, or more successful, or more rich. Distinctions, in terms of that deepest of all attributes, personal worth, are crucial. Against the potential superciliousness of others, the sense of self-worth is far more significant than the colour of the skin. The school system is encouraged to thrive on this. The telling phrase is 'I'm not good' compared to others, putting oneself into a category that could become defensive or assertive, like being good at other things. 'Doing something wrong' is a barrier against the collective expectations of society, another isolating experience. That sense of failure is reinforced by repetition. Children look at 'other people', the successful in their own terms. The rich might be an arbitrary choice, but when it comes to the diurnal experience of school, differences are essential. It is in this atmosphere, formal as well as informal, that prejudice against groups and against individuals, can thrive.

Keeping up with the group or dropping out

One of the issues in this competitive atmosphere is the relationship of speed to neatness. Children are aware of two conflicting pressures: to get the work done in the allotted time and to make sure it is good enough. They do not want to hold up the class, to be singled out for the teacher's attention. To get the task done at all costs is one clear impulse. Throughout their comments we constantly hear the echo of the teacher's phrase 'do it again'. Neatness, or striving for perfection, can take time. But so does staying behind. No wonder children wish they had the facility to do work easily as well as fast.

> I like doing my work neatly and they do it or not very neatly. I do feel terrible when I'm not the best at something because I always go last. Terrible, because I would never get my work done. It would take me probably all week.   (boy, 6)

Here it is not a question of ontological belief but a realization that the standards he is supposed to attain are not his own. He is slow. In the system he works in this is 'terrible'. He is compared against a group norm. The majority of children feel they are not as successful or as clever as they would like to be. Even if it is in only one subject that they feel this they all share a lack of confidence. They see others who are doing better, pleasing the teacher more and, it seems, finding the set tasks easy to achieve. Sometimes this sense of not being good enough is the result of coming to a new school and having to make new comparisons. But in any school comparisons of success and failure are paramount.

The reason I'm last is because I'm slow because I take it nice and calmly but all the other ones are so good at it. They do it really fast and it's good. But I don't. 'Cos I'm not very good at stuff.   (girl, 8)

When I've just been off school and I'm better and I come back and they've gone ahead of me. I try to work as quick as I can. Well, I just mainly try to keep up.   (boy, 8)

I have to learn everything so quickly to get with them. I've got to do that and like that because they've done plus and minus and all of those. And now I've got to start and do add and sharing.   (girl, 8)

The strong urge to keep up or catch up with others shows how children feel the constant pressure of the school system. They are urged to complete work, do set tasks and generate activities. The pressure on children goes deeper than their performance against a set of criteria, or key stages, and deeper than pleasing the teacher. Children are aware that they are in competition with each other. They do not want to appear to be slow or stupid. They constantly compare themselves to others: they understand not only the differences, the groups, but the way these relate to the large issues in society. Can they find their place? Will others usurp them?

They just might be a bit cleverer than me. And if they're getting things quicker than me, they're just going to be cleverer than me... sometimes when I do any work quickly I'm really bored afterwards. And so if you finish slowly you won't be bored.
Once I did my sums, one of my sums quite quickly and then another person started going really quickly so then I had to catch up with them. And it was a race, like we were running to the teacher and trying to show her.
Sometimes they say that I'm slow at things and that I'm not clever or anything.   (girl, 8)

There is always that sense of comparison, of self-doubt against self-belief. It is like a 'race' for attention and for achievement. At one level the concern is with success, for producing the finished product. At another it is a matter of innate abilities. In these terms children find themselves labelled: some are able and others not. In the academic life of the school this distinction is crucial. The pupils are left wondering why some should find it so much easier to fulfil all the set tasks than others. What are the personal characteristics that some bring to bear that make them so much more successful? What connection is there between the character and the outcomes? The sense of competition derives partly from the race to finish first, but it is underlined by its association with ability.

> Sometimes when you're doing maths things you have to do it quietly, sit on your own, with books around you so that no one will copy you or you can't copy them. I start sweating and feel 'Oh I'm not going to be able to do this, and everyone's going to finish before me' and things like that.
>
> (girl, 8)

To keep up and know what is expected is the important demand, both from the teacher and the peer group. It comes much more easily to some children than to others and this is closely observed. Pupils assess their own abilities against the performance of others, and take a critical look at any limitations they might have compared to others.

> I don't like myself because I'm not very good at maths... I'm not sure that, well, what divide and times means. It's just like they're on another thing and I'm stuck with that. And they've got it all right and they're on this other thing.
>   I'd like to be the best at sums and I'd like to be the best at... I'd like to be the best at lots of things.
>
> (girl, 8)

The assessment that children make of themselves often depends on how they rate their ability to fulfil set tasks quickly. This draws attention to the fact that some children have a natural facility to work with ease; the gap between effort and ability is the more marked. Even if it might be boring to do work that is undemanding, the real dread is not keeping pace with the others, of being some kind of drop-out. There is always a latent possibility that they will be left behind, be ostracized, will no longer be part of the mainstream. If this happens do they look for an alternative psychological institution?

Finding the middle way

Children want to be able to do work easily rather than be the cleverest for its own sake. Indeed, a number of them point out that they do not wish to be the best, any more than they wish to be the worst, lest that might make them arrogant or a show-off.

> No, because you would be called brainy and perfect. I'd like to be a stage where you're not someone who needs help but someone who's not a brainy but not having difficulties.
>
> (girl, 8)

> I don't really mind if I'm not first but I don't really mind if I'm last but I
> hope I'm nearer the first one.
>
> My best friend, he might have done it before me and I think I'm going
> to be really embarrassed.   (boy, 8)

One important factor in the relationship between peers and the formal curriculum
is not to stand out: to be part of an homogeneous group that has no particular
attention drawn to it. For all those who wish to identify themselves as belonging to
a distinct group, there are many more who wish to remain anonymous. They
eschew the alternative to invisibility and keep their own counsel and their own
reflections. They do not want to be seen as different, as too clever or too stupid, for
either way leads to teasing, being picked on. This is not to imply that they want to
be completely left to their own devices. They wish to see teachers give all people
equal attention, even if this is impossible, given the assertive attention seekers.
They vie for position in front of the teacher. The majority manoeuvre themselves
to be *outside* the notice of the teacher, but they are never invisible from each other.
They can hide from a teacher's attention but not from the awareness of their
friends. Sometimes their friends can be a distraction.

> Some people like whisper to me and that and I just whisper back and they
> keep on doing it. And I just keep on doing it. I don't get my work done.
> Sometimes she says 'That's not a lot, is it?' And things like that.
>
>   (boy, 8)

Unfairness is sometimes an inadvertent mistake, and sometimes a deliberate individual act. It can also be systemic. When the private cajoling causes public problems then the sense of the importance of unfairness becomes the more strong. It is
then the system that is personalized.

Children's concerns about their own abilities stem from the comparisons they
make with other people. Usually it is other pupils in the same class. It can sometimes be their own family. The sense of sibling rivalry, and the distinctions of
position and attention are turned into a more public status of achievement and
success.

> It worries me because my mum and dad they're quite clever and my
> brother's quite clever, so I'd think I'm not the same. I don't like to be the
> smallest unclever. I like to be thought of as good.
>
> I like to be good at work because I come from a working family really.
> Everybody does their best in our family.
>
> There are certain people who think they're better than me and they
> don't show it. So when we're in maths and things and we're in the same

> group doing the same things, they're always going [noise of hurrying] and
> I say 'I know you're copying me' and they go 'No, No, No, No'.
>
> (boy, 8)

There is no doubt that comparisons are not only being constantly made and observed but talked about. Labels are freely put on people, and those who think they are clever are disliked for that fact. Ability and performance are one of the starting points for teasing. Part of the culture of the school rests on competition and this is to some extent apparent in rewards, in the recognition that something has been well done. But stronger than praise, and a far stronger motivating factor, is fear of failure. Children are afraid of what others will say if they do not work successfully, the teacher with 'do it again' and the other pupils with teasing. For every word of praise there are likely to be five of admonishment, if not delivered by the teacher then nevertheless felt by the pupil.

Those who conspicuously do well are not singled out for praise by their peers.

> Sad because they think like 'we're the best'. They say like 'I know more
> things than you' and stuff like that. And I sometimes say 'So what. At least
> I'm good at writing and better things than you', like football and things,
> like sports things and protecting myself, like judo and stuff.   (boy, 8)

Those children who stand out tend to be 'picked on'. This term can mean a variety of things from subtle teasing to outright bullying. Being picked on can mean unwelcome attention from the teacher as well as from other children. The term covers the sense of hurt felt by the recipient, whether the perpetrator means to hurt or not. There are few children who have not suffered from it, whether through the subtle forms of teasing about being stupid, or by being told off for being too clever and therefore a show-off, or because they are victims (or perpetrators) of physical assaults.

Groups, prejudice and enmity

For many children school can be an uncomfortable experience. The intensity of school lies in the mass of complex relationships. Friendships are being tested.[20] New groups are being formed. There is admiration for some and quarrels with others. School, in fact, provides for an intense social and emotional life that enters through competitiveness and working with friends and being distracted by others from the formal curriculum. There are all kinds of relationships taking place and judgements being made. There are distinctions of behaviour as well as ability. There are remembered relationships, and a sense of being wrongly singled out.

There are insecurities in relationships. But at the core there are awarenesses of groups – not of their own making but of success or failure.

> He's not a very nice boy because he used to be not very nice to me in the infants. But actually now when we're in the Juniors he's been quite nice to me. I've been playing with him.
>
> Sometimes I push people over by accident and they say I did it on purpose so I get annoyed. And sometimes I get in trouble and I say 'That's not fair!' and things like that. And I think I shouldn't do that but I can't stop myself cos they push me over as well sometimes. But I still don't swear.
>
> Sometimes this girl at school called Beth, she's nasty but sometimes she's nice. So I can't make up my mind. She sucks her fingers, and her friend call Kirsty, they're really good friends because they've known each other since they were in nursery and they both suck their fingers and thumbs. Sometimes they don't let me play with them, so I don't. And then later on she says 'Do you want to play with me?', so I say 'Oh, all right'.
>
> If they were first all the people were first and I was last I would have to stay in when it's home time and I would actually like to go home. It's just that they're better than me and someday I'll learn more than them. I wouldn't be good at a lot of things and I wouldn't be able to move to seniors very quick and I'd be the last person and things like that. There's, um, two boys I know they are very good at writing, spelling. One's called Martin and he's a very good runner and things like that as well and he knows virtually about everything.   (girl, 7)

Here we see many of the threads of school life woven together. Judgements are made of character and ability. Relationships are volatile and friendships easily made and dropped. There is violence and accusation. There are temperamental changes, with insiders and outsiders. There is self-consciousness and worry as well as admiration. Nothing is completely stable. At one stage there is a sense of belonging to a group, but this is unreliable. What is being learnt is the importance of belonging and the fear of having enemies. The instability, the essential insecurity, stems from the uncertainties. The same individuals are 'not very nice' at one stage and 'quite nice' at another. There are false accusations that are 'unfair'. Sometimes she is allowed to penetrate an inner circle and play, but all the time comparisons are being made. The most potent group is of those who are cleverer than her.

At the heart of such a mass of experiences there is a desire to be liked, to be popular. One of the great fears – together with being stupid or being bullied – is to have no friends, to be in a group that does not belong, that is not recognized as a coherent whole. To be isolated, alone, is the ultimate sense of being the victim of prejudice, the final infringement on self-worth.

Anyhow I haven't got them much friends. I don't know. I got no friends except for Daniel. That's only one friend. I wish I was different.

(boy, 8)

People leave me out of games and they don't really play with me much. Like today I won't mention who the people are but yesterday there's a new girl called Catharine and, um, well, Mrs B told me to go out and play with her... well N came up and, pushing me out of the way.   (girl 8)

Usually at lunch times I don't have anyone to play with. I do feel terrible when I'm not the best at something because I always go last.   (boy, 8)

The phrase 'nobody likes me' is redolent of something deeply felt, of a sense of isolation, of being cast out. It can also be a collective feeling, as in the case of a closely-knit gang. In the small institutions of school the sense of the personal and the collective join easily together. The individual only matters as part of a group, a group of success or failure. Either there is the awareness of attainment, and praise, or the contrary sense of being a failure. If the feelings are personal and leading to a sense of loneliness, the most obvious, indeed inevitable, response is to find others in the same position. Isolation is unbearable. Forming a group from those who are equally disgruntled or insecure is a form of self-protection. The groups or gangs that are formed in school are usually of those who feel academically excluded, who need mutual support in rejecting the collective ethos and demands of school.

Schools create a connection between shared relationships and the formal social curriculum. It is well known that underlying any academic success is the ability to make relationships, to understand social forms and to create dialogue.[21] Motivation is a key factor. This is affected by the way children relate to each other as much as by the way they relate to the teacher. Attitudes towards their abilities stem from their observation of other children as well as their ability to carry out set tasks. The security and the insecurity of school are dependent on the feeling that pupils have friends of like mind, that there are people to play and work with. When the two become out of joint then there are difficulties, and the temptation to play truant and form alternative patterns of friendship becomes the more strong. When, as in the case of a child wanting to join in and being rejected, there is no obvious place for them in school, children are bound to seek alternatives. They try to force themselves on the attentions of others, so that the rejection is felt the more strongly. We see, in these patterns of commentary, the beginnings of social alienation, of truancy, and of aggressive behaviour. Prejudice is turned from a sense of personal isolation into an atavistic fear of others, of exclusion. The personal experience becomes a pattern.

Every school experience provides the opportunity for a variety of relationships. Pupils become popular or unpopular, or do well or badly. School highlights those who are misfits, who go against the collective ethos. Not fitting into one set of values leads to fitting in to another. If the ethos of the school – working hard, obeying the rules and pleasing the teacher – is rejected, it is usually for the sake of an alternative style of life. The gang-leaders need to have an audience as much as the 'joker' – the pupil that plays the official school system.[22] The gangs want the approval of their peers; the others need the approval of their teachers. For most children there is no need for a clash of cultural systems. They adapt. They make sure that their private experience is kept separate, and they relate one to the other. But there are those who clash with the collective system. These are the ones who need to collect a group of like-minded peers, who together see a value in an alternative system.

The fear of getting into trouble

All children are aware that there are 'naughty people' in a school. They do not observe uniform conformity, or all pupils doing what they know they should. They also realize that schools vary.

> There's this naughty boy. He doesn't go to school. He throws stones. And he's rudeness. I don't like living there.   (girl, 8)

Children do not merely observe others who are naughty any more than they remain quietly distant from those who bully. Naughtiness is closely linked to 'getting into trouble'. It is something that affects all.

The potential contamination of being with the wrong people leads children into becoming aware of the differences between schools and their reliance on certain neighbourhoods.

> My mum wants me to get away from this school really. My mum doesn't want to talk about it but she might take me away from this school. She doesn't want me to be with Greg. He's the one with the black hair. We get in enormous trouble.   (boy, 7)

> No, don't like school a bit but my mum wants me to go to – school. I dunno. My mum just wants me to go. You get all these kids beating you up every day.   (girl, 9)

Children are aware that they are easily affected by the people they are with. Just as teachers try to rearrange seating and groups so that children do not cause each other trouble by leading them on or distracting them, so children almost helplessly observe and are affected by the same phenomena. There seems to be a fascination with the alternative culture, of paying attention to other children rather than the teacher. They are worried by the competition to do well and by the potential disturbance from other children. This feeling of being caught up in events is a strong one: it means not just working less efficiently but getting into trouble. This is the shadow of school life: the real possibility of failure both social and academic.

> I just don't like the other children. I only like my friends. They pick on me. They're rude. They say naughty things. It's just a habit. I always get told off. The dinner ladies. 'Cos I always get the blame by Johnny… He said I pull his trousers down and go to the head. I'm the last person to finish.
>
> (girl, 8)

Children feel contaminated by the presence of naughty ones. They also feel threatened. It might be tempting to join in the pranks that other pupils play, but children also are aware of the effects of others on them whether they like it or not. It is as if they cannot really keep completely clear of the alternative culture. The symbol of this alternative social system is the bully. Much of the expressed anguish of school life derives from competition, from comparing themselves to others. Underlying that is a more complex, more volatile system of developing and changing relationships. This goes beyond expressions of friendship or admiration for particular prowess or particular charm. It comes through the vulnerability that children feel in their reactions to others, from getting into trouble to being picked on.

The threat of bullying

The children uniformly mention bullying in one form or another as part of the everyday life of school. Like getting into trouble, children find themselves personally caught up in it. It is for some a developing mixture of reactions to other people and personal initiatives. The justification is 'sticking up for yourself' in the face of other people's physical or verbal attacks. But it is very hard to see the distinction between provocation and defence. What is clear is that physical violence becomes a form of life within the social ambience of the school:

> Some people don't like me probably because, like, if they start kicking me and that I just get hold of them and throw them across the playground or something because I get annoyed. If only people wouldn't come up to me and start kicking me and that. When they start if I can catch them I just get up and swing them round me and make them go spinning round because I

get so annoyed with them. They do it to some other people and call them
names. Like really horrible names. The one that does it to me is younger
than me but I'm taller than him. Sometimes I just walk away but he comes
back at you and that until, like, you just get hold of him and just throw him
across the playground kind of. He just kind of smiles and then because he
knows that I don't like swearing... he, I don't do it back and that's why he
can get me back. I just try to forget about it and the next day, sometimes he
comes back on it and that. My dad told me somethink to say to him and he
said 'I don't care' which was a bit naughty.   (boy, 8)

The mixture of frustration, anger and provocation are all finely balanced. Out of a
sense of isolation, of not being liked, comes the violent response. The very fact that
he is so easily provoked, his inability to cope with teasing, and the automatically
aggressive response make him an obvious target. Those who are not good at making neutral relationships are vulnerable to provocation. In this case is he concerned
just with one boy or with all the others?

No, as long as he isn't with a gang of people though. Some other people bigger than me. 'Cos they're a bit stronger than me and I don't like it. Not
frighten me but I just like, they all come at me and that. I try and run away
but they just get me and try and like beat me up and that. They throw me up
in the air. They like lift me up and then wing me like that. It's really horrible.
                                                    (same boy, 8)

The 'gang' of people makes the sense of personal identity, in a negative sense, the
stronger. This boy is isolated by his ability to be provoked, to retaliate. Personal
relationships become a collective norm. The concept of protecting oneself is seen
as necessary against those who either form gangs, or are stronger, or both. The tendency to hit back, to be provoked, itself singles out the boy as a victim as well as a
bully. Even bullies know the extent of their own faults.

It makes me sad when my brother gets beaten up or something. So I go
and have a go at the people who beat my brother up and then they regret it.
    The people that come back at me and start punching me and that – I
don't like people that want to come back at me.   (boy, 8)

There are two clear symptoms of wanting to control: to make sure 'they' regret it
and the attempt to stop them 'coming back'. It is as if the bully felt it was his duty to
punish anyone who stands up to him. Through these isolated incidents arises a
more generalized perception of others and themselves: people who need rejecting
as well as those who deserve acceptance.

Fighting is an undercurrent of school life which depends on how much control is held over the edges of relationships, of rivalries and power. The pupils are aware that they lead each other on, that one thing leads to another:

> I haven't got too many friends in this area. Because I fight. I just join in one. If Daniel gets beaten up I beat them up. I punch them. They're in my class really. And some are in a different class. I punch. And I beat up my mates. Like David – we usually have fights.   (boy, 8)

Fighting – with 'mates' included – is not just a simple matter of bullies and victims. It is a pervasive part of the experience of children, out of school as well as in, and both more influential and harder to control than some of the analyses of bullying might suggest. For many children there is a palpable sense of threat. Fighting might seem a natural sport for some, but for all, fighting means the most obvious form of bullying.

Children see bullies as a regrettable fact of school life. They are the ones who demand attention as a group, and as people who can single out the individual for attention. They bring pressures to bear that cause the response of personal assertion or the camouflage of invisibility. Bullies are observed to find the appropriate victim: the one who stands out or who 'asks for it'.

> There's quite a lot of Chinese people here. My friend, Di Wan she's Chinese and people pick on her. They go like that [pulling eyes] and everyone says where's the Di two and three? I feel quite sorry for her. I still wouldn't really like to be Chinese though. I don't really like their eyes myself really. And I don't like the way they speak really. They speak really fast.
> (girl, 7)

Whilst this girl feels to an extent protective of her friend she understands completely the point of view of those who would find foreigners a matter for teasing. Even the person who is teased for being different understands why.

> That I've got curly hair and stuff. It's not my fault that my hair sticks up, is it? Because they're all white here and there's no browns. And they think that my clothes are funny but they're just the same as theirs… In [the other school] there was Elizabeth and Sarah. And they were black. There's about three or four. When I started this school it's hard to make friends. When I started there it was all right because I had a friend that had already started there but then when I moved I haven't seen all these people before and I get left out and stuff with all the games.   (girl, 7)

The obvious starting point for racism is the fear of those who stand out. Whilst this might be a matter of intellectual prowess, the more visible differences are physical. There are many other prompts for teasing and bullying – matters of personality, like 'showing off' – but physical impressions, being tall, or having red hair, or wearing glasses or wearing braces on the teeth, are all matters of self-consciousness in the child and a point of comment to his or her friends. The sense that there are typologies of differences, often obvious, is pervasive. Once a rumour of an attitude against an individual is set up it spreads easily. Children, like adults, are easily led. Even against their better instincts they 'lead each other on' and they *know* this. This is why the different cultural systems of the school are so important. Underneath the victimization and the bullying there is a certain sympathy for those who are hurt. Even the bullies realize what it is like to be on the other side. Nevertheless the symptom of difference leads to what seems like inevitable teasing. Let us take a complex, but typical, example of a person who is teased and who reacts badly to it from the point of view of her mentor.

> People leave me out of games and they don't really play with me much. Like today… and, well, Nabila came up and she wasn't treating me very well in the game and pushing me out of the way.
>   She's been through a rough patch. Nearly everyone keeps on saying that she's, um, that she looks like the colour of poo, just because she's black. Since then, whenever somebody's not nice to her or they don't want to do things she always takes, gets a bit frustrated and angry and takes it out on everyone. And she thinks they actually try to say to her that they don't like her because she's black. But that isn't always true.   (girl, 8)

What this girl sees as true is more complex than a matter of simple racism. She understands the ways in which girls fight for friendship, for recognition from each other. She sees the significance of the 'rough patch' that leads to suspicion of any offer of sympathy. And she acknowledges the inherent sense of frustration and weakness that leads children to take it out on others. The generalization of what others might feel is separated from the individuality of understanding. But the actual feelings about the cause, like having a rough patch, do not lessen the personal hurt of rejection. The groups that cohere and disintegrate remind one of the essences of prejudice.

> It wasn't just Nabila in the game. It was everybody else. She didn't make me very happy and when I said I'm not playing they all said 'good'. And even Catharine said it. And well, when I'd gone off Nabila was gone off as well. She was crying. And so was I. And then I went over and Catharine came to me and said 'What's the matter?' and I said 'I'm just not playing.

I'm fed up'. And Catharine just went off. And Nabila came up to her and she's just taken over Catharine now. Catharine does not like me any more.

I've got plenty of other friends.

I feel a bit sorry for her 'cos sometimes when I say I like her she doesn't believe me. Like, well, when everyone is being horrible to her she says 'No one likes me. I haven't got any friends'. And I say 'I like you Nabila. You're my friend'. And she just walks off in a huff and says 'You're just pretending. I know you don't like me because I'm black'.

People, they say that to her so maybe she feels that no one likes her at all. Because one person started it off saying she was black 'cos she's the colour of poo. 'Cos they just want to cause trouble and be spiteful. Some children have been through a rough patch themselves, so they take it out on other children. It makes them go through a rough patch just because they've gone through a rough patch at home.   (same girl, 8)

The 'rough patch' is the explanation for bad behaviour to others. The assumption is that there is an emotional cause, a personal sense of weakness, for acting against others. Moods dominate actions, and moods are volatile. But there are already psychological and social explanations for behaviour, like having a rough patch at home. It should be noted that children think of adults as essentially temperamental; beneath the role they play teachers are assumed to be very moody.

The tensions and conflicts between children derive from their strong desire to be liked – as they want to be loved by parents – and the realization that there are temptations to be nasty that are difficult to resist, as in sibling rivalry. So much depends on the subtle influence of the peer group. Children both understand what it is like to be victimized and find the pleasure of joining in almost irresistible. For most children this tension is sustained: one is balanced by the other. For a few children the sense of personal isolation is never overcome, whether it comes about for superficial reasons like physical appearance, or deeper traumas that derive from the home. But for most there is a sense that isolation, of being outside a normative group is permanent. Once set in a certain direction it is easy for all kinds of factors to reinforce it.

Children realize that being different means being marked for attention. This difference does not have to be a weakness. On the contrary, it can be the very fact that there is someone better, cleverer, or prettier than the others.

Whoever's the best in the class is usually bossiest and everyone doesn't like you very much because they're jealous of you being the best. And they think you're bossy, like Eve. She used to be in our class and she was the best at everything. And she had loads of boyfriends and everyone hated her because she, she didn't really care. She was mean to everyone. Bossy, unfair and cruel and well, everyone thought that she was the prettiest in the class and they were so jealous of her, really. So they were all being

horrible to her but she didn't care. She's left and now she's gone off to travel round the world.
(girl, 8)

Competition, on a number of levels, is very important to children. They would like to be amongst the best without standing out. When someone *is* the best in every way and doesn't mind standing out, that is a cause for jealousy. But that is also a sign of invulnerability, and the majority of children who fear becoming victims do so either because they fear being teased for defects, or physically attacked because of weakness.

People teasing me and calling me names.
(boy, 8)

It is as if difference is interpreted as potential weakness. Many girls fear being teased just as many boys fear being attacked or 'beaten up'.

The anxiety of being victimized

The fear of being physically or mentally hurt is a pervasive one. It appears in all kinds of statements, in all kinds of contexts. It has been noted that this is like an accepted part of the social culture of school. This does not imply that it is acceptable, nor taken for granted by children. Physical attacks are the most visible sign of what makes children anxious. Their trepidation in the world is a lack of confidence that they will be safe at school, in the street or even in the home.

Some things make me sad like people being horrible and saying 'No you can't have that' and I say 'Well they mustn't like me or somethink'. Like you say 'No, you can't have that' and then I just feel a bit upset.
(boy, 8)

Whilst children think of school and home as two distinct worlds, there is a far greater distinction between the formal life of the school – the obeying of rules and the recognition of propriety – and the more fluid, more dangerous, more volatile and unrestrained world of friendships and enmities, of peer groups for the individual or against. The desire to be recognized, to be nurtured and supported binds all these worlds together, but each has its own potential to disappoint.

The simple worry that children have at the heart of all this, wherever they are, is the fear of being 'beaten up'. It is part of a suspicion of the outside world and it is also a part of school life.

Stephen beats me up. He's in Miss P's class and he beats me up.

(boy, 8)

I don't like it when people kick around and that. I don't like it when they kick me.   (girl, 8)

Sometimes these big boys come up and bully me but apart from that it's good.   (boy, 8)

'Apart from that': it is clear that in school and in the friendships made at school there are many moments of great pleasure, of having fun, of carrying out success-ful enterprises and of feelings of fulfilment. But that is not the whole of school life. In the centre of their experience children form a view of the world. They find themselves vulnerable to others. They learn what it is like to hurt and be hurt. There might be many moments of unsullied joy, but these are like a distraction from the formative experiences they are undergoing. An essential part of their experience is the realization of, and apprehension of, danger. This links school with the outside world.

When I go to the park, there's always bullies there and when we're on the swings they climb over the walls and scare us off.   (girl, 7)

There are two ways in which schools inadvertently help to foster the sense of per-sonal identity in competition against others. One is the idea of achievement and its association with ability. It means that some stand out as being more successful, as better than others. It means that there are particular pupils observed as being picked on. Thus, inadvertently or not, schools develop a sense of distinction, of groups to be emulated or avoided, which explains why prejudice grows over the years.[23] The other way in which schools foster differences is in the more hidden curriculum, the painful hurly-burly of bullying and teasing, of strained relation-ships and new friendships. The sense that there are particular groups who stand for distinct attitudes, which can be either attractive or repellent, develops rapidly in places where there are so many people brought into varying places, shifted around, divided and organized but always into classes and groups.

To some, the development of these generalized distinctions might be simply an inevitable part of socialization, but it should be remembered that the crucial disso-ciation of ability from hard work means that there will be those who feel disenfran-chised and who feel estranged from the larger social world. The hierarchies of competition within or between schools foster prejudice. It might not always mani-fest itself in particular racist attitudes but it suggests a way of seeing the world not just in stereotypes but in ways that foster suspicion and antipathy. In the case of those who play truant and who become excluded, the sense of being outside success, and personally vilified, is strong.[24] The formal demands of society are rejected, and the attraction of a particular peer group or gang becomes a counter or alternative social position. Ultimately all interactions with others, even with the roles played by teachers or the police, are taken personally. The psychologically excluded want – they demand – 'respect', being treated like an individual, being seen for what they are, not what they do or how well they do it. It is the insecurity and the demand for more personal control that not only gives them an oblique and uncomfortable view of themselves, but asserts their own differences against particular groups of others, be they official, like teachers or the police, or unofficial, like gangs or types from elsewhere.[25]

The ontological insecurity of being individual

Most children do not want to stand out from the norm. They do not want themselves too clearly defined against the shared characteristics of others. Any individual characteristic, physical, emotional or mental, that makes them distinct and draws attention to them is to be avoided if possible. They prefer to be invisible.[26] They prefer to remain, for the most part, anonymous. They accept a certain normlessness, a fluidity of identity, unassertive in the adaptability to the social order. There are, of course, some who become accustomed to standing out from the crowd. These assert their distinction by dress or behaviour: they define a stereotype of the conventional world and set themselves against it. This prejudice either for or against convention is one of the most pervasive. It can be directed against particular groups, or other nations, as well as against society as a whole. But the majority of children do not wish to be conspicuous. They want to avoid extremes, even of doing too well and therefore being stereotyped. This also applies to the way in which they imagine their own futures. There is a sense of unusual relativism as to what they might or might not do.

One would have imagined that children would be tempted to fantasize about their own futures, that they would have huge ambitions. We do see occasional glimpses of this but even when we do they are undercut by realism. They know that the rewards will go to those who work, that life is competitive. For the most part children hope that they will do enough to survive, to have enough money, and a good enough job. These children have their fantasies but they also have their expectations. When confronted by their *real* futures they think of themselves as leading an ordinary enough life, of being one of the 'normal people who walk their dogs and stuff' (boy, 8).

Children are aware that fantasizing about the future is nothing more serious than that. It would be nice to be rich and famous, but it's unlikely. They know that some become pop stars but they do not expect it to happen to them. And yet one is free to dream, to imagine.

> I like to think about being a good footballer.   (boy, 8)

> I love to imagine myself in the future and famous but this always leads me to feel worried.   (girl, 7)

> I like to think about what it would be like to be a millionaire.   (boy, 7)

Liking to think about imagined possibilities heightens their sense of realism. It is pure thought, pure fantasy. There is no sense, when children show a streak of ambition, that they are unaware of potential failure, of the fact that to achieve such an ambition entails luck as well as hard work.

When children talk about their futures they think about them usually in terms of employment. Domestic circumstances are involved, like having children, but when children try to explore their futures they are bound together with a sense of realism. They see their future lives as ordinary and as unremarkable. In the illustrations of these attitudes we will see a complex relationship between desire and reality, between the need to work hard for success and the fact that such success is by no means guaranteed. Children share both the desire to seek pleasure and the desire to do good. And yet these desires are normally contained within a far more routine sense of what is possible, let alone beneficial.

> You'd grow up to get a good job and earn quite a bit of money. You wouldn't get that good a job and you'd end up quite poor.
>
> If I learn quite a lot and learn how to read and write properly I think I'll have quite a good life. Like being a builder, or a computer maker. Archaeologists would be a real lot of money.
>
> Well, I wouldn't mind to be an archaeologist or in the army but I would like to be in the army more. Because, one, you can discover things from the past and in the army you feel quite special 'cos they help people from dying, protecting them.
>
> Problems about jobs because sometimes they don't get enough money.
>   (boy, 8)

The first requisite is getting a good job, defined by providing enough money. The second requisite is being able to perform the tasks demanded by school. The third, more fanciful, is to do something that you would like to do. Some children link what they are good at in school with their futures but, like outstanding musicians, they are rare.

> You can get much more jobs being good at maths, than you can for any other things that I can think of. You would be a shopkeeper. You could be a plane flyer. You could be a teacher. Things like that.
>
> It's important if you are really good at the violin you play in the concerts and get lots of money and things like that. I want to play in concerts in my spare time but be a rally, um, racer. It's more likely that I'll be a musician 'cos I don't really know as much about cars as I do about music. But I do know quite a bit about cars.   (boy, 8)

What is possible, and what is likely, are two different things. On the one hand is the prospect of being a shopkeeper: what might be achieved with good mathematical results. On the other hand is the fantasy of being a rally driver. But the link is also made with actual knowledge and the real possibility of playing the violin in an orchestra. Even this is a long shot, and recognized as such. Possibilities and desires always seem to be mitigated by what is more likely.

> You need to be good at writing and stuff 'cos you need a job when you grow up.
>
> I think I want to be a runner. I could work in a bank. 'Cos you can get quite a lot of money for that.   (boy, 8)

> I'd like to be a vet. And I'd like to be a show jumper and I like watching my mum work in an office.   (girl, 8)

> Get a good job and earn money. I might even get my own business. I'd make a pop song. Be a pop star. Or even just work in a café and have my own café.   (boy, 7)

There are categories between different jobs but also between fantasy and reality. Realism and the domestic ideal is placed against the possibility of something better. This is an uncomfortable juxtaposition. Children know that in different circumstances, not just through their own hard work, the outcomes might be different. Certain people will be lucky and achieve what they desire. In other countries things would be different, and often worse. The sense of relativity is important. It is as if children hold two beliefs at the same time. They are encouraged to imagine what life *could* be like and what life *is* like for some people as seen on television or personified by the seriously rich. On the other hand they see the ordinary realities of every day, the jobs their parents do. They are aware of the tension between the two.

> I would like to be an actress. I just like doing plays and things. Lots of people want to do it and not many people get to.   (girl, 8)

The typical connection between wanting to be an actress and enjoying acting in plays gives us a glimpse into the way that children connect what they observe in school with what might happen afterwards. The fact that children believe that the purpose of schooling is to prepare them for jobs is well established.[27] But so is the fact that there seems little connection between the curriculum as presented in school and subsequent employment. All the skills so emphasized by schools and the national curriculum are never closely related to their subsequent uses. The key stages of the curriculum are presented for their own sake, as targets suitable for testing. It is no surprise that young adults who have not done well in the academic system look back on their schooling with dismay, not only as a lost opportunity but with a sense of disappointment that the purpose of learning was never explained to them.[28] The attitudes of children to their futures reveals that they see the world of school as disconnected from the adult world.

The domestic realities of the future

The long-term vision of success, depending on the hard work of school and passing exams, is seen as a competition in which some will have good enough jobs to earn lots of money and others will be unsuccessful. Children do not want to compete or stand out any more than they would at school. They want to have a secure place. The connection between immediate success at school and *some* form of job and security is clearly made.

What children desire in their futures is a job that pays well, which can be translated into security. They are more concerned with that than with a job that is exotic or fanciful. The distinction between the fantasy of future life and the reality of what is perceived is strongly made. 'When I was younger I wanted to be a clown' (boy, 8). Children's real ideas of the future are actually realistic, even ordinary.

> I think I'll probably live in a flat. Because if I'm not very rich I'll probably live in a flat. 'Cos they're a bit cheaper than houses.   (boy, 8)

This realism imbues much of their thinking. It is only when they either have far greater ambitions, and greater disappointments, or when they feel they are inherently at a disadvantage that they feel that society, or a part of society, is against them. This realism leads most children to suggest that although they have preferences for certain kinds of employment, they know that the chances are that they will end up taking very ordinary jobs. They might want to be air hostesses but assume they will probably work in a shop.

Children's views of their future are based firmly on their own circumstances, and this includes the fact that all the people around them, including their parents, have ordinary jobs.

> 'Cos it's, if you wanna get a good job, but, um, like if you wanna get a really bad job then I wouldn't go for it, but if it's good I would go for it. But if there's really good ones I would just go into the shop and then say 'How much would you owe me if I joined this job?' And they would say how much and then if there's, and then I would just go for the shop with the more money.
>
> Like a sweet shop. Just a normal job. But it's getting hard.
>
> (boy, 8)

The desire to fit into norms, to be ordinary, is very strong. Security, from the point of view of those at school, is an essential. There is little desire to be confronted by the challenging or demanding. It seems as if school experience has caused them to settle into the most pervasive of norms, not to stand out, not to attract attention or single out the unusual. Avoidance of other people's prejudice is also a recognition of its potential.

> I'll work in the restaurant. I want to be normal – a normal person. Like I don't want to wear make-up or anything. I want to work in the restaurant because it's my mum's restaurant. I help her with the glasses and plates on the tables. I want to live in England with my mum. I don't want to live on my own.   (girl, 8)

> I'd like to be a vet, but no, because I'm not very clever. Work is something like a supermarket or somewhere.   (boy, 8)

The children's vision of their own futures is both unambitious and realistic. If they do begin to fantasize they soon correct themselves. They have a clear sense of their own talents, or lack of them. The futures that they map out are very much like the present. There might be a range of possibilities and these connect to present interests, but always they return to the outline of *actual* jobs:

> I like digging up things and I like history a lot. I would like to illustrate a book maybe and maybe I'll work in a factory or maybe I'll work, maybe I'll be a manager. Or maybe I'll just work in a business.   (boy, 8)

Working life, central to their interpretations of their futures, is the main but not the only concern. They have few social goals or political ambitions. They are, however, aware of domestic realities. They speculate about being married and having children. They have ideas about how many children they would have, and why, and see their domestic futures as realistically as their working lives. Safety and security, as well as fulfilling norms, are important. One of the safest and deepest senses of groups is the ordinary and the everyday.

> I would like to have two nice children and I'd like nobody to get hurt in my family and I'd like to have a long life and a happy life… I like the fact that you'd have children to keep company and to help.   (boy, 8)

> I want to have, to be married, and to have a child, but I don't know how many. I just want them.   (girl, 8)

The domestic future is as plain to children as anything else. They do not want to be lonely, so they wish to have a family. They also think of what fun they could have with their own children, partly as a symptom of their own nostalgia and partly as if children were seen as playthings. Their analysis of their own futures reflects their own personal experiences of the home.

> I would have a husband and I would have two children. I would have them. I don't know if it will happen but I would like to have a girl and a boy. I'd call them like Amanda and something else.   (girl, 7)

The future is seen as essentially a mirror of the conditions in which they now live. The cultural milieu is well defined, in terms of food, furniture and housing. It all centres on having enough money to pay for the essential requirements; not too much and not too little. This is why having a job, indeed having a good job, is so important. But there are also some glimpses of other possibilities in the future. Even a boy who talks about wanting to go to university and have quite a lot of money speculates about an alternative scenario.

> I might when I'm older, I might hang around with some boys who'll get me into trouble and I might go to the police 'cos I'll be old enough to go to the police.   (boy, 8)

The social realism is strong. Whether it is a sense of personal ontological relativism, a perception of belonging, or a matter of insecurity, remains an open question. We might speculate in which direction the individual might develop, between the definition of the self against others and the ironic detachment of their own position, but to the children themselves it is unclear. The ambivalence between an acceptance of relativity and a sense of its unfairness still remains. Prejudice, whilst part of experience, is not at this stage the atavistic need to give their lives a meaning.

Children see a strong connection between the present and the future. Their parents' circumstances and outlooks appear to form their own aspirations. This offers a certain kind of mediocre security, but it does not suggest that they are pursuing long-term plans or that they have long-term fears. Life is usually seen as going on much as before. Whilst there are just occasional glimpses of different levels of speculation, as about death, for the most part the children's outlook on the future is very much a matter of the ordinary and the everyday – the 'normal people who walk their dogs and stuff'.

All this suggests a kind of tolerance, an ability to accept and to find their own place in the world, modest, quiet and undisturbed. There is a contrast with the world of academic competition. Indeed, such views of the future are also an escape from the stresses of school. Security is all. In school, between the pressure of exams and expectations and the threat of so many other people, security, like moments of daydreaming, is highly prized. A classroom can be a safe and peaceful place. There are corners that become havens of security. There are moments of escape from the bustle and harassment of the everyday.

Tolerance has all kinds of aspects, from understanding to indifference. The sense of personal relativism, of modest self-belief, does not in itself mean that all other people are seen in the same terms. Intolerance is born in insecurity. Prejudice emerges from a sense of difference. It is when realization of other people's success or prowess is juxtaposed against personal anxiety that the trouble starts. Whilst there is modesty and a lack of self-belief about the future, and a desire for what is imagined as normal security and ordinariness, children also possess strongly held beliefs about themselves. One of these is of their own inadequacies against other people. They all express levels of discontent that to them are significant, even if these discontents appear to rest on what could be interpreted by others as trivial, like wearing glasses or having curly hair.

Self-esteem is a characteristic much studied and highly valued in the development of personal, social and educational achievement. When failures occur they are often the result of a loss of belief in an individual's ability, an absence of motivation as a result of some kind of trauma. But the ways in which people look at themselves is, of course, far more complex than self-belief or its absence. Everyone has a tension between confidence and insecurity. Arrogance is often a disguise for a lack of self-worth. The way that people see themselves is therefore always changeable. At one level it is pragmatic. We are who we are with all the egotism that goes with our own point of view. But we might not necessarily think that we are the best possible of human beings and we all wish that circumstances were different in one way or another.

The way that self-awareness grows is a delicate matter, depending not only on temperament but chance, on accidents of incidents and relationships. The dependence in young children on the ability to formulate relationships through dialogue is well documented. So is the fact that self-awareness and awareness of other people as distinct entities with their own points of view develops very early. The Piagetian assertion that only young children are autistic in their egotism is now seen as nothing more than a myth, because of children's ability to see other points of view and because of the realization of the inevitable self-centredness of anyone's point of view. The Berkleian conception of the world as one formed by the sensory impression on the mind, and that we can only know as reality what we see and feel, has an ontological truth to it that is at least one layer in the conception of the world.

The sentimentalized picture of childhood – naïvety, innocence, selfishness and optimism – depends on a false adult nostalgia for those periods of play without responsibility, for the knowledge that others would be there to protect and support. (Of course, it is not only adults who feel nostalgic for the past.) The rationalization for this nostalgia has been to conceptualize childhood as a period of unbounded optimism, of looking forward with profound belief in the future, as well as relishing the security of the immediate. This implies that children remain unaware or untroubled by the world around them, a world that is constantly before them in the media, especially on television. This is clearly not the case. Nor, as we have seen, is childhood a period of untroubled bliss. Even in the microcosm of the home and school, let alone through the intrusions of the wider world, there are traumas: quarrels and disagreements, jealousy and discontent.

The pragmatic side of Berkeley's world of sensory intuition is the fundamental philosophical acceptance of the individuality of the self, the inability to do anything but see outwards from within. This is an obvious fact, but it has profound implications. As children clearly realize, the way you are, like the language you speak, depends on where you happen to be born. They know it would be perfectly feasible to have been born in Africa or the United States, and that might have been a better or worse fate. Instead they accept where they are as arbitrary. They might like or dislike the fact, but that is the given case. There is no divine right that dictates that children are born into the best of families in the best of times in the best of countries. One can detect such notions in the literature of the past, especially children's literature, but it does not affect these children. They have a more pragmatic sense of themselves, a pragmatism that not only makes them look in an almost detached way at their circumstances but which compares their own way of life with that of others.

Ontological insecurities

Children are aware of the limitations of their own circumstances. They can cope with this, just as they can complain about the weather, contrasted against the holiday sun, but have to put up with it. What they find they cannot cope with but still have to accept is certain characteristics in themselves, like their appearance. Girls, especially, are conscious of their appearance, and rarely happy with it. There are two kinds of self-consciousness. One is about anything that makes them different – being tall, or wearing glasses – the kind of distinction that attracts bullying or prejudice. The other kind is to do with the way they look or speak. They wish they were more like other people. The type of hair that they have can cause a strain of resentment or puzzlement.

> It feels, it seems funny 'cos you know my mum has straight hair and I keep on asking her, 'Why can't I, why haven't I got straight hair?' Well, my dad's, you know, has those fuzzy hairs like… and I've got really fuzzy ones and it all sticks up and I hate having my hair washed. I want it to be straight but my mum says I look lovely like this. My mummy says 'I have to pay sixty pounds to get it like you and it just falls out in the morning'.
>
> (girl, 7)

Whatever the encouragement by the mother and the suggestion that she has a natural perm there is no question that she wants anything but straight hair. She is teased for having such tight curls. She is not the only one who wishes her hair were different and more like other people. The difference of appearance is translated into a realization that this can attract prejudice. Looks or intelligence or behaviour can all go against a norm. The desire to avoid attention, from teachers as well as fellow pupils, becomes the stronger for having some kind of mark of distinction.

Children take a close critical look at themselves and do not necessarily like what they see. There are often two levels of dislike: wanting to have something that is within reach – like different clothes or a different hairstyle – or things about which little can be done, and which makes them different. This can be a simple matter of wearing glasses, or their voice.

> Having to wear glasses. Well, you haven't really got your natural self. You're here and all your friends are here. Separate.   (girl, 8)

> My voice. I don't like the sound. When I record something when I say something my voice sounds funny.   (boy, 7)

They are also unhappy with some of their personal characteristics. These can range from simple shyness to characteristics of which they disapprove in themselves.

> Sometimes I'm a bit shy on assemblies with talking.   (girl, 8)

> I'm naughty. I lie. 'Cos I punch. And I beat up my mates. Like David. We usually have fights. I lie so I don't get into trouble. So the other person gets into trouble.   (boy, 8)

A deeper level of disturbance comes through children's emotional experiences rather than their self-criticism. This is not just a matter of the suffering that comes from incidents of being bullied, or losing friends. Those troubles of childhood are well documented elsewhere, and whilst one should never underrate the effects of traumas on children – on all children – it needs to be borne in mind that emotional troubles come about not only as a result of difficulties like academic underachievement or being picked on but through a more troubling awareness of a general unhappiness with themselves. Children know the particular events as well as the particular characteristics that make them unhappy, but they also express a more steady and long-lasting unhappiness. This is not just a matter of being lonely at times – ' I like to play lots of games and I don't like it when my friends are off and ill, so I don't have anyone to play with' (boy, 8) – for this is but a passing problem. Children express more steady-state discontents as well as momentary ones. It is as if children would actually like to be someone different. They accept who they are, but they do not necessarily like it.

> I wish I could have more patience and not argue so much.   (girl, 9)

> I would like to have the personality to make people laugh.   (boy, 7)

> I would like to have a personality that makes a likeable person.   (girl, 7)

> I would like to be the sort of person with lots of friends.   (boy, 10)

They so badly wish to be liked, and to be admired.

All the incidents of everyday life, having to do extra work or being teased, remind children that the potential for unhappiness is always with them.

> There is not always anything to be happy about.   (boy, 10)

Childhood is not a time of simple and unalloyed bliss. Children do not think of what makes them unhappy as an exception. More general characteristics of frustration and anger are presented. We see some of the underlying alienation from home and society expressed by a boy who gives all the symptoms of getting into real trouble later on.

> Sometimes I throw things even if people are there, like last night I threw the chair really badly and I nearly hit the TV and I dared to throw it through the window or something. 'Cos I get really angry sometimes.
> Sometimes I used to steal as well.
> Some people don't really like me and be nice to me or anything.
>
> (boy, 8)

Anger is an expression of a form of self-hate. This goes deeper than reflections of their characteristics or the desire to have more attractive personalities. Some children express a deep discontent.

> My mum keeps on saying I'm sort of like different. See, when I have assemblies I like running away. They're boring.
>
> Q: Do you like anything about yourself?
> A: No.
> Q: Nothing at all?
> A: No.
> …
> Q: Pardon? You'd like to be a horse?
> A: Yeah. 'Cos they're nice creatures. They're nice animals.
> Q: Do you like being you?
> A: No. I never do nothing when I go home. I just watch telly.
>
> (girl, 8)

Are these just the characteristics of being bored, both at school and at home? Boredom itself is a symptom of a lack of self-belief, or the creativity that arises from a mind unencumbered with anger and frustration. Some children view themselves as ordinary, as not standing out. They also do not rate themselves as special.

> I don't like being me. I want to be in a different school… I want to be a person like, richer than I am.   (boy, 8)

The reality of children's lives includes more misery than the nostalgic view of adults would suggest. Perhaps seeing children playing seemingly without a care in the world gives an optimistic gloss to this vision. Certainly nostalgia is an emotion shared by children. They too look back on younger days as if they were happier then.

> I'd like to be changed back into a baby again, because whenever I go to my friend's house, which has a little toddler or child that's one or two or three

years old or something I love the toys that they play with because I always like playing with the musical toys.   (girl, 8)

I am not always happy any longer. I was happy when I was younger.
                                                                                (boy, 10)

The question remains how such a sense of insecurity will be dealt with. It is not put on for display, or seeking attention. It is a mark of negative distinction, to be unhappy, to be discontented. There are many structural reasons for being so and all are due to comparisons between their own circumstances and those of others. Differences abound, in the home and in school, in their experience and observation of society. And differences also pervade the world.

References

1. Cullingford, C (1991) The Inner World of the School, Cassell, London
2. Anderson, K and Gale, F (1992) Inventing Places: Studies in cultural geography, Longman Cheshire, Melbourne
3. Titman, W (1994) Special Places: Special People. The hidden curriculum of school playgrounds, World Wildlife Fund, Godalming
4. Rapoport, A (1977) Human Aspects of Urban Form, Pergamon, Oxford
5. Hart, R (1979) Children's Experience of Place, Lovington, New York
6. Moore, R (1986) Childhood's' Domain: Play and place in child development, Croom Helm, London
Cullingford, C (1995) Children's attitudes to holidays overseas, Journal of Tourism Management, 16 (2), pp 121–27
7. Matthews, M (1992) Making Sense of Place: Children's understanding of large-scale environments, Harvester Wheatsheaf, Hemel Hempstead
8. Kahn, P and Friedman, B (1995) Environmental views and values of children in an inner-city black community, Child Development, 66 (5), pp 1403–17
9. Cullingford, C (1996) Children's attitudes to the environment, in Environmental Issues in Education, eds G Harris and C Blackwell, Arena, Aldershot
10. Mayall, B (1994) Negotiating Health: Children at home and primary school, Cassell, London
11. Woods, P (1995) Creative Teachers in Primary Schools, Open University Press, Milton Keynes
12. Chawla, L (1986) The ecology of environmental memory, Children's Environment Quarterly, 3 (4), pp 56–71
13. Ouston, J (1999) School effectiveness and school improvement: critique of a movement, in Educational Management, Redefining Theory, Policy and Practice, eds T Bush et al, Paul Chapman, London
14. Aitken, S (1994) Putting Children in their Place, Association of American Geographers, Washington
15. Cullingford, C (1992) Children and Society, Cassell, London

16. See all the literature on sink schools.

17. Cullingford, C (1999) *The Causes of Exclusion: Home, school and the development of young criminals*, Kogan Page, London

18. Sluckin, A (1981) *Growing Up in the Playground*, Routledge and Kegan Paul, London
Meason, L and Woods, P (1984) *Changing Schools: Pupil perspectives on transfer to a comprehensive*, Open University Press, Milton Keynes

19. Blatchford, P (1992) Academic self-assessment at 7 and 11 years: its accuracy and association with ethnic group and sex, *British Journal of Educational Psychology*, **62** (1), pp 35–44
Stipek, D (1981) Children's perceptions of their own and their classmates' ability. *Journal of Educational Psychology*, **73** (3), pp 404–10

20. Davies, B (1982) *Life in the Classroom and Playground: The accounts of primary school children*, Routledge and Kegan Paul, London
Pollard, P and Filer, A (1996) *The Social World of Children's Learning*, Cassell, London

21. Wells, G (1985) *Language Development in the Pre-School Years: Language at home and school*, Cambridge University Press
Richman, N, Stevenson, J and Graham, P (1982) *Pre-School to School: A behavioural study* Academic Press, London

22. Fransen, A (1981) On qualitative differences in learning: effects of motivation and text anxiety on process and outcomes, *British Journal of Educational Psychology*, **47**, pp 244–57

23. Toivonen, K and Cullingford, C (1998) Racial prejudice in a liberal democracy: a case study, *Politics, Groups and the Individual*, **7** (1–2), pp 45–56

24. Cullingford, C (1999) op cit

25. Williams, I (2000) *Adolescent Estrangement from Society*, Huddersfield University

26. Pye, J (1989) *Invisible Children: Who are the real losers at school?*, Oxford University Press, Oxford

27. Cullingford, C (1991) op cit

28. White, R and Brockington, D (1983) *Tales Out of School: Consumer's views of British education*, Routledge and Kegan Paul, London

6

The world in its place: nations and nationalities

Neutral discriminations

Categorization is both necessary and the first sign of the grouping of habits and experiences into a personal and unique typology. It is the basis for discrimination. It applies as much to social as to objective distinctions between what is important and what can be ignored.[1] Almost as fast as the classification of objects comes the classification of people, the discrimination between the individual welcomed and the individual seen as a potential threat. What later transforms itself into a highly cultivated set of social nuances and niceties, in familiarities and snobbery, in exclusivity and a sense of belonging, has its beginnings in the need to make order out of information. Discrimination is essential, but in its earliest forms it is neutral and objective. It does not start with the sense of 'us' against 'them', or appear trailing a host of emotional associations. The first signs of the learning of categorization are objective.[2]

This capacity to make order out of a proliferation of information, to structure it, to make what is seen, heard and felt fit into a meaningful shape, develops early.[3] Words themselves place disparate objects or types into categories and are, in one sense at least, examples of what could be called stereotypes.[4]

The young child looks on the world with a gaze that is both objective and untrammelled.[5] But it is also a complicated gaze, an active process of making sense of things. Even when we are comfortable with our habitual sets of associations we realize that these operate on a number of different levels. Certain words or images will trigger a whole set of different reflexive responses, emotional as well as intellectual, critical and self-conscious as well as nostalgic. Whilst young children are learning the characteristics of the physical world, and the categories that make it intelligible, manipulable and manageable, they are also learning about its changeability and mutability. Nothing is static. There are many concepts that need to be learnt, from the reality of objects that are hidden or out of sight, to the distinctions between 'tall' and 'high' or 'big' and 'wide'. At the same time that children develop their conceptual plans of the environment they are also reacting to it. This implies making judgements.

The early gaze of children is neutral and objective but it soon progresses to discriminations which include either threat or security. The sound of a particular voice or the pattern of a particular face is not only extracted from the mass of information as unique but also placed into a particular meaning. At first the human voice stands out against other sounds, then certain human voices, and later the tone of that voice. That sense of objective security in seeing the peopled world not as a potential threat but as a neutral ground for the sharing of relationships to some extent remains with children for years. But it is also coloured by their ability to make more complex and refined social distinctions from an early age.

If the natural world with its changeability and mutability and infinite variety is a complex one, then the social world of people, and groups of people, is even more so. One of the earliest concepts that children learn is the distinction between truth and falsehood.[6] Even before they are able to articulate it, children learn to recognize that people each have their individual point of view, that there are inconsistencies and disagreements as well as shared knowledge. They see that people hold on to what they believe is true even when it contradicts the point of view of others. The most powerful form of categorization is the realization that categories are fluid and can change, once they are associated with a human agency. Thus the known objective world has falsehoods as well as truths, and is visibly constructed differently according to the point of view of each individual in it. Long before there is any awareness of the meaning of the word 'epistemology' children are deeply embedded in its understanding.

In order to survive and make sense of the world in which they find themselves all human beings have to take a great many things for granted. Everyday actuality is something all accept as fact.[7] At one level, therefore, children, like adults, see the world not just as a personal construct but as a consistent set of shapes, categories and meanings. At another level children are aware that the cultural as opposed to the physical meanings of the world are both more complex and more lubricious.

The seeds of children's neutrality and relativity and the seeds of prejudice and stereotyping grow from the same soil. The necessity to categorize, as in language, might begin with a sense of objective reality, but it is also a reality consciously and idiosyncratically imposed. The point of view might seem at first purely egocentric, and in the most extreme forms of nationalism it appears to be so, but young children are not born egocentric in that way. They see their environment both more objectively and with a greater understanding of the differences between other people's mental habits. Just as a mass of complex information is simplified by the perceptions in order to make it comprehensible, so do people develop habits of simplification over the years. The narrowness of the point of view is not innate but develops as people learn to treat new information in a familiar way. On the one hand, therefore, the idea of prejudice is one both familiar to everyone and to that extent inevitable. On the other hand it is something that can be so fine-tuned that it is never a necessity. Neutral categorization might be close to emotional associations but it is not the same thing. The relationship between the two is constantly undergoing change.

The judgements that young children make are based not only on their immediate environment. Just as they discriminate between truth and falsehood, so they see the impinging of the world outside. They have to develop a sense of place, of their place in the world. They are mental geographers realizing the significance of different spaces, even if they do not always understand that significance. Confusion over distances, however, does not imply that the concept of differences, in people and places, is any the less significant. The experience of differences in people and groups of people comes as early as the recognition of the importance of other people. There are distinctions of size, between adults and siblings; of tone of voice, between fathers and mothers. Thus different characteristics are then attributed to larger groups, together with an awareness of the significance of groups themselves.

Young children are aware of the multivalent nature of groups, insiders and outsiders, those who belong and those who do not, from the moment they see the operations of their family. They might not always be able to articulate what it means to belong to a particular social group or nation, but they are aware of its existence. Their understanding of the world as a whole, and their place in it, develops not as a series of stages in acquisition, but as a personal sense of the need to give both experience and information some shape. When it comes to the concept of nationality, therefore, the attributions that children give to different countries are as significant as their knowledge of them. Long before the physical and economic geographics are formally presented to them, children have their own distinct ideas of what different countries mean to them. They have their favourites and they have some they fear. The judgement of a country and the associations they hold are strong and dependent more on general association than on fact. On this basis children hold consistent and shared views of the world they are in.

The world divided into categories

The concepts that children have of other countries consist of a string of different types of association. In order to make sense of these they can be divided into five levels of distinction, although it must be noted that all of these overlap. The first level is that of the simplest of binary divides, the rich countries and the poor, the attractive and unattractive. The second level is an extension of this divide, into those countries that seem threatening and those that appear more friendly. The third level involves the inhabitants of the countries, those who seem to be 'nice' and those who seem 'nasty' according to the associations with the characteristics of the country they represent. The fourth level consists of a range of symbolic associations that carry cultural stereotypes with them, like food and dress. The fifth level is that of personal experience, through overheard anecdotes, through travel and through meeting people.

All these influences and associations form a mental map of the world, but a map that is not precisely laid out in spatial terms. The sense of distance and place is often shaky. Comments made about travel reveal how difficult it is to be precise about what it means to 'go abroad'. If the awareness of time and distance seems blurred and even arbitrary, the overall sense of distinct countries, of other places, with alternative climates, languages and cultures is firmly embedded. From the awareness of distinctions of groups and hierarchies there develops a clear idea of the larger conglomerations of countries and peoples, an idea that dwells on differences and a sense of otherness.[8] Within this developing sense of the contrasts between peoples form the ideas that suggest that there are clear preferences according to personal affinity. Familiarity with a way of life, especially if it relates closely to the children's own, suggests something to be approved of.

Children's early understanding of themselves as belonging to a distinct place or region appears to be muddled, but this does not suggest that they are unaware of the fact that they are in a unique place. Their sense of relativity, realizing that they are placed in a distinct context, is joined by their awareness of a whole hierarchy and variety of places, of ever larger boundaries. Their awareness of the nature of the world before being able to map it can be likened to an awareness of the infinity of the universe without being able to conceptualize it easily in terms of time and distance. Young children interchange their identity with a place and a country, citing themselves as belonging to a town or region as readily as to a country.[9] But the imprecision about location does not infer a complete lack of awareness of the essential differences between sizes of location. It is obviously difficult to grasp the different political and geographical conceptions behind as complicated a place as the United Kingdom. There might be stages in understanding that Glasgow is a distinct place, that it is in Scotland, that it is part of Great Britain, but the essential knowledge of a locus, a place that is wrapped around both the individual experience and that of others is there long before it is expressed in political terms.[10]

Before children express the notion of a hierarchy of places – city, county and country – and long before they are taught to define the distinctions, they are aware that they exist. What they do know at the age of three and four is that there are countries with different peoples in them and that some are preferred to others.[11] The artefacts of different cultures are easily conjured up and places that form a conceptual world of differences evoked, from Spain and France to Africa, America and Australia. We see certain countries or continents, like Africa, constantly mentioned with clear mental pictures of what they are like. There is a group of countries as significant that are far more rarely mentioned, like any part of Eastern Europe, or China or the Philippines or Japan. Some of the gaps in knowledge seem to be surprising, but they show the unsystematic way in which children need to put together their own conceptions. Rather than peruse the globe and place precise configurations on continents, children have emotional associations with certain places. The image of the United States on the one hand and Africa on the other is deeply embedded. Even Piaget acknowledges the fact that children have their favourite countries, even if they seem to be chosen on a whimsical basis.[12] But children also are aware of places they associate with negative characteristics. Distinctions precede definitions.

The cultural dominance of the United States

The subtle definition of place, with nations and countries and continents, is not the first thing that children learn about the contrasts of the world. Political boundaries are less significant, even if real, than the sense of groups of people, some of whom are seen as welcoming and some of whom are to be avoided. On the one end of the scale of contrasts lies the United States. For nearly all children, the United States is the promised land. It symbolizes plenty. As the sense of its identity develops, so there is increasing citing of its richness: the possessions, the large size of everything.[13] The country symbolizes the attractions of wealth. But even before the particular images of ownership are defined as the most potent of characteristics the United States is held in warm regard.[14] It is a place that is associated with friendliness as well as riches.

It is significant how homogeneous this picture is. There could well have been counterbalances to this theme of the attractions of wealth. The fact is that there is widespread social deprivation in the United States. The conditions of many groups, especially those of minority ethnic origin, and the circumstances of certain ghettos, like those that surround much of Manhattan, are well known. Indeed, they are often a background to the series of popular Hollywood films-noir, with police involved in corruption, with drug dealing and car chases in locations chosen for their urban squalor. And yet this side of the United States, witnessed by all through the medium of film, elicits barely a mention. There are great contrasts within the country, and often displayed in film. But it is only one side of America that is remembered. Instead of a contrast within a country children use the United States as symbolic of all that is best in capitalism in the developed world. Countries are contrasted against each other rather than seen as containing contradictions within.

The United States is often associated with examples of blatant excess, as if wealth were to be flaunted through any means possible, including the absurd, like stretch limousines. Whereas the children are suspicious of the very wealthy in their own country since they associate them with showing off and snobbery, they seem to take on the more distant image of the United States as if wealth there were either acceptable or ubiquitous. Whilst they see themselves as treading the middle way between fear of poverty and suspicion of excess, they see their own country as relatively modest, as if they were the normal condition, thankful to avoid the threat of the extremes of poverty.[15] And yet their attitude to the rich of the United States, unlike their attitude to the very rich at home, is one of unmitigated admiration, even envy. Somehow the picture of the world as a whole, with its vast and distant contrasts between rich and poor, is one that is considered both inevitable and static. The fact that the United States is rich makes it blatantly attractive.

The key note that is persistently struck for the image of the United States is riches:

They're really rich and they can buy really good cars and stuff.   (boy, 8)

It's a richer country than this country. 'Cos its a big country. They have loads of money. And they buy things.   (girl, 8)

Riches in this context is directly linked to valued possessions, rather than with the unnecessarily excessive. You buy things that you want. The sense of instant gratification is strong. Whereas the strongest desires at home are for more space, whether in terms of more rooms or the freedom to roam, these things seem to be taken for granted as already existing over there. The connection with secondary desires, like possessions, is immediate. It is perhaps this association of an abstract concept like money with something palpable – the desirable possessions that are so assiduously marketed – that makes riches in the United States more acceptable. As with geographical exactitude, children do not know the minutiae of what can be bought for different amounts of money. They are vague about the difference between five, fifty, five hundred and five thousand pounds. But they know what money *does*. They are aware of what it can achieve. They understand its power. And they know the alien currency well enough.

'Cos everyone's rich there and the same in New York, 'cos everyone's got about three hundred million dollars.   (boy, 8)

The amount might be deliberately exaggerated but the insistence on everyone being rich is significant and ubiquitous. For some reason, perhaps because of the way that the United States markets itself, there is a subliminal belief in the generalizability of wealth. This also demonstrates a particular way of simplifying an association. Countries, or continents, have prime symbolic values that underlie all other details. The contrasts are reduced to what are, against realistic analysis, powerful simplifications.

This symbolic world of contrasts between countries has a number of specific conceptual attributes that surround the core association. In a divided world it is the contrasts themselves that count and that lead to certain outcomes. The riches of the United States are seen not so much in terms of generalizable power as in the personal ability to acquire possessions. Money is not an abstraction but a means to particular ends. Ownerships, buying things, especially toys and, later, designer clothes, are real experiences. The desire for gratification includes possessing things, so that financial riches have palpable results.

> It's a good place and you get so many things. Skateboards are made there. Really good ones like mountain bikes and you know, really good things. I've seen programmes...   (boy, 9)

Toys are known to be made in the United States, the begetter of so many film-linked crazes. The result is a scramble for possessions and pressure on parents to spend money. These objects are advertised in two forms, both directly and as part of the Hollywood 'scenery'. The idea of a good place is directly linked to the acquisition of good things. If some of these things are obtainable over here, is the implication, think how much better they are over there. Just as the United States symbolizes 'more' and greater wealth, so it is seen as being full of better and bigger toys.

Part of this sense of awe stems from the fact that so many fashions directed at children emerge from the United States. Designer wear for adults might still be linked to London or Paris, but for children the trendy clothes, from Levi's to Ralph Lauren, are American. The annual Christmas fad of a particular toy or model that everyone *must* have is almost always of American origin. This suggests that in young people's minds wealth is directly linked to a sense of superiority: wearing better clothes, being in the lead in fashion.

> A lot more expensive clothes. 'Cos a lot of things like movies and new things come out first in America, before Britain, so I can imagine American people wearing the latest fashion.   (girl, 9)

Fashion and expense are closely linked and it is interesting to note the extent to which children are nurtured in such an attitude. Whilst some forms of influence might seem to be inadvertent – Judy Blume's books are designed to *reflect* teenage tastes whilst they help form them – there are so many of them, it is as if the importance of fashion, in language and behaviour as well as in possessions, were being deliberately orchestrated.[16]

Children are aware of the source of many cultural artefacts. They are highly tuned to the 'American' way of life, not only absorbing many of the attitudes they see in situation comedies (if not the accents, except when singing pop music) but realizing how influenced their own way of life is by another country.

> They got dollars and I like dollars. They've got different cars on there and they have different all kinds of stuff there. They get really big pizzas about *that* size. In Pizza Hut. And they have french fries. And chicken McNuggets.
>
> (boy, 8)

Whilst fast-food outlets abound in their own country they are still seen as part of an imported culture. The awareness of different origins of cultural habits could hardly be more explicit. Restaurants exhibit different ethnicities in their foods, separate cultural hegemonies. But 'American' food outlets are also a culture of a style of eating, an approach to food that is still associated with a cultural fashion, one that children, whatever the best intentions of their parents, feel is attractive. Fast-food chains are associated with their origins, a place where 'they' have big pizzas, or cars. The differences are noted whilst being absorbed. The mighty dollar is invoked as a currency to be preferred for its symbolic value if not for its meaning in financial terms. What is it about the selling of America that so many children admire the dollar long before they are told about exchange rates or even the price of things in relation to annual incomes? Perhaps it is because of the link with size – 'bigger' suggests 'and better'. There is an atavistic sense of greed.

> It's good because there's lots of places. It's big. It's got big houses. Big cars. Better houses, better because most of them are bigger and they've got different styles. There's better films that you can watch. There's bigger playgrounds. Lots of things to do.
>
> (boy, 9)

Part of the sense of relativism comes about because of the awareness of a 'better' place elsewhere. Different begins to be associated with bigger and better.

The United States is marketed not just through brand names and fast foods but through the world of entertainment. All are symbolized in Disney World theme parks, where exciting activities are associated with Hollywood characters.

> I'd like to go to the sunny place 'cos there's three different Disney Worlds in America. All the people there are like modern fashioned and they're really cool kind of sounding like... I would like to be really happy and swimming and they have really nice clear water.
>
> (girl, 6)

The sense of 'lots of things to do', vast possessions, and the most modern of fashions are all intricately linked. Although there are theme parks, even a Disney World, in Europe, the original source of such entertainment is still rated more highly than any domestic equivalent even if accessible. One reason for this is that the marketing of these figures and activities is done in a cheerful way. America is not just presented as bigger and better but as a friendly place. Their approachability and openness are often remarked upon.

> They say they're really friendly and sometimes they come up to you and go 'Hi!'. They just walk up to you and go 'Hi!'. (boy, 8)

This invocation of the notion of friendliness to go with size and riches reminds us of the end of W H Auden's poem *On the Circuit*:

> God bless the USA; so large,
> So friendly, and so rich.

The image of the United States has remained constant for years. The impact of Hollywood films and the merchandising of so many things as distinctly American has directly influenced the opinions voiced by children. The United States is seen as an entity that provides distinctive and desirable experiences as part of its cultural inheritance. Its presentation, particularly on television, is constant and even if not uniform, results in an overwhelmingly favourable image. Children are conscious of the experience of seeing its display.[17]

> It just sounds rich and it looks quite rich on TV. (girl, 8)

The rich countries and the poor

The United States is clearly associated with riches. This is in marked contrast to other countries, particularly the developing ones. Such a divide is absolutely clear to children.

> Some countries are poor and some are rich like America, you get very rich, some by oil and everything and they have a lot of money, and it's completely the opposite in Ethiopia. By oil, and other things like, because they're big business. (girl, 9)

Nothing could be in greater contrast than the attitudes children express towards the poorer parts of the world, especially Africa. In place of admiration and the familiarity of cultural artefacts we find fear and loathing. This might be inevitable, given the actual contrasts of the world and the constant reminders, as in Oxfam campaigns, of the sufferings of the people in this part of the world. That children absorb these images is also inevitable. What is interesting is how they react to and internalize them.

The first constant portrayal of the African experience is of people starving.

> The children, well, they're brown and they're not well fed and they're small and they're skinny because they haven't got enough food and some die of, um, water and hunger because they haven't got any food to eat.
>
> (girl, 7)

> Africa, children dying and that. There all elephants around. They're brown. They have no clothes. They live in little blanket tents. You only starve and you die.
>
> (boy, 6)

The Oxfam image of Africa, designed to evoke pity, is reproduced here. The brown children, naked and helpless, skinny and pleading with the large eyes, keep recurring. There is a clear awareness that they are suffering and that suffering is a result of lack of food, plentiful elsewhere. But there is little sense of outrage. This is how it is. The picture remains a picture rather than a cause.

> And countries which have no food and have no clothes. Africa. Some of them have no clothes and you can see some of the people there shivering. Some don't have clothes and some just have rags and things like that.
>
> (girl, 6)

Deprivation is presented as a characteristic of such places. The people they see have no clothes or rags or strange clothes of a primitive kind. That seems to be their way of life. The contrast with the privileges of the children's own circumstances leads to a certain distancing, the noting of all the signs of poverty of their circumstances.

When children learn about Africa through domestic sources of information the picture is of complete deprivation. There is no explanation of difficult climates or a lack of a manufacturing base to account for why the people are poor. Poverty is imbibed as a way of life. It is as if the fact that there are large cities, with skyscrapers and traffic jams, were either withheld from children's attention or ignored. African houses, as evoked in educational programmes, are of a distinct kind, and uninfluenced by modern technology:

> Like some houses are made of straw. And, um, I think in Africa they're made of cow's muck and they wait 'til it's dry and then they go and they build houses with it.
>
> (girl, 9)

Just sticks. And they have lots of cows and cow-pats. They pick them up in big trolleys and then put them and then splat them on their houses to make the cracks all get stuck. And so it's all stuck. And they have to get right round near the ground so there are bits on there and then it goes at corners. So it sticks it in the ground. Sticks and cow-pats.   (boy, 6)

These descriptions sound like the result of lessons on different cultures, but the source is not the school but what has been seen on television. This is how 'they' build houses, with sticks and cowpats. It is depicted as a way of life but one that is adapted to particular circumstances. The way of living is closely associated with difficulties, of soil and climate, as if culture were an almost exact equivalent of the environment.

The imagery and the facts of deprivation are constantly being reinforced. The picture of the child so weak that the flies seek moisture from the eyes is often evoked.

They were black. They had flies all round them. Some of them had wounds.
                                                                            (girl, 8)

What is taken from a picture of famine is the sense that in *that* place there are 'loads of flies' and in *that* place there is not enough water.

Really, really hot and they don't have much water. They have to dig to get the water and then you get dirty water to drink and sometimes it's poisonous… they hardly have any rain. And when it does rain, they put buckets out and dig holes… the places that are starving, they've only got like big sticks with cloth at the top and leaves.   (boy, 8)

The poverty of Africa, so often stressed, presents itself as a structural, permanent way of life, rather than as a temporary aberration caused by war or drought. The people *never* have enough water, and have 'only got' primitive kinds of shelter. There are people forever benighted, poor, in need of pity and charity, permanently in need of help. Either the perceived inevitability of this needs more attention or it is put aside as a fact of life. The world will from this perspective remain divided.

The sense of Africa, standing as it does as representative of the whole of the developing world, is one of permanent poverty and backwardness. Aridity of climate is associated with primitive ways of life and with 'blacks'.[18] The imagery is always negative.[19] Nursery children already associate Africa with starvation.[20] Indeed, any pictures that children are given that contain black people or arid countryside were immediately associated with poverty.[21] This is the case despite the fact that in their own classes and schools there are considerable numbers of black people, let alone actors and reporters on television. The association of blacks and Africa, blacks and starvation, prevails. This is partly because the television pictures, especially on the news, are so powerful. They become generalized.

> Because on the news it showed what they were eating at the moment and what the trucks were bringing over to them.   (girl, 8)

> Sometimes when I'm watching programmes like *Newsround* and *Blue Peter* things like that… just poor places that they've gone to… food problems and these people just crowding round, starving.   (boy, 9)

What television shows as news is repeated often enough for it to become associated with a way of life. There is no surprise that children would be alarmed and distressed by the pictures of suffering, but this leads to a negative view of the developing world. Despite all the efforts of charitable agencies to present a more constructive view of the rest of the world, and despite their efforts at promoting policies of self-help that are sustainable, the understanding of Africa as dependent permanently on charity is ubiquitous. Children, like adults, are supposed to react to pictures of the starving with pity and charity, but they respond to the pictures rather than the message. Whilst they are shocked at the contrasts between the very rich and the very poor, they grow up to believe that this is how the world is. And whilst some of them mention particular countries like Zimbabwe or Kenya, or those most recently on the news, they all talk of Africa as if the picture were always the same, forgetting the contrasts of climate, culture or environment. Their generalizations are steady and permanent.

It is worth noting that the imagery of Africa, in terms of screen time on television, should be that of nature programmes, but despite the occasional mention of an elephant, the equatorial forests or the 'jungles' are rarely mentioned and then only as a background to the central social image. Children do not lack an interest in wildlife. On the contrary, exotic animals are a source of interest. Their image of the world is still centred on people and on what people do, and how they live. The ephemeral images of the television, as news comes and goes, becomes a fixed one. Those who look on distressing footage become capable of dealing with their distress; they have to learn to be inured. But they also learn that such distress is constant, often repeated, sometimes in other places, but also always in 'Africa'.

Reactions to poverty

Images of poverty can have an alienating effect. There is a certain irony that one effect of the global village, when television brings pictures of distant places into the home, is to create an enhanced sense of separateness. The sense of Africa evoked by the children suggests no desire to go anywhere close, in contrast to the United States. Despite the many attempts to evoke sympathy and interest that could turn to action, as in the missionary endeavours of Church or school 'Tear-funds', there is a sense of estrangement rather than closeness.

> Because I remember at my school we were having this fund-raising appeal, so if they went to the doctor they had to carry their pills home in just tissues and they just disintegrated by the time they got home because of the heat. They just didn't have anything. And they all made that trip. Sometimes they walked just about hundreds of miles for water. It's stupid.
>
> (boy, 9)

The frustration of helplessness does not lead automatically to suggestions of greater involvement. What remains in the mind is seen as so absurd it is just stupid. In conditions like that is it even worth giving charity? Nevertheless, charity is presented as the one source of potential well-being. The assumption is that 'they're not rich enough to feed themselves'.

> They're not as fortunate as us. They haven't got a lot of money or food…
> like England sent over some doctors to get them well again.   (girl, 8)

Children have to make sense of all the imagistic information by putting it into an homogenous pattern. All has to be connected by some kind of emotional as well as intellectual thread. Poverty is associated with a certain style of living, as famine is associated with the weather. It all seems inevitable. The explanations that they give for their idea of Africa centres on the climate. The peculiarities of the environment are assumed to lead to a particular way of life, and this is looked on with a certain distaste. Just as the African way of living is visualized as centring on straw and mud houses, so the people's habits are considered both endemic and distasteful. What they eat, whether they have to or choose to eat it, is unattractive.

> They eat what things move, like beetles and snails and slugs.   (girl, 6)

> They haven't got proper food there… they eat like mud and horrible stuff
> like that.   (girl, 7)

But despite the 'horrible' experiences, which could be a result of circumstances, the divide between the styles of living, including eating, go deeper than that. There are other reasons that they do not have proper food.

If they had burgers they wouldn't have nothing to cook them with. No cookers and don't have proper food to eat. They don't use cookers. They use, they light a fire. They get two woods with one going along and up and the other one going up and one do the same the other side and get a metal bowl and put the burgers in.   (boy, 9)

The sense of contrast between 'us' and 'them' is very strong. All the familiar accoutrements of normal life which are so taken for granted that they are rarely considered suddenly become the more valued. Normal houses and normal burgers and shops to buy them in: all these are missing.

If they didn't hunt to look for their food, um, they would be like... well, how could they eat if they didn't hunt? Because they might not have any money or anything to give to the shop people. The shops are not like shops here. Like you just go through a door and you can have a look around and say 'mm, that's nice!' Well, they're not like that. They're, kind of, you know, the greengrocers and that, they're kind of open like that.
                                                           (girl, 8)

The strangeness and the horror of the extreme strikes the children forcibly in pictures of poverty, but what also lingers in their minds in the absence of the familiar. Whereas the familiar enhances what is valued in the United States, the familiar is missing entirely in pictures of Africa. The defining characteristics of their own way of life, from clothes to hi-fi and television, is substituted by living styles on which the children look with almost anthropological distance. All the artefacts, all the possessions that define their own culture, are missing.

Things like plants and three piece suites and television and things like that. And transistor radios and personal stereos and things... not proper houses at all. Sticks and bits of material stuck together.   (girl, 9)

The contrast could not be greater. How could people live without their three piece suites?

The promotion of difference and familiarity

That sense of distance is enhanced by the association of Africa with being peopled by 'blacks'. Coming from a multi-cultural society these children observe the images that are presented to them and store the facts. The starving babies are 'black and skinny'. They 'look like they're from Africa'. Despite their own experience 'there's black people there and white people in England' (boy, 7). All the negative associations, of mud houses, lack of food, and harsh conditions, surround the 'blacks'. Indeed, the occasional witness who has actually been to Africa notes the distinctions between the living styles and standards of the 'whites' and those of the 'blacks'.

> There's quite a lot of whites as well... They live in quite big houses with big gardens... The other people live in huts and things or small little houses.
>
> (girl, 8)

The great divide is, then, not just a matter of money but of colour.

One of the important effects of the depiction of other countries is the reinforcement of the value of the existing culture in which people live. The familiar becomes the more important. What could be taken for granted, like eating certain foods at certain times, or the utility of modern conveniences, becomes a cultural icon. Certain habits are seen not to be generally shared. They become the more valuable for not being inevitable. The sense of the ordinariness of the familiar becomes transformed into a mark of distinction. Alongside the neutral relativity of accepting what is there, the description of what is, the everyday, is marked with a cultural value. The concept of hearth and home, and of the significance of the neighbourhood, becomes allied to value. The familiar can become the more important, a middle way: the right one.

The imagery that makes up the mental pictures of Africa and the United States is like the reduction of a succession of pictures to their simplistic essence. Whilst there is a hint of envy in the one case and a touch of horror in the other, the way in which they are described is not strongly emotional. It is rather a laconic statement of fact. But countries are not always treated with such clear objectivity. They are also associated with being friendly or with being threatening. At another level of analysis children suggest a more emotional engagement with what countries signify: war as well as poverty, the threat of war as well as terrorism. The savagery of terrorists or the sufferings of people in war are at a different level from a status quo which can be avoided. Terrorism signifies personal threat. Those countries that are unstable, and threatened by war, or which threaten other countries with war are mostly at a safe distance, but, unlike those suffering in Africa, are seen as a potential threat. Some countries 'might have a war. They just put a lot of things too far' (boy, 9).

As well as rich and poor countries, then, there are good and bad countries, bad ones suggesting war or political instability. There are glimpses of the fear of Russia.[22] This is because what is presented on the news is not the individual circumstances of people, but the political issues.

They weren't free like us. We can do anything except murder people. But there, they had special things like the Catholic church that was different to us. People weren't allowed in there unless they were strict Catholics, proper strict Catholics, unless they had permission by the people at the gate, at the door. And if they tried to get in without the people at the door saying they couldn't, and um, they tried to get in, even though they said they couldn't and they were shot. I heard it on telly.

It's very strict there, and they take people easily to prison and they have the black market and if you're caught buying from the black market you could be in prison... They're strict there, like I said before. That's why I wouldn't want to go to Russia. I wouldn't like, 'cos they've got harsh rules like if you're caught doing something wrong, you get sent to prison.

(girl, 9)

Some of the facts might be muddled or mistaken, but the imagery is linked to the sense of threat, of people trying to go where they are not allowed to, of an oppressive police force, of social rather than natural disaster. The sense of police control, of 'strict' rules as well as the black market all leads not only to *not* wanting to go there but of a more pervasive idea of an oppressive state.

Such comments show clear awareness of political tensions associated with particular countries, as if some suffered either from a controlling government or from external threats.

They're terrorists there. I think they're a bit like Arab people. I think their habits are different maybe, but I don't really know. They wear sort of long sheets wrapped round their heads to keep the heat off them. I'm afraid of the people there. (girl, 8)

On the other hand there are countries that are seen to be distinctly friendly. Australia, as presented on *Neighbours*, an all-white suburb of domestic material bliss as well as argument, is one such.

I'd like to be Australian as well sometimes... because I just like their accent and things like that... it's hot. A bit like Zimbabwe except they don't have black people. And there's a big enormous bush as well. It's a very big space. And it's got a big sea all the way round. (girl, 8)

Australia has two essential attributes: size and friendliness. It also has two extra ingredients, a warm climate and exotic animals. The warm sea and the bush make it pleasantly different. The Aboriginals are not mentioned. Instead we find the attraction for wanting to *be* Australian.

> I would like to live there because it's quite a nice country and lots of people who have been there have told me about it. One of my friend's has actually been to quite a lot of the schools there because she's part Australian and they're a bit more educated than our schools.   (boy, 8)

As is the case with the United States there is a desire to live there, but expressed on a more domestic scale. There is a strong tendency for children to say they would like to visit the United States, but they would like to be Australian. They like the accent. They have relations. The world of *Neighbours* is closer to their own and has all the warmth of the familiar. Whilst girls in particular cite *Neighbours* as a source of awareness, there is a general confirmation that they learn about Australia through personal contacts as well, like the friend who has been to a 'more educated' Australian school. They have heard others' enthusiasms.

This suggests something about the different sources of knowledge. As other research also demonstrates, the presentation of a country cannot be separated from the medium of knowledge with which it is associated. Russia is known about through the news, the United States through entertainment and Australia from other sources.[23] The news about Africa is, of course, reinforced by the charitable agencies. The binary divide between the good and the bad, attractive and unattractive is made the more subtle by additional associations of threat or friendliness. The world then is seen not just in terms of static, permanent attributes but in terms of volatility or potential volatility. The sense of engagement with another country can become more personal.

Nations and national characteristics

One country that is clearly associated with a sense of fear or threat is Germany. In the minds of many Europeans, Germany holds a unique place because of the Second World War and the Holocaust. The way in which nationalism was linked with racism is still a strange manifestation of wickedness that will continue to perplex those who study human nature.[24] This is because of the way in which ordinary people were willing to carry out the cruellest of deeds in an organized and efficient way.[25] Ethnic cleansing, the massacre of other tribes, killing in the name of religion are the terrible stuff that fills newspapers. Attacks on nation-states abound, from the ancient war between the Chechen people and Russia, through the nineteenth century, through Stalin's mass murders, to the present day. What makes Germany an unusual case is the way in which violent prejudice was so closely linked to political and economic organization, and the way in which the past is still a source of fascination, and constantly recycled in films.

Comparisons between Stalin and Hitler are often made, but the reaction to the people they ruled still differ. It is with the Germans that there is a lasting association of behaviour with race. We have already noted the complex reactions to Germany during and after the Second World War. Should they all be put down? Is there something genetically wrong? Or were they the victims of the extremes of human pathology, a lust for violence that was allowed to get out of control? Young children in their attitudes towards other countries either see the harmless stereotypes, or they see the way other people live, as manifestations of the inevitable, where poverty is seen as both pitiable and fearful. The person is never separated from the nation, or place.

British children's attitudes to Germany is uniquely negative. They are not, of course, alone in this. Those brought up on the unselfconscious chauvinism of children's literature still manifest a great suspicion of the Germans. The negative feelings are due to a blend of the stereotypical image and the actions that express that image. Here we will summarize what has been dealt with more fully elsewhere.[26] Whether it is due to all the films that rely on Germans as the enemy, parents' memories, or shared histories, Germans are assumed to be war-loving and brutal.

I'm afraid they might be nasty. They might kidnap you.   (boy, 7)

... because they are wicked... whipping people and shooting people.
                                                                (boy, 8)

I think they were quite mean. They must have been 'cos Hitler was. Hitler was very violent and also very, very aggressive.   (girl, 8)

The transference from an individual to the many, and the association of historical fact and latent and continuing characteristics are typical. The most famous German, despite the fame of certain sports personalities, remains Hitler.

Nations and stereotypes

There are many levels of reaction to other peoples and other nations. There can be fierce prejudice and fear. There can be envy and admiration, a desire to be elsewhere, as if the security of being oneself were essentially displaced. And there are many lighter touches in between. The sense of other people's characteristics being eccentric rather than threatening, stereotypical in image rather than behaviour, is also widespread. France is a good example of this lighter, equivocal, more ambivalent series of labelling and making distinctions. There are many Francophiles and there are many invocations of 'Frogs' if there is an argument about trade. But generally the French, unlike the Germans, do not pose a threat. They have peculiar habits, not vicious ones, although this does not prevent the stirring of passions if there is a call for it.

The stereotypes of the French are a mixture of personal experience, and the images presented through the media.

> Snail's shells and frog's legs... they usually sell them in stores and some-times in restaurants. My dad's eaten some of them in Paris. Frog's legs and snails. Some people are artists. They sometimes wear blue striped jump-ers, T-shirts and a blue hat with a little, a tiny knob on it. I've seen it on a programme on television.   (boy, 7)

The question is whether secondary experience remains a separate image or whether it colours personal knowledge. The idea of the beret and the striped jumpers is one of those generalizations that fit the much-expounded image of a nation, like bowler hats and pin-stripes. They are labels, even if they are no longer current. Years after their establishment, school textbooks and plays still invoke the same picture. But frogs and snails prevail.

> They eat snails and I think they eat horse. And they eat French bread. 'Cos when we went there we went in this shop and I saw some snails and they eat octopuses. I didn't see so many wearing berets... [my sister] got me one and she told me that they do.   (girl, 7)

Personal experience is bolstered by being told what to notice. Berets might not be seen but are still looked for.

The amount of information about other countries and other people is enor-mous and is constantly having to be sorted out. The way this is done is by the acceptance of images, by association with past experience, by critical analysis, or by a combination of all three. It is as easy to dismiss the latest pictures on the news as distant and irrelevant as to be shocked and horrified by them. But they all have meaning. They are part of the discriminating activities that are not limited to early learning but continue to be applied. Children are influenced by personal experi-ence, overheard remarks or anecdotes and by the reports of what is happening else-where. Other countries are associated with tourism or terrorism. They are friendly or dangerous places. This sense of place is also a sense of other people. If one coun-try is dangerous it is because of the human activities that take place there. It is not just a matter of circumstances but of will.

All experience is made personal and recorded emotionally in some way or another. Some incidents might stand out and leave a distinct impression, but it is the accumulated evidence of association that create prejudices. One scene can then be generalized into a bias.

People in Germany, most of them, they're not very nice. They're kind of
shouty and rough... when we were in Germany we went to the Rhine
      Falls and they were all shouting and everything. And one actually
kicked a person and tripped him over.   (girl, 9)

If there is a prevailing view then anything will be interpreted in experienced light
of that view. Conversely, a particular experience can trigger such a general response
thereafter.

When children talk about other countries they do not only describe. They
always reveal attitudes and judgements. Nothing is neutral. Whilst on the surface
there might be a description of what people wear, or what they eat, objectively
observed, there is underneath a judgement, positive or negative, on whether that
seems similar to their own habits or experience, or alien, something to be emulated
or despised. There are associations of symbols and peoples. Thus Hitler stands for
Germans. The particular image is representative of the sense of massive support.
There are places where things happen, like war and famine. But it is almost impossible to dissociate events from the people involved. Take, for example, the prevailing image of Iraq.

Dead people everywhere. Massive vans everywhere and these guys with
guns. Cruel, violent, savage... not all but most, like Saddam Hussain and
other ones. Like the troops, you know. I think they're a bit violent as well.
Go around destroying everybody for nothing.   (boy, 9)

It is not only the figurehead who is seen as cruel ('I'll punch him his head in. He's
so cruel, you know') but the supporters. There might be only one image but it pervades others, even if there is a sense that this does not encapsulate 'all'. The visual
images of guns and dead people are followed by what they mean: mankind's inhumanity to man. The question is whether that is confined to one place, or pervasive.
That it exists could be understood by children to be a unique characteristic of a
group of people, or a general symptom of mankind out of control. They personally
experience unkindness and intolerance almost every day. They also see the contrast between the relative peace of where they live and the unbounded cruelties of
war. Certain things happen everywhere; and other things only happen elsewhere.
How they understand the difference is crucial.

Whilst there are violent images of war, and the people associated with them,
these images are also supported by the sense of difference, of estrangement. It is
impossible not to be aware that there are cultural habits that are also expressed in
the pictures that are seen. A war is peopled.

On the television you see all smashed up homes and it's quite hard to see
what they are... I've noticed the women wear dresses, like of, like white

dresses and black shoes and black kind of scarf round the head and then covered to their eyes. And some even have it round their eyes... if you like cover your face it wouldn't feel nice... you wouldn't feel right. You wouldn't feel free, I think... because of their religion.   (girl, 8)

The images of war are not just of arbitrary brutality. They include innocent victims, the people characterized by their circumstances. They might be the dying poor of Africa, or they could be the culturally defined peoples of a particular region. There is talk of religion, but has this ever been explained? Have there ever been real explorations of the diversity of cultural circumstances or the common concerns of humanity? The images of the 'black kind of scarf' are associated with discomfort, with the alienation that is provoked by the sense that what someone wears is imposed upon them; the black hats, the goatee beards, the side-locks, the yarmulka...

Children are prevailed upon with a sense of 'them'. It can be neutral or it can be threatening. What they are sorting out is how to make the choices between those places and peoples that are friendly and accommodating and those who are inimical, that are to be avoided. Even on a holiday, observations concentrate not only on the pleasures but the differences, on cultural selectivity as well as generalizable habits. The 'they' can be deemed to be a friend or an enemy. After a holiday in Greece, all modern conveniences and great pleasures, a boy recalls all the details, from the weather to the accommodation. He appreciates the beach and the food. He is, up to a point, caught up in a package holiday. But he also observes, constantly.

They wear hats a lot and they speak a different language. And they are usually rather plump... I'm not sure if they grow oranges. They certainly grow nuts... The sort of crops they grow aren't the sort of crops we grow. They wear different things. They look different. They are used to different things... they don't have very good schools. Not with a very lots of people in. Not with posh furniture and things like that in.   (boy, 8)

Difference is a neutral term. It can remain so. Or it can be a mark of ontological distinction. It can be positive or negative. But the marks of distinction, of 'them' and 'us', are deeply embedded. Now they begin to have cultural meaning. And this can be good or bad, tolerant or prejudiced.

Children have a mental map of the world that is full of contrasts. In place of safe or threatening places, and extending the idea of rich and poor, they project an awareness of the contrasts of the world, of other peoples. They associate them with artefacts and emotions. And they are aware of what they prefer. They have a sense of their own circumstances, and the pictures of other countries gives them a stronger awareness of what is familiar, and ordinary and everyday. This makes their own security all the more important. It is not something taken for granted.

References

1. Bourdieu, P (1984) *Distinction: A social critique of the judgement of taste*, Routledge and Kegan Paul, London

2. Bruner, J (1996) *The Culture of Education*, Harvard University Press, Cambridge, MA

3. Sugerman, S (1983) *Children's Early Thought: Developments in classification*, Cambridge University Press, Cambridge

4. Bates, E (1976) *Language and Context: The acquisition of pragmatics*, Academic Press, New York

5. Cullingford, C (1999) *The Human Experience: The early years*, Ashgate, Aldershot

6. Flavell, J *et al* (1990) Young children's understanding of fact beliefs versus value beliefs, *Child Development*, **61** (4), pp 915–28

7. McGinn, C (1993) *The Subjective View. Secondary qualities and indexical thought*, Clarendon Press, Oxford

8. Reay, D (1995) They employ cleaners to do that: habitas in the primary classroom, *British Journal of Sociology of Education*, **16** (3)

9. Piaget, J (1929) *The Child's Conception of the World*, Routledge and Kegan Paul, London

10. Jahoda, G (1962) Development of Scottish children's ideas and attitudes about other countries, *Journal of Social Psychology* (58), pp 91–168

11. Lambert, S. and Wiegand, P (1990) The beginnings of international understanding, *New Era in Education*, **71** (3), pp 90–93

12. Piaget, J and Weil, A (1951) The development in children of the ideas of the homeland and of relations with other countries, *International Social Science Bulletin* (3), pp 561–78

13. Jahoda, op cit

14. Jeffcoate, R (1977) Children's racial ideas and feelings, *English in Education*, **11** (1), pp 32–46

15. Cullingford (1999) op cit

16. Cullingford, C (1996) *Children's Literature and its Effects*, Cassell, London

17. Nightingale, V and Troyna, B (1981) Watching the world go by, *New Era in Education*, **62** (4), pp 126–30

18. Graham, J and Lynn, S (1989) Mud huts and flints: children's images of the Third World, *Education 3–13*, **17** (2), pp 29–32

19. Yungkunz, M (1988) *Children's Attitudes to Developing Countries*, Centre for Development Education, Oxford

20. Lambert, S and Wiegand, P, op cit

21. Graham, J and Lynn, S, op cit

22. Nightingale, V and Troyna, B, op cit

23. Ibid

24. Arendt, H (1989) *The Banality of Evil: The trial of Adolf Eichman*, Secker and Warburg, London

25. Goldhagen, D (1996) *Hitler's Willing Executioners: ordinary Germans and the Holocaust*, Little, Brown, London

26. Cullingford, C and Husemann, H, eds (1996) *Anglo-German Attitudes*, Ashgate, Aldershot

7

The world and the individual's point of view

Nations and nationhood

One of the tests of knowledge as a sign of being well informed that predates the National Curriculum is the ability to name countries and capitals. The ability of children to demonstrate this rudimentary geographical awareness is patchy but quite impressive. When asked to name countries, the children between them come up with a long list: Abu Dhabi, Africa (sic), Albania, Algeria, America (sic), Andorra, Antarctic, Arctic, Argentina, Australia, Austria, Bangladesh, Barbados, Belgium, Bhutan, Borneo, Brazil, Canada, Chile, China, Cyprus, Czechoslovakia, Denmark, Egypt, England, Ethiopia, France, Gambia, Germany, Greece, Greenland, Honduras, Hong Kong, Hungary, Iceland, India, Iran, Iraq, Ireland, Israel, Italy, Japan, Kenya, Korea, Kuwait, Lebanon, Malaysia, Malta, Mauritius, Mexico, Namibia, New Zealand, Northern Ireland, Papua New Guinea, Paraguay, Poland, Portugal, Romania, Russia, Saudi Arabia, Scotland, Singapore, South Africa, Soviet Union, Sri Lanka, Sudan, Swaziland, Sweden, Switzerland, Thailand, Togo, Tonga, Trinidad and Tobago, United States, Turkey, Uruguay, Wales, West Samoa, Venezuela, Yugoslavia and Zimbabwe.

Within this list, however, lie great variations. Several of the least well-known countries are mentioned by just one boy who considers himself to be an expert on the names of countries. Several countries, like Turkey, are mentioned just once. Nor is this list, the one closed question given to children, supposed to be comprehensive. As one seven-year-old girl says, 'I've heard of lots but I can't remember them'. What is more significant is the fact that there are certain countries mentioned by either all or most of the children: Africa, as if it were one country, America (meaning the United States), France, Germany and Australia. Other countries, like Spain, Italy, Greece, Scotland, Iraq and Russia are mentioned quite often. But the significant knowledge of the names of countries ends there. In this context of naming places no mention is made of Norway, Finland, Holland, Bulgaria, Libya, Peru or Columbia, to name some one might have expected.

But this is mere knowledge. Much more interesting and revealing is what children think a country consists of and their attitudes towards it. There is a difference between the awareness of the names of countries and their reflections on these countries. There is also a difficulty in defining what a country consists of. There is, after all, especially in the case of Africa, a difficulty in separating the idea of a country from the concept of a continent.

> I think it's outside – I don't know if it's in Europe or outside Europe. It's in, er, the sort of same bit of land as Europe. But I don't think it's Europe. [Germany]   (girl, 7)

The definitions of territory overlap. The concept of Africa, like that of Europe, is constantly evoked. Where boundaries begin and end are hard to define, but the fact that there are territorial boundaries and defined nations and nationalities is understood early. The difficulties of definition, as in the case of the United Kingdom, should not obscure the essential grasp of the fact of different peoples within different states. The concept of belonging somewhere is firmly embedded. There is a tendency to name the town or city they live in as well as a 'country' for each town, defining a particular community embedded within another.

> Like Birmingham's a city, England's a country. So all the cities are the places in the country. So the country's the main bit like England.
>   (girl, 8)

Difficulties in definition do not imply ignorance. There can be muddles. Countries that are cited include Cyprus, Crete, Alaska and Hawaii. But very few suggest that they have no idea of what a nation consists of.

> It's a place where – I don't really see any difference between a country and something like a continent. It's just like one big whole world.   (boy, 9)

This boy showed in his discussions of particular countries that he is aware of their distinct and separate characteristics. The neighbourhood has its own defined space, and beyond that there is a sense of belonging to an inherited cultural entity, defined by accent, or language, by building habits or house styles.

Children find the concept of a country difficult to define, but, as we will see, their very difficulties reveal ways in which they form their mental maps of the world. Many find the concept difficult because they wish to define a country in geographical terms: as a distinct space, smaller than some spaces, bigger than others.

> Some countries are sort of like islands. And you get continents with loads
> of different countries in them like Europe. Like the Soviet Union. That's a
> continent. It's got loads of different countries in there like Asia and that.
>
> (boy, 9)

The sense of a country as a tract of land leads to some interesting misconceptions:

> The North Pole isn't a country. It's just ice, loads really.   (boy, 8)

Again, this is a matter of definition. Children's sense of countries as entities is
strong even when they make mistakes between continents or towns. One good
example of this is following misapprehension about the meaning of China as a
country.

> I think I might live in China because when we were in America, in Florida,
> we walked all the way up the hill to where a place called China was. And it
> was quite a nice place. We saw a few white people. Everybody else was sort
> of browny colour. Because we've been walking around China when we
> were in Florida. And daddy's gone – well, I think I've heard of India as
> well. It's quite near Bangladesh. But India's quite a funny place to live in
> because you would be in wigwams. I've seen them on telly and I've seen
> people like in India and I've seen people in China. China's quite a nice
> place to live. When we were in Florida we saw, we went into Mexico.
>
> (girl, 6)

Here we see the difference between analytical knowledge and the real awareness
and experience. This girl has tried to match her own experience to the terms that
she has heard, finding her own way through a mass of information. A country
becomes a cultural milieu. It is transferable, a symbol of clear characteristics.

'Us' and 'them': the closeness of association and the distance of place

If the concept of a country is difficult to define, it does not prevent the formation of
attitudes towards particular countries. Before the development of knowledge
comes the forming of opinions, in which some countries are preferred to others.
Difficulties of definition do not prevent children having a very clear idea of the *fact*
of different countries, and the concept of space. There are many other countries
and they are some distance away.

'Cos I expect, well, when it's night-time for us, it's morning there, I think. And when it's morning for us, it's night-time there. And when it's summer here, I expect it will be autumn there. A long way away. [Germany]
(girl, 7)

'A long way away' is a phrase often used, although there is also a realization that distances are comparative.

Germany; they are quite close in miles. I know it's quite far away but we're both in between the equator and the North Pole. So the homes are probably the same 'cos the temperature, it's cold in winter.
(girl, 9)

One of the central perceptions of the 'otherness' of other countries is that they lie 'across the sea'. There is a widespread awareness of the significance of the English Channel in particular, so that travel to other countries entails something more complicated than driving in a car.

I know where Germany is. Our seafront is across there. You know there's loads of water. You go right down there in a boat, backwards, right and if you go really far, the next morning you might be there.
(boy, 6)

The awareness that travelling to another country involves something more than everyday transport is a phenomenon of an island people and the mention of the sea even helps define the concept of a country. Although both Wales and Scotland are mentioned as countries, there is not the sense of their being foreign. A country is a place that is far enough away to entail serious travel.

It's a part of the world that people live in and if you want to go to another country, like Mexico, you gonna have to get a boat or an aeroplane.
(boy, 7)

You have to take… you can go by car or train or plane to get there or you can go by boat… It's a little way off. Sometimes it's over some sea and it's different from us.
(girl, 7)

Children's first idea of a country is as a geographical entity, a place that is distinct, that somehow is a piece of land and either joins on to another or is an island. They make many attempts to explain the phenomenon of a country as a distinct entity, based on scientific or historical reasons.

It's a bit of earth. The country floats on the earth. And, er, it stays on when it goes upside down because there's something called gravity.　(boy, 7)

For most children, however, a country is a piece of land where people live. It is a larger manifestation of the group, separate and distinct. At the same time that they are perceiving both hierarchies of power and control, and the formation of relationships in their schools and communities they realize that there are larger manifestations and consequences of groups.

A country is a place to visit as well as a place where they live. The assumption is that each country will be different: it will have some distinct physical appearance that is unfamiliar, just as the people are assumed to be unfamiliar.

> It's got trees and it's got, sometimes, long grass and wild animals. Some other countries have got sort of yellowy grass, long sort of grass, but only yellow. And some have got green grass that's very short.   (girl, 8)

The pictorial imagery varies but the assumption is that each country will look different with separate characteristics of weather, houses, vegetation and people. Separation is essential. They could be visited on a holiday but that is often linked with an almost objective and temporary scrutiny of what is visited.

In defining the characteristics of other countries, children are influenced by where they themselves live. The idea of travelling by sea or air, and the idea of a country as a piece of land is influenced by their experience and observation of the British Isles – in themselves a difficult set of countries (or country) to define. The difference between a 'place that's joined to another place and an island [as] a place that's on its own' is clear, but many children associate countries with islands. Thus, a country is a 'sort of place with water all around it' (girl, 6).

> It's got to be quite big. It's got to have water around – it might not have water around it because you can have a big place with a line through it so you can get into one country or another without going through the water.
>   (boy, 9)

The children realize that when they look at a map, a country can be in the same land mass as another with borders clearly marked, but this is not their own experience. Sometimes this influence is so strong that it is difficult to describe another country in any other way.

> I've been to France. It's a different mass of land. It's broken off from one big place and it's fallen out into the sea and, er, just stayed there.
>   (boy, 8)

The way that children acquire their knowledge of other countries is significant. Public information, especially on television, is balanced by personal experience. Children have to make their own sense of what countries are like. Information is not presented to them in a systematic fashion. They look at maps, or collect cards, or show a special interest in a book and through that accumulate knowledge. They never mention school as a source of knowledge. Instead, for this kind of awareness, they seem to be left to find their own means of discovery.

> 'Cos in 1990 I had a World Cup sticker book and I know most of the flags.
> (boy, 8)

> Well, I've heard of nearly all the countries in the world 'cos I've got a game and it has all the countries in the world and their export and their capital and the things like that.
> (boy, 8)

As a result of such detailed knowledge, some unusual or obscure countries are mentioned, such as Bhutan, Swaziland, Tonga and Andorra. It seems that the acquisition or collection of knowledge is something that arises from other interests. This explains the mixture of erudition in the cases of some children and the case of shared knowledge centred on a few countries.

An awareness of a particular country can arise, then, not only from the amount of material presented on television and personal anecdote, but from chance. It can be the result of an interest in sport, or in collecting things, or emerge from reading.

> I think it's West Samoa. They were playing rugby.
> (girl, 8)

> I've heard of Egypt in a Bible story.
> (girl, 6)

The way that children learn about other countries is arbitrary and, it seems, rarely formal. Their knowledge of what a country is – not an easy definition, even if revealing – depends very much on their own construction of information. One underlying theme that unites all attempts to define is that countries are *different*. In one sense that is part of the natural definition: they are distinct geographical entities. But it is the difference between countries, in terms of culture and style as well as natural resources, that children repeatedly stress.

> People eat different ways, people walk different ways, they run different ways. Some people, sometimes they treat their houses different ways.
> (girl, 7)

The crucial difference that children see lies in the people. Nationality – the definition of cultural uniqueness – is a concept that children understand early, even when they have difficulties in defining it.

Germany's near France. The country's after France. And some of them
are like English people and some of them are like French people. And
some of them are like French and some of them are like Spanish.

(girl, 6)

The reason that children are so familiar with the concept of nationality is because
they are aware of their own distinction in relation to other people. Children are
self-conscious, defining themselves in phrases such as 'I am British'. They have a
greater sense of both relativity and distinction. The very fact that they were born
and live in a particular place is both arbitrary, a matter of chance, and an essential
defining fact. They know that they would be different had they been born somewhere else. They appreciate the relativity of their circumstances. They find it perfectly feasible to imagine living somewhere else. They might be familiar with, or
prefer what they are accustomed to, but this does not imply an immediate sense of
superiority. At the same time they are defined as who they are in a group against the
different characteristics of others. Whilst the sense of relativity smacks of benign
nationalism, it can easily be manipulated in different ways. Any form of prejudice
rests on a perception of the 'other'.

There is nothing parochial about children's sense of identity in relation to others. They see the mixture of people that make up the world and witness contrasts
in language and pigmentation. In addition to the individual differences that are
always observed, children are aware that being from a different country is just one
such strand of difference. This is partly because the children either have had, or
have spoken about, personal experience of being abroad, or have mixed parentage.
The cross-cultural experience of children is widespread whether their background
is privileged or not. They are aware of the concept of nationality quite objectively.
The grounds of knowledge, the understanding of difference, begins as essentially
neutral.

I'm Scottish because both my parents are Scottish. But I was born here.
It's better being different from anyone else.   (girl, 9)

Children show an interest in where their families come from. They can talk about
their parents or grandparent's origins as matters of fact. They are aware of their
own complex backgrounds.

I come from England. My dad comes from Coventry and his mum comes
from Scotland.   (girl, 7)

I'm half Barbados and English.   (boy, 7)

I'm quarter Irish. Well, I'd rather be more Irish than English.   (boy, 9)

I'm half Italian.   (girl, 8)

My mummy's Japanese and my daddy's English.   (girl, 8)

When there is a chance to show a difference in their inheritance, children reveal that it gives them a distinction. It is not only other nations that are different. They show an awareness of the distinctions between living in a country and belonging to it.

> Half English, half Australian. My dad's Australian. We're going to go and live in Australia next September, so, sometimes, I think of myself, when we were in Australia I thought that I was Australian. 'Cos I caught the accent. Now we're back in England I think of myself as English.
>
> (boy, 8)

Indeed, the greater the mixture of their background, their roots, the more it seems to interest them.

> Well, I'm part German... I'm American, Greek, English, Czechoslovakian and German. I'm American because I've got an American passport. I was born in England but I've got an American passport. My mother's American. My dad's Greek.   (boy, 9)

> I was born in France, but, um, my mummy wanted to come back to England. She's all English and half French. She can speak French very well.
>
> (girl, 7)

Children know about their own backgrounds and talk about them as a natural part of their individual identity. Many parents will be occasionally embarrassed by the very openness of their children's remarks. The facts are themselves of interest rather than potentially awkward. It is only later that people grow more secretive about their personal circumstances, their inheritance and private concerns. Children are also aware of other people's different identities whether in their own class, or seen on television. One clearly observed difference that they take for granted as well as accept is that of 'blood'. When they talk of their mixed nationality they imply that there is some genetic inheritance that makes them out, far deeper than colour.

> I've got different bloods. I've got lots of different bloods inside me. I haven't got one, not just English. I don't know what kind because they are all different kinds. I know I've got, I think I've got French and, of course, I've got English, Portuguese, Chinese, but I don't know the rest really.
>
> (girl, 6)

'Not just English' is a phrase that uncovers children's sense of a richer trans-national inheritance. They describe themselves as a mixture of peoples, and the use of the word 'blood' demonstrates that distinction between being English because they live there and speak the language and being English because that is in their 'blood'. They sense the arbitrariness of fate. They *could* have been born anywhere else. There is no sense of immutability of their circumstances.

I live in this country… Being English is all right. But I'm not really. I don't have much English blood though. I have Greek blood, half Greek blood.

(boy, 7)

One of the clearest signs of differences between people of different 'blood' is colour. This is part of children's immediate experience as well as their view of the world as a whole. It is easy and normal to point out this distinction between people, and they do so as a matter of fact, rather than as an immediate sign of superiority or inferiority. After all, they see their own colour as an accident of birth.

I'd be black like the other people or brown or white. (girl, 7)

Some people have got brown skins and some people have got white skins. If I stayed in Africa I could have brown skin. (boy, 6)

Despite the fact that all these children have experience of ethnic minorities within their school, there is an association of blackness with Africa.

Like in Africa it's people live like brown and in Great Britain people, most people are white, sort of… some people that I know are brown.

(boy, 7)

The children are, of course, being questioned about other countries as well as their own, not pressed for views on ethnic minorities. But the image of Africa, like that presented on television news, represented by the suffering of black people, is strong. Generally, the children talk about differences of colour as matters of fact. It is very rare even to be able to read any incipient racism into their attitudes.

I don't know where Shahida's come from. I don't know where she's come from but she's in my class. Some are coloured. Some are normal.

(boy, 8)

There is no indication that colour is a latent excuse for racism, or that different ethnicity is an issue. It can be used, like any difference, as an excuse for bullying or teasing, and it can be a matter of self-consciousness, and even self-abnegation, but in these cases it is just one in a choice of any number of excuses. Seeing differences does not automatically mean not accepting them. There is a fine balance between the easy acceptance of distinction and the moment it becomes associated with enmity and threat. Prejudice can be ambiguous, arbitrary as well as changeable. There is nothing automatic or even atavistic about racism. Usually children see blackness, like nationality, as an accident of birth, rather than an abnormality. It is a condition of where you come from.

> Some people are black because they live in very hot countries and they might get burned.
>
> (girl, 8)

Skin colour, like blood, is just one differentiating factor. It is noticed but not of high salience. There are other distinctions that are seen as far more important. After all, they see a mix of inheritances in themselves, even if these are usually European.

> I'm half-caste because my daddy was brown and my mum's white.
>
> (girl, 7)

Distinctions of culture as well as place

The most significant differences between peoples, as outlined by children, are the differences of culture and language. They are aware that they live in a pluralistic world, with countries that have different habits and other ways of life. There is no sense of an homogeneous culture, even within Europe.

> Some people have five meals in their house a day and some people have four. And some people, they usually wash their hands before dinner and some people don't.
>
> (girl, 7)

> Some people kick people out of their homes. Some people don't. Some people go to church. Some people don't. Some people work. Some people don't.
>
> (boy, 8)

The differences between styles of living are as true within the country as beyond it. It is as if observed contrast were extrapolated into their interpretation of the world as a whole.

> Some people have got short tempers and some haven't. And some are nice and some aren't. Some have got a different sort of voice and different hair

and eyes. And things like that and skin colours. Different skin colours and
different accents.   (girl, 9)

The stress is again on the differences between people which are at a variety of levels, from appearances to houses and habits. How people behave is an important as
their looks. Different temperaments, including their own, are seen to be significant. The world is divided into a series of differences.

> Some people speak different, some people look different. Some people are
> a different colour, some people eat different things, some people live in
> other countries and the countries are different to the others. I might be
> black and your face would be much more different.   (girl, 6)

The awareness of differences that children perceive is coupled with a readiness to
see that living in a particular place or country affects the person. The relativism
they express is clear. This means that they acknowledge that things *could* be different. Some countries are seen to be preferable to their own, just as others, like some
in Africa, are associated with nothing but discomfort. The children acknowledge
that the personal experience of each country is different, and that it makes a difference to the way in which people behave.

> I'd be growing up and I'd learn a different language and my school would
> be different. Much more different because you normally, every school,
> you have tables in each spot but schools in different countries, you have
> your desks in line.   (girl, 9)

> I might be adopted because my, one of my friends is adopted. And I might
> not have any pets 'cos there might not be any, um, things like cats and dogs
> in that country.   (boy, 8)

The most significant sign of cultural difference for the children is language. It is
the closest that they get to a sense of personal identity, as if 'I am English because I
speak English'. People are defined by the language they use, and language is a
strong interest for children.

> A country is a big, big group of people, like they're all different and speak
> one language. And then you get another country that's a big, big group of
> people and they're all different but they speak a different language to the
> other country. That's my idea of a country.   (girl, 8)

Being different and speaking a different language belong together: language is a
sign that is both immediately recognizable and which suggests something personal.

Not only does language inform a style of thinking, but it also cuts people off from understanding each other. People in other countries are difficult to communicate with.

> A country is, it's called a name because other countries haven't got the same language quite as that country. Like British is not the same as French.
>
> (boy, 7)

Children do not, however, suggest that those speaking other languages are inferior as if 'they can't speak properly'. Instead, they see the variety of languages as just another aspect of the many differences that make up the world as a whole.

For this reason, there is even the suggestion that the Tower of Babel was a significant event:

> I think God was the one who separated a country because what I've learnt in school was, this wasn't that long ago. The people where God lived, they were building a big tower up to heaven and he stopped them and all separated them into different languages and countries. I think that's how countries became but I don't know that. It's just that the teacher tells us and the teacher doesn't know that either.[1]   (girl, 8)

Language divides people, and is one of the main cultural differences. But children also show signs of recognizing the differences between countries in terms of religion and politics.

> Some different places believe in different gods.   (girl, 7)

> It's a big land of mass which is ruled by one person like a king or a queen or president, or something like that. Islands are just surrounded and they're not always linked to another country.   (boy, 8)

Added to the idea of a country as a geographical entity rather than replacing it, and linked to the idea of an autonomous culture, the concept of a country includes the centralized state, being ruled by one person.

> A place where a lot of people live and you have someone leading it. And it's smaller than a continent, bigger than, sometimes, an island. And it holds a lot of people.   (girl, 8)

> Mainly it's just a government with, who have the most power sort of thing, with maybe a king or queen, or, if not, a president... just a lot of houses, a lot of people.   (boy, 9)

There are a number of ways of defining a country and it is interesting to see in what kind of priority children place the distinct aspects of a country. It is clear that in addition to the geographical completeness the children see countries as different in politics and culture, with people of different languages and habits. The picture they have is either of a place that is in complete contrast to their own country – like Africa – or as a place in which the everyday business of people sums up their own way of life.

> Cities, parks, various buildings. Lots of people generally doing kinds of work and all the simple things in life. A place producing various amounts of produce and electric things, stuff for electricity, things like game boys and things.   (boy, 9)

Definitions of different countries show that children are aware of nations and the fact that they themselves happen to live in one place. Some difficulties of definition do not preclude a clear sense of where they live, from street to town to country. The very way they describe distances shows their grasp of the concept of a big, varied and complicated world.

A map of the whole world

When children put their impressions and information about the world into a coherent structure they conclude that the world is full of contrasts. They see the distinctions between rich countries and poor, between those that are technologically advanced and those that are primitive. Their picture of the world recognizes the extremes and simplifies to the extent that it is assumed that whilst there are contrasts within their own country between rich and poor, most other countries are either one or the other.

Beneath this clear contrast, however, other characteristics emerge. Particular countries are associated with their own styles of living, with different eating habits and clothes. In fact, some of the stereotypes that are one level of recognition of a multi-cultural world, from chopsticks to saris, are clear clues to differences. But children are also aware of other more complex facts about the world. They realize that there are differences because of war. Some places seem peaceful, and full of holidaymakers. Others present pictures of poverty as a result of violence. The world is seen as a dangerous place in parts, and in other parts as a place to be explored.

This picture of the world might not seem very sophisticated but it does show a kind of analysis that is a true impression of the information children receive. They are aware of dangers, dangers that need to be avoided if they cannot be ignored. They are also aware of the ways in which cultures are presented, for good or bad.

They are sensitive to the consequences of such contrasts between the rich and the poor. The underlying contrast is a significant one for the political future of the world. Such a division is an important dimension to the way that children might think about the world as they grow up.

> My mum used to live in South Africa. It's a lot different. Because it's more hotter, and it's got rain forests and it's got different wildlife, got different people. They're black. And some of them are white. The whites, they've got guns and they can kill rabbits. The whites, they can kill deers, and lions when they attack them. But the blacks have only got spears and bows and arrows. Whites have got machines and the blacks haven't. They've got machines that build the guns. To protect them... it's nice there.
>
> (boy, 7)

From the tone of these remarks it is difficult to assess whether he thinks of such divisions as inevitable, or good or bad. At this stage, such a phenomenon is observed without a clear moral directive. What is clear is the assumption that modern technology belongs only to one group, and primitive bows and arrows to the other.

In children's mental maps of the world the sources of information are particularly important for the influence they bear. The kind of impression that television makes is at a different level from personal experience or even stories told by travellers. Bad news, in the form of negative aspects of countries, tends to be conveyed by television. Leaving the United States and Australia to one side, children tend to rely on television to tell them how bad things are elsewhere: wars and famines, terrorism and flooding. 'Good' news, in the form of seeing the good things in other countries, is often based on personal experience. Many of the children have, after all, gone on holidays abroad, and they associate them with all the pleasures of travel. They would not have travelled to the places that are depicted on the news. The quality of the descriptions and analysis, therefore, varies with the source. Those descriptions that rely on television depend on visual images, selected often by chance. There is a different level of analysis and personal involvement in the actualities of travel. One girl, for example, has been to Japan, but then goes on to describe what she knows about Greenland as seen on a television programme. First Japan:

> They look different. Their eyes are smaller and they're a bit longer, and their faces are rounder than ours. And they, some of them are quite old, but they don't look that old. They have different kinds of food. They did have McDonalds and things like that, but the food was normally rice. Normally, like they don't have things like we do, they have rice with, um, and they have a kind of soup.   (girl, 8)

Then Greenland:

The homes are a bit like Japanese ones but their roofs are much smaller, and, well, one house had steps going up to the roof round the side. And they hunt seals and they make, um, this boy's grandma had to make him some new seal-skin boots. And they do have videos. They have these big fluffy coats like Eskimos and I think they wear trousers... They might eat seals because I'm not sure if they would just waste all the flesh 'cos they used up all the skin.

It was about a boy that lived in Greenland.   (same girl, 8)

Both the similarities and differences are interesting. In both, quite an impressive amount of information is conveyed, although there is more personal anecdote to come about Japan. But the girl makes attempts to generalize from the experience, to sum up, to pick out salient features. On Greenland she keeps reverting to a particular feature; the 'one house' and 'this boy's grandma'. The question is how images become generalized. We know that one picture can dominate an impression of a country. In the case of her personal experience she is more aware of what is normally the case and the generalizable distinctions are clear.

The most difficult concept that children have to deal with in understanding other countries and peoples is the balance of sameness and difference. All people are similar at one level, and different at another, in terms of language and culture. To measure exactly in what this difference lies is complex, and will be taken up later. It is possible for children to hold both distinctions and similarities in their minds at the same time. This contradiction is typical. On Greece:

The snails, and I think they eat more fish... they're quite the same really.
The women usually wear big dresses... I can't remember anything else.
They're just quite different.   (girl, 7)

This is true: they are both the same and different. The similarity is sensed most firmly by personal experience, by being engaged with meeting people and living amongst them. In those conditions, both distinctions and common habits are observed. On television, however, it is the dissimilarities that are far more forcibly conveyed. The less familiar the place, the more the differences are made clear.[2]

The world of conflict

Nothing expresses the central imagery of television news coverage as clearly as war and violence. Other countries, like the Middle East or parts of Africa, or Bosnia-Herzogovina, are clearly depicted as war zones.

Dead people everywhere. Massive vans everywhere and these guys with guns... cruel, violent, savage... I wouldn't like to meet any troops because they'll probably, you know, kill you.   (boy, 9)

On the television you see all the smashed up homes and it's quite hard to see what they are... I don't particularly like war because it's, like, it's quite scary. And I just don't like it.   (girl, 8)

When these pictures are presented on television, however, children also notice details. Images of war are precise and include people. The children notice the kinds of dress that people wear – again, differences – in the middle of the common cruelty of war.

That children are emotionally affected by what they see is clear. The images of famine are treated with a comparatively laconic distance. They are part of the constant symbolic world of television. But war, violence expressed in a more dramatic way, is seen as affecting people more directly. It is more arbitrary, less part of the whole primitive state.

I didn't want to see them when they kept on killing people, so I went like that [pulling hands over eyes].   (boy, 6)

I feel sorry for all the people that were in the houses when they got messed up. There are people who have lost their houses.   (boy, 9)

Despite the news coverage, children remain uncertain and uninformed about the causes of war, or the political background. What they see, and what they talk about are the repeated images. War is the final, most organized, form of collective prejudice. The images of violence abound. These are powerful but not necessarily different according to the place in which the violence takes place. War, and the effect of war, is the most abiding image.

It's not that good because it's all been bombed. Most of it's been bombed. And some people have died. And probably all the buildings are broken down.

Most of it's been bombed and it's not nice 'cos it smells because some of it's dirty. The people have left all their rubbish.   (boy, 10)

The world includes many unsafe places, with too many wars in too many places for analytical attention. Children are not shielded from pictures that depict quite clearly what war really means. After all, as in the case of famine or floods in Africa, the presentation of the stark reality is supported by a sense of duty to convey the truth and to elicit help. These images are of people suffering in the face of natural disaster. Just as often people are seen to suffer as a result of cruelty and hatred. The question is what connection is made between these acts of atrocity, with their political justifications, and the more mundane, if far more personally damaging, bullying.

Children are no longer unaware of the conditions in which others live. They are not in a state of innocent ignorance where the world is a safe place and optimism prevails. Their attention is focused on suffering children, whether in Africa or Romania, according to the story of flooding or orphans.

> It's a very, very poor country and they haven't got much food or anything like that... And they look very sad, sometimes, too. They haven't got any food or anything like that. That's the main thing. And we've got lots of food... They don't have any food and it wouldn't be very nice wishing you'd have some food, sometimes, and not having any and being all cold.
>
> (boy, 8)

> They haven't got food in Romania. And they haven't got clothes. And sometimes they die because they've no food.   (girl, 8)

Just as the charitable agencies communicate their needs by sharing harrowing pictures of suffering, so case studies are made of the plight of children in other countries. Until such a universal system of communication, children would not necessarily be quite so familiar with suffering as part of the human lot. They would have been aware that some political regimes were worse than others and some countries undeveloped, through reading magazines such as the Boy's Own Paper. Heroes, after all, had to have enemies and needed to be in danger. There were, therefore, tales of war, of smuggling, of slavery. But there was never such a dwelling on misery, let alone the opportunity to bring pictures straight from the heart of darkness to the security of the living room. Earlier, children recognized the world as only partly civilized and looked on unexplored continents as comparatively primitive. One wonders whether such a simple distinction has really been overcome.

The imagery of suffering is vivid and takes many forms. It is by no means confined to the developing world as comments on Romania reveal.

> They're probably one of the poorest countries in Europe, because of those little children there who've got something wrong with them and nobody wants them. And they try to get attention by banging their heads in their horrible cots and stuff and making big bruises on their heads.
>
> I've seen some on charity-raising things, and I've seen some on TV.
>
> (boy, 8)

It is the foreground, the actuality of what is happening that is noticed and discussed, rather than the reasons, the politics or the economics. This does not mean that children are insensitive to political issues or unaware of politics. It means that children are seeking their own explanations, having to construct a meaning on which to build their interpretation of the world.

The majority of countries of which children are aware are the countries that appear most regularly on television, through the news or through entertainment. Those countries that are large and significant but rarely appear in the news, like Canada, are rarely mentioned. Japan is occasionally mentioned, and not only by the girl who has been there. When it is mentioned, the stereotypes of cleverness and kimonos make an appearance.

> They're very up to date, probably are different to us. I know some women wear kimonos and things like that.   (girl, 9)

> I like the language and I just think they're generally a very clever type of people. They're OK at sport. I like their rugby side. They got crushed by Scotland, but they can run really fast.
> ... ladies can wear kimonos, but men have these sort of robes. They're similar to kimonos... The currency is sort of higher. It's 124 yen or something for, like, one pound. I wonder how they got it up there in the first place. They've got higher expanding the education which I like.
> (boy, 9)

Again, one detects the influence of the news: Japan is significant in the financial world and in technology.

The personal experience of other peoples

The other way in which children learn about countries is, of course, through personal experience. A few have lived abroad, or paid visits to relations. Almost half the children have been abroad on holiday. This is where they learn that there are good things to be said for other countries, that differences can be beneficial. After all, there are countries that have good beaches and where the sun always shines, as in Barbados.

> It's sandy and it's got a warm sea like the Indian sea and we, me and my brothers, we used to catch crabs in the sand... They're black. And they always wear necklaces. They have these bracelets... I think it was because of the fashion.
> (boy, 7)

Children's descriptions of countries in which they have had holidays reveals the balance between the experience of one or two incidents, and their more general observation. They have particular and piecemeal memories rather than the absorption of characteristics. From particular experiences generalizations can be made. Switzerland is depicted thus:

> We stayed in a house next to the clock which went dong every – it went every half past and o'clock. All through the night as well. They have this lorry which went to every town on the mountain and then, and inside the lorry was this shop and it was really good. (boy, 7)

It is the small details that children recall, like the shapes of shutters, or the shapes of buildings, like the kinds of cars, or the kinds of clothes.

> They dress like their children like anything. When they're babies they have earrings on them and the plaits in their hair and I don't quite like that much... They have different kinds of bottles for coke and things like that. They don't have plastic bottles. They have glass, real glass. [Spain]
> They have two windows joined together in this funny way... and you have to undo this and then undo that and then these two windows spurt out and you can hardly get them back in again. (girl, 9)

So much depends on the place in which the children stayed, on their immediate surroundings and on how they spent their time:

> It's very hot and there are flat houses with very high roofs. And there's stone walls on the roads, and in the village we lived in, the houses weren't like that. You went down the main road and lots of little passages turning off. So you went up one and the other person went up one and you went, er, where am I? And you couldn't find a way, it's like a maze. [Greece] (boy, 8)

The kind of view children might have of Spain or Greece can be limited to the holiday site, but they do show greater interest and curiosity than that. Their observations might be based on the particulars of their chalet but they do reveal the ability to take in other things, too. Thus, the same boy will talk about the 'nice beach' and the houses.

> They're rather shady and there's usually a balcony. And, as they are rather far up, usually on a hill, you have a very good view when you look out of the window. Except you can't look out that well because there are fly shades. (same boy, 8)

To this observation and experience will be added a more negative note:

> They're not, they don't have very good schools. Not with a very lot of people in. Not with posh furniture and things like that in.   (same boy, 8)

Experience teaches children to extract details that have struck them as significant, from windows to the view. They relate their new experiences to those with which they are familiar. They do not approach holidays as an opportunity just to relax on the beach. Indeed, when they say 'all we really did was go to beaches', it is more a sign of disappointment than of a satisfying holiday. Even holidays can have *longeurs*.

> It was very hot and I liked the beach and everything like that. And we kept going on all these walks and I wanted to get back. I was really bored most of the time 'cos I was only about six then.   (girl, 7)

But on the whole, the holiday is enjoyed as a time in which a new place can become familiar and certain freedoms, like space, pursued.

> I like the hotels which I stay at… it's quite small. And if I stayed in a hotel with my parents, Adam and I would go down to the shops 'cos the shops are only a little way from where we stay there. It's got a swimming pool. It hardly ever rains. I just like it there.   (girl, 7)

In such an experience, the question remains whether there has been much scope for understanding a different country, whether the immediacy of the experience is placed in any cultural context. Visits are supposed to foster tolerance, but they also point up the differences.

Ever since the Grand Tour, there has been an assumption that travel broadens the mind. More recently, however, there have been grave doubts as to whether the average package holiday gives any insight into a different way of life. Similarly, the concept of television as a means of communication of such power that the whole world becomes a global village, or culturally homogenized, has held sway over thinking for many years. But differences, great and small, continue to abound. Understanding has not replaced wars, and communication systems have been used merely to make aggressive acts the more systematic. There are also doubts about whether all the nature programmes, the documentaries, films and news have done anything more than football matches to foster understanding and the overcoming of chauvinism and prejudice. The evidence that children present does not fall into any simple category. There is no doubt that children are observant of things when travelling, but what they observe depends on their particular experience. When asked to piece together their thoughts and experiences, it is the incidents and pictures that stand out. To say they have learnt nothing is untrue. They might not have placed information into categories or generalized from their experiences, but they are affected by them. Similarly, they have been presented with a series of images about the rest of the world on television, but what they see fosters an awareness of difference and distance far from the global village or one dominant culture.

At one level, the reflections that children make on their travels are arbitrary. They happen to have been in a certain place at a certain time. But at another level, such experience is crucial in forming their sense of their own identity. It is their own perspectives on themselves in relation to others that they are creating and inventing. These perspectives are not thrust upon them, nor are children helped to articulate them. This is why some of the images they present are so extreme. Nevertheless, as they reflect on what they have seen and done they begin to discriminate clearly between what they see as good or bad. Italy, for example, can be seen in different ways.

> Most Italians love children. And I love the food and all of that. I don't know the language of it and the food's great as I say. I just love it... They are loud, cheerful, interesting. They have big voices, most of them... They make better fashion. They make more jeans. They have sort of, like, gold buttons all the way round the waist... they laugh a lot. More than we do.
>
> (boy, 8)

Many of these assumptions about Italy, love of children, fashion and food, are universally shared. They are the standard view, as sung on television. But this boy has experienced Italy and discriminates between his generalization about Italians and his own experience. Is he, therefore, reflecting a true or given stereotype? Certainly, he is looking for things to like.

Italy can also strike the visitor in a different way. After some praise of the beaches and the beauty of the Roman architecture, a girl reflects

> They're kind of like... as it's hot, they kind of, like, have to wear different clothes. In the actual city of Rome, they're not very nice to other people and things. And they are kind of, like, horrible. Kind of, like, burn other people's houses and things like that... In the mountains they're very nice.
>
> (girl, 8)

Here, again, we have the contrast between the town and the country. It is not only in Great Britain that children associate the city with decay or pollution. The personal experience gives a more complex understanding that is not always purely positive. But it does tend to be more positive than the kind of information gleaned from television.

The Tower of Babel

What makes countries distinct? This is a more complex question than it first seems since it embraces a range of cultural factors and habits that are not only the product of distinct societies but are influenced by international events. Children are all aware of the existence of different nationalities, just as they are aware of different groups. They know that places such as Germany have different parts, that the French have different habits and that the person living in a developing country is presented in a different way. But to define what their differences are is a more complex matter. After all, real differences are not just a matter of political boundaries. Nothing could more clearly demonstrate differences within a political society than the United Kingdom itself. And yet there are such things as nations within their own football teams and flags, and there are some that contrast more strongly with others.

At any subtle level, therefore, national characteristics are difficult to define. There are, however, some seemingly obvious things. One difference is the weather and the impact that it has on people. Another difference is the physical appearance of people whether they be white or black. Yet another difference lies in the way of living, in the contrast between the rich and the poor. However hard to define, children know that difference is there: in the use of shutters, the chiming of a clock or the type of food.

But it does not need the Tower of Babel to remind us that there is one characteristic of peoples that seems to children the most significant: the fact of different languages. The idea of God stepping in to divide people into different countries might not be believed, but the fact is that countries are defined by their separation into their own languages. This is the most important characteristic that defines, in all the children's minds, what makes people 'other'. It is their inability to communicate in the same language, the impossibility of 'us' communicating with 'them'. This is more important than the colour of their skin or the houses in which they live. For all the global systems of communication language is still perceived by children to be a great barrier between people.

Children show an ambivalent attitude to languages. They are all interested in the differences and in the varieties, in the sounds and in the difficulties. They also realize the great variety of tones and accents. All these differences strike them as being both fascinating and threatening. After all, one of the greatest difficulties in their experience is not being able to communicate. On the other hand, what would other people prove to be like if you were able to understand them?

Their own language is a matter of sensitivity. They have the same laconic acceptance of it as they do to the other facts of their circumstances. They recognize that had they been born somewhere else they might have acquired a different language, but English is what they have got, and that is therefore the one they like.

I don't like different languages. I only like English language. Things that my mum and dad can understand. But my dad knows a lot of French, so I could speak French to him.

I like, as my friends are the same language as me. I like that they understand me.   (girl, 7)

I like the way how they talk. And I like how they say their letter threes. Like, if you say 'three'. I like to say 'three' because it's a good idea in English, because I like when I say three, I like it. It makes my tongues, I like getting my tongue feels good.   (boy, 8)

I don't talk like other people might because they come from a different country. I think it might be hard. But I know it won't because it's their language, but I still think it will be hard. I like being English 'cos I'm used to the English language.   (girl, 8)

There is a clear awareness, in confronting another language, of the distinction between phonetics and semantics. The children react to the sounds of different languages, but realize what language is really for. They can readily contemplate learning other languages, but for the most obvious reasons find that a real challenge. They are comfortable as they are. Sometimes other languages can seem like a threat.

I just don't like it when other people talk other sounds. They speak different.
                                                                                       (girl, 8)

Friendliness on holidays abroad is, after all, associated with the ability to speak English:

They're friendly, very friendly. And most of them speak English.
                                                                                       (boy, 9)

The ability to communicate is clearly seen as of central importance. This is not surprising. But it helps to define what children see as different in other people: they have their own world but there is no easy way to penetrate it. If they could also speak English, then many things could be possible. Talk is what makes friendships, and children feel they must talk to their friends. This reaffirms the distance they feel to those from other countries who cannot communicate.

'Cos I don't have to say all those funny words and stuff like that. And if I'm not English, no other people can understand me.   (girl, 7)

I feel if I was in a different country and I came to Britain for my holiday, I wouldn't quite understand the other children if they tried to make friends with me. So that's why I like being English.   (boy, 7)

They don't speak the same as me. Because if I wanted to talk to my friends, I wouldn't be able to if I couldn't speak English.   (girl, 7)

If I went to a different country on holiday, everyone would speak in a different language and I couldn't understand it. So I wouldn't be very happy 'cos I wouldn't know what they were saying.   (boy, 8)

This acceptance of the importance of speaking the same language as other people is a form of nationalism without the chauvinism. They *want* to be able to understand others but cannot. Liking being English means liking being where you are. It is unfortunate if others cannot speak your language. This fact leads the children to appreciate when others *can* speak their language and show their friendliness.

Well, a lot of other countries speak English as their language, so that helps a lot when we go abroad. They have got a German language but I think a lot of German people do learn English, because so many places speak English.
                    (boy, 9)

You can meet lots of friends because you can speak English and you can say to them 'Will you be my friend?' or something. You can go to schools and you can understand what the teachers are saying because they're speaking the same language as the children.   (girl, 7)

Speaking the same language as other children is far more significant than being a particular nationality, being British. There is no such mystique in these children. They can imagine being elsewhere. The significant point is that they and the people around them speak the *same* language. That is more to the point than which particular language that is.

If I was German and my family wasn't, I'd have to live in Germany and if I spoke German and my family spoke English, I couldn't understand them.
                    (girl, 7)

Having said that children accept the fact of different languages and the need to communicate in any of them, that does not mean that they *like* all the languages that they hear. As is the case with accents, they clearly prefer some to others. There is, for instance, a tendency to like the sound of French and not to like the sound of German.

They speak a different language. Oktletkt, something like that. If there
was a person who can speak English, I would have to say what it means.

(boy, 8)

They say 'merci', that's 'thank you'. We had a French person over, I like it
because they speak nice.   (girl, 6)

The Italian language I think is more easier to understand, even for English
people, than German. They get a lot of 'g's in German, don't they. As I
said, their language is horrible. I don't like their language.   (boy, 8)

Part of the consistent, if comparative, dislike of German is, of course, a result of the
association of it with the 'guttural' commands of German officers. It is a language
exploited by films and television as an example of brutality and command. More
striking, perhaps, is the genuine interest in other languages of a kind less connected
to films of war. Some really appreciate the different sounds that people make.

Of Bajun: 'They talk funny. Wicked. A wicked sort of language.' A language is a
style of sound, a way not of communicating, of creating 'speech acts', but a way of
revealing something different, something other:

I don't like being English. It's so horrible. I wish I was France. The way
they speak, that's it.   (boy, 8)

There is always a tension between the phonetics of a language, its tone and rhythm,
and its meaning. Children are from an early age sensitive to the tone, recognizing
particular voice qualities before they interpret meanings, and they remain interested in and responsive to the different qualities of sound, which is why they like
some languages so much more than others. At the same time, this awareness of
phonetics, analogous with phonetic awareness in neonates, depends on the distinction from semantics. Naturally, they are aware of the meaning of their own
language, and whether it is aesthetically pleasing is of secondary importance. Listening to other languages without understanding makes them concentrate on the
sound. The frustration of *not* being able to understand is very strong.

I don't make any friends there, really. There wasn't any people, only my
aunty, that we knew, but nobody else. I couldn't speak to them because
they speak a different language and they couldn't understand us. I would
have made lots of friends.   (boy, 7)

In France I went to this hospital and they were horrible about it because my
dad was trying to explain what was happening and he said 'I know, I know, I
know' in French and he was kind of being really horrible.   (girl, 9)

There was these waiters. They were kind to me and they spoke to us, but we couldn't understand them.   (girl, 10)

The experience of frustration, of not being able to understand other languages, or for other people not to understand their own, is not limited to those who have been abroad. All the children are aware of the importance of understanding and of the divisions brought about by failure to communicate. They recognize that all social relations depend on sharing a language, which is why 'foreignness' is defined constantly in terms of the identity of a language, rather than by physical appearances. They stress the central importance of being able to communicate.

Being able to talk to people so they understand you.   (girl, 8)

I just like people can understand me and because we understand the language.   (girl, 8)

It's because when you speak a different language to what you normally do, it's quite hard to understand what you're saying. And when you go to school you sometimes learn different languages and all sorts.   (boy, 6)

Strongly to the fore in the children's minds is the difficulty of not understanding. This is almost like a cultural unfairness. The difficulties of understanding interpersonal relationships is transmuted into more collective acts of frustration. The subtle differences in tone, in teasing or command, give way to a more general inability even to attempt to communicate and accept. The children are aware of what it would be like if they spoke French, if they were suddenly deprived of the possibility of speaking to their (English) friends. Whilst they are aware of the cultural relativism of languages, and the fact that if they lived, or were born, elsewhere they wouldn't speak English, their first thought is what it would be like if they were deprived of their friends. They see themselves transported abroad but they do not see themselves at first as having a parallel milieu with a whole alternative set of friends. What they at first reflect is the confusion. Language is what binds people to their friends. Communication is all. What then do they do, deprived of that essential need?

Other languages are different from each other but they all have the problem of being other than English. Children are aware of the variety of different languages, sometimes to the point of confusion.

They speak funny, the Germans. Like, um 'oui' and 'bonjour' and, um, 'deux', 'trois', 'cat'. That's up to four. I go to French Classes. [German?]Um 'oui' is 'yes' and 'bonjour' is 'hello'.   (boy, 6)

I know some words in German. 'blumen' means flower. A different language, Spanish. I don't understand what they're speaking. And they're speaking Germany. If I came from Germany, right, they wouldn't understand my, um, language. I'd know their language, right, but not that much though and they wouldn't understand our language. In German they speak like German. Pakistan speak their way. Germans speak their way. English speak their way. And, um, Americans speak their way.

(boy, 8)

Like in this country we say 'd's but in French they use 'd's for two, and for 'a's in their country they use 'n's for ones.   (boy, 8)

I speak in [Italian] quite well. And also my mum does Chinese, so she brought me her book all about China. I know a couple of words in Chinese.

(girl, 8)

There is a shared awareness of the variety of different languages, each with its own system, and most, except to the few who can speak a second language, are only similar in their impenetrability. There is a sense of suspicion at some of the differences.

Them Spanish, they can't talk properly.   (boy, 6)

When you write it you don't have to do like French. You don't have to do little squiggles or anything like that.   (girl, 8)

Any suspicion and any confusion arises from the fact that the children are aware of the difficulties posed in trying to understand other languages. Not to be able to communicate is worse than awkward. They are used to their own language. They see other languages as being difficult. They cannot quite imagine learning other languages in the same way that they learnt their own, even if, at another level of thought, they acknowledge that if they lived elsewhere they would. One of the most powerful messages that children receive when they travel abroad is the fact that they are isolated in their own language, that the most significant point of familiarity, security and inner safety is denied them.

I can't contact people if I live somewhere else. Because you can't speak to people if you go abroad. You can only speak to the people that take me.

(boy, 8)

When I'm going to my other countries. Holland and Scotland. It's difficult to learn how to speak like that. It's difficult when my nanna in

Holland, when I ask for a drink of lemonade, it's difficult. She doesn't know what it means. I have to go and run up to my dad and ask how you spell lemonade in Dutch.   (girl, 7)

The difficulties of communication are felt more strongly than the possibility of learning another language. Far from believing that they live in an age of communication, children see themselves facing many barriers.

Like, if you were, like, a different country you would come into school and if you came from a different country and when you talk to the teachers they don't know what you're talking about. Because they talk different and, like, if somebody's French, they talk French and we're trying to understand them and they're trying to understand us but we can't... if they speak a different way and I speak English then, really, I wouldn't understand and I wouldn't understand and I wouldn't know if they're nice or not nice.   ·   (girl, 7)

There are few glimpses of the possibility of translation and the other forms of communication. What children stress is the confusion. This suggests almost a subconscious resentment of other languages. This suspicion emerges when they describe both the difficulty of communicating and their connecting disparagement of the sounds of the language. Any language sounds the more difficult just at that point when a person is desperately trying to make out what is being said.

The only thing is me and my dad went to this shop and, um, the Greek lady was asking us something and we couldn't understand anything she was saying. 'Cos she was Greek and we weren't. She was speaking all these funny things and we didn't know a word she was saying.
[The Chinese]. I don't really like their eyes myself, really. And I don't like the way they speak. They speak really fast. Their own Chinese language goes bl, bl, bl, bl, bl. And, um, Di Wan, she can speak English and she goes kind of like she doesn't go 'do they' she goes 'du du'. It just sounds really funny. I still like her though.
We've got a French girl next door to us. All she can say is 'hello' [said with contempt]. I'd hate it if I lived in England and I was French and all these English people. All she can say is 'allo' and when I say 'Do you want to play with me?' she goes –. I'd prefer it if I was English and they were all French people. Still, I wouldn't really like any of it because I'd be really bored and I wouldn't have anyone to play with because I couldn't speak their language.   (girl, 7)

There are many different challenges set up in understanding other languages and children are aware that their own language is like a warm set of clothes, surrounding them, protecting them from the outside world. They can understand, without particular empathy, the difficulties of being a foreigner in their own land. With more empathy and experience they acknowledge the awkwardness of being abroad and unable to communicate. They are also aware of how much of their own personal and cultural identity is created by language. Their interest in foreign languages, however, is one that is shaped not only by their awareness of the difficulty in communication, of understanding, but also by their sensitivity to the wide range of sounds that different languages can produce. Clearly, the preference for one language over another is biased to a small extent by the association of a language with what is considered an attitude. German, for instance, as a vehicle for a formula of Nazi phrases on television, is far more disliked than others. But children do talk of sounds and accents; they are sensitive to the noises made by people, whether in person or through television, that denote that they are speaking a different language. An incomprehension of what is being said draws attention to the way it is said.

Language as a national barrier: dialect as a local one

Children can become confused between a language and an accent: 'the Americans speak their way'. To a small extent, this might be a confusion about terminology, but more significantly it shows an awareness of tone, of the sheer sound quality of what they hear and the differences between one and another. Other people within their own country speak with an identifiable accent: this is also a demarcation line that reveals outsiders. People sound different whether they come from another part of the country and can be understood, or whether they come from elsewhere and cannot. Again and again, there is an overlap between the two:

> They've only got a different accent from us really. They talk the same as us but got different accent.   (boy, 7)

Here, there is a clear awareness of the distinction between accent and language. But the distinction is not always so clear.

> Americans talk a different language.   (girl, 9)

After all, people talk in different 'voices'. These are dependent on a range of factors like status and circumstance. There are private and public means of communicating. Each country has its own uses of English, as programmes from the United States and Australia make clear. Differences are both of language and accent.

> Different because they [Germans] speak a completely different language. [Americans] Their voices, like, their voices are different. I think your voice would be different... like an American type of voice. A different type of voice...
> (boy, 9)

This is a sign of the fact that different languages are tuned to children's sensitivity to different accents. It is clear that they know the differences in status given by the ways in which different people speak, but they are also aware of regional differences. They are aware of the uses of accent for purposes of snobbery or humour, which are often at the heart of television entertainment. They also show marked preferences for some accents and dialects rather than others. This is not just recognizing that some 'can do the police in different voices', but in reacting to them with firm biases.

> I like the Scottish accent. I think that's kind of good.
> (boy, 9)

> I like Sweden because they do talk, but they kind of sing when they talk. I like their speaking.
> (girl, 7)

A distinct liking for a sound of voice is, however, less immediately apparent than the reactions against certain dialects.

> Liverpool. I don't like their accent. I hate it. It's horrible... and it's quite cold there as well.
> (girl, 7)

Some children are made to feel aware of their own pronunciations.

> They do ask me where do you come from because I speak a different language than them. They speak funny up here to me. And I keep telling them that I come from Manchester, Manchester, Manchester. But they keep on saying 'where do you come from?'
> (girl, 7)

An accent is, in certain circumstances, a difference that can be picked on. But generally the children are more neutral about accents; they know that English is spoken in a variety of different ways all over the world.

They've got a slangy accent. They have some different words in America than us, like faucet and elevator.   (boy, 8)

Sometimes I think of myself when we were in Australia. I thought that I was Australian 'cos I caught the accent.   (boy, 8)

Sometimes when I go to a different part of England they kind of speak like that but in a different, a bit different language.   (girl, 7)

They speak a different, they've got sort of like an accent. They speak different words but they still mean the same thing. They say it differently in different words. 'Cos they were born there and they know all the words and, like, they copy from their mum. Different 'cos they're brown. They're not different but they've different colour skin. They've been in England a long time now. Most of them have got rid of their accent, if they had one.   (boy, 10)

The most significant difference between people lies in the way they talk and the language they speak. This is seen as more significant than the colour of the skin or the shape of the eyes, although these are also clearly observable as a difference. Observations of people's appearance as a mark of difference are very few compared to the concentration on language. Language is, however, both a matter of sound and a matter of communicating. Children might prefer some accents but the regional dialect rarely causes problems of bullying. The question is whether this is because of the speed with which children adapt their accents to the circumstances in which they find themselves. It could be that of all marks of distinction the tone of voice, the being 'branded on the tongue', is the one that is most sensitive. The association of an accent with a particular class or background can cause all kinds of resentment, of frustration with not being able to understand or anger at feelings of implied superiority. Communication is all, but what is often conveyed are matters of style, background and cultural, or class, assumptions which are more powerful than words.

The hegemony of one's own linguistic identity

What do children make of learning other languages? Clearly they are frustrated if they are not able to understand, and also disappointed when people do not speak English. But they do not make an automatic assumption that everyone *should* speak English. Their sense of relativism is too strong for that. They do not express that extreme linguistic self-centredness so often satirized from *Our Mutual Friend* onwards.[3] Not being understood is a real problem that needs to be overcome by learning, and not just assuming that others should learn.

> It should be important that everybody in the whole world should learn about different languages.
>
> (boy, 9)

Children indicate that the ability to speak more than one language is a desirable state.

> The ones that know a bit of English I think are all right, because they can speak it very well – my au pair could. So I could understand my au pairs 'cos most of them know how to speak English very well, really, because they live quite near... I can speak Chinese and I can speak Portuguese, French and English. Only a little bit of each though. But I can speak the whole of English.
>
> I think of myself English mostly because it's better, because I can speak more English than anything else.
>
> (girl, 6)

Language is an identity and a means of communicating. Each person has a given language, but wishes to understand others. This tension between the difficulties of speaking other languages and the acceptance that they have one language that belongs to them, between potential frustration and the acceptance of how things are, is one of the reasons that children are aware of language as a personal marker and a definition of otherness. They would, therefore, like to speak another language even if they have little opportunity to do so.

> My sister has, she'd learnt French in one of the classes she's been in and she might teach me. I'd be able to learn different languages. 'Cos sometimes I get bored with saying things that I normally say. And I always get bored with saying the same thing all the time.
>
> (girl, 7)

The ability to use other languages is one that children would like, but they know that it is difficult. There are, therefore, one or two of them who do slip into a defensive mode, seeking the untroubled safety of their own language and seeing other languages as no more than a threat.

> I've done about English quite a few years now and I don't think I want to change because I'd have to learn different words. I wouldn't speak the same.
>
> (boy, 9)

The fact that people speak different languages is accepted. So is the notion of a language as an indication of an accident of birth. This is part of the children's relativism, their acceptance that things are as they are according to their circumstances. There is no sense of the egotistical sublime that they feel they are special for being where they are. There is a sense of pragmatic sophistication, a realization that other people all over the world share their own separate individual outlook and that each is different. The differences are specifically linguistic, a mark of cultural relativism.

> I'd probably speak a different language. And be a different colour, but I can't think of many things that are different.   (girl, 7)

> They speak different languages, because I would speak a different language. And the people in England wouldn't actually understand me.
> (girl, 6)

> The language would still be the same. Because if you were born like your mother, your mother lived there, it means you've got some blood in the country you were born in. So you speak the language.   (girl, 8)

Blood might seem thicker than the environment, but whatever the influence, it is the language that is seen as being more significant than colour or clothes. Relativism in terms of the arbitrariness of the language they speak is one side of the understanding of the world as it is. The other side is the significance, within that, of the cultural hegemony of linguistic understanding. We are what we speak, and what we are able to communicate.

Social life, instruction and communication are recognized as depending on language.

> If it was a country where you learn a different language and my mum was speaking it, then I would probably learn it, too.   (girl, 7)

There is a consistent acknowledgement that language is acquired because of the environment, even if these children are most aware of the immediate environment of the home. They cannot envisage speaking anything else than their mother, as if they have always known their own language and cannot remember having learnt it.

> German? I think that they speak funny. But if I try it and I was born there I might learn the language there and I might probably get into the habit of saying it. Because I was only staying at my friend's in Scotland a few days and I kept talking like this and my sister said 'Stop it, you're talking like they talk' and I said 'Well, Zoe, I've got a habit'.   (girl, 7)

My country right or wrong?

Whilst language is relative, the sense of patriotism might seem to be anything but. Some languages are preferred over others, but mostly because of their utility. What reasons should there be for preferring one's own culture? There was a time when children were encouraged to feel and express patriotic fervour. The literature written for children during and between the two World Wars expresses, consistently and strongly, the sense of superiority of the British over other nations, whether in Europe or beyond. The assumption was made that each race had particular characteristics, like laziness or untrustworthiness, whilst the British stood for gentlemanly virtues, a sense of duty and fair play. There are, of course, many nations that still attempt to foster a sense of pride in their country, whether this is linked to moral virtues or simply an attempt to promote economic self-interest. Saluting the flag, singing the National Anthem: there are many examples of nationalism promoted. The idea of moral superiority has, to an extent, been replaced by flag-waving and rooting for particular sporting teams. The sense of patriotism, therefore, should be expected to persist.

The pragmatic outlook of children has already expressed itself very clearly in their attitudes to their environment. It is equally strong in their sense of themselves as people living in a particular place at a particular time. It also manifests itself clearly in their views about the country they live in. Children accept the fact that they like where they are for reasons that could equally justify other people feeling the same, wherever they live. There are few hints of the moral superiority of being British, let alone flag-waving. From the children's point of view, they consistently share a sense of comparison; they like to be where they are, generally (though some don't), but they are equally certain that the liking of one's circumstances is directly attributable to the fact that that is what they are used to. If they lived in a different country, they point out, they would feel differently. This is very different from any sense of immutability, of being in the right place, of belonging, by some divine providence, to a superior race.

> For me this is the best place, but some people might say other things. I expect it's because I've been here a long time and I've just got used to this place and I just like it. Because I've got a lot of friends here and that. Some people living in other countries might think 'Oh, that doesn't look like a nice place to live'. But when you've been here quite a long time it's quite a nice place to live. They might not like it because they haven't got any friends or whatever. Or they just can't afford enough to buy a house if they sold their other home.

> Somewhere like France, places like that. 'Cos I went there on my holi-
> days. We went skiing and it had just started snowing over there. And it was
> quite nice.
> It's OK, but I just like this place a bit better, really, 'cos I've lived here
> longer. If I got used to them then I think that it would be the same as this. It
> would be nice to see what, to get used to another time line and not have so
> much traffic if you went to another country where there's no roads and that.
>
> (girl, 8)

The sense that they like where they are because they are accustomed to it pervades
the reflections of children. They are aware both of the fact that the place they are living in might not be the best possible – and this comes from someone who is affluent
enough to go skiing, and not only from those who live in 'inner city' conditions – but
the fact that everyone else will have an equal loyalty to his or her place. A place you
like is the place you know. It is a place where there are friends, and familiar customs,
where there are things that you like doing. This ambiguous cultural relativism
means that there is no deep-seated or carefully promoted sense of shared national
virtue. There is no divine providence behind the fact of their circumstances. There is
no ontological security of a shared spiritual home. Instead the very fragility of their
conceptual grasp on their facts of existence means that children are the more vulnerable to threat. The very fact of cultural diversity leads them to think of the peculiar
set of their own circumstances, the more distinct for being arbitrary.

The sense of the comparative, the non-egocentric and the relative is strong.
Others, outsiders, strangers, could view the place you live, and the conditions in
which you live, with distaste. Or they could simply be lonely, be strangers, cut off
from normal discourse by differences of language or cultural possessions. Children
are aware of the possibility of culture shock long before they themselves undergo it.[4]

To that extent, they are aware of an international point of view, a relativism
which puts all people in their place. This is chance, not providence; circumstance,
not consequent superiority. And this sense of the relative is formed of clear binary
contrasts between the rich and the poor, between affluence and starvation.
Children are glad that, comparatively at least, they are in the middle.

> I like the football team in England and I like the name of the team – it's
> quite nice. And just like Britain. I don't know why. I like it. Probably if I
> was from France, I would probably like France. But I don't know that for
> sure, do I?
>
> (girl, 8)

Being in the middle is to be aware of the threat of the possibility of all things being
epistemologically different. Others have their own meanings. Children are aware
that however strong their own point of view, others might have their own. They

give no sense that their world, seen from their perspective, is the one that has most to recommend it.

> Well, they, the Egyptians, might look funny to me, but I suppose that's because I'm not really used to it.   (girl, 8)

Everyone has their own point of view. This suggests an awareness of perspective, of a developed sense of seeing other people's point of view, that gives no automatic right to inner satisfaction or complacency. Whilst there are clear contrasts – would anyone wish to be in a famine or a civil war? – it all depends on the place from which you start.

> I'm not really sure 'cos I quite like every country. Except for poor coun-tries, because I wouldn't like to… Can I choose my own country? Proba-bly England. There's all greenery and it's all sort of different. It's got sort of like everything.
>
> You bring children up in different ways in different countries. Because you have different experiences from bringing up the children. [Spain?] I'd look like a tart. I'd have ear-rings all round here and loads of plaits and bows in everywhere. I'd hate to look like that.   (girl, 9)

Stereotypes and prejudices might persist, but such images are placed in a context of comparatability, of relativity; the assumption is that other people look askance at the way they live. Their own lives are as alien to people from other cultures as the other way around. The experience of travel itself endorses the sense of possible alienation against the feeling of being at home.

> I like being Italian. Here I like the sea, the cold nights, 'cos I don't like hot and stuffy nights. The food is nice here, but I do like Italian pastas. I think I like living in an island because you are nearer the sea. If they're doing some-thing serious, then they are much like us. They all have different opinions and the look isn't much because it doesn't matter how anyone looks.
>
>   (boy, 8)

The ontology of friendship as belonging

All people have different opinions and different tastes. If there are advantages to being in one country, these advantages are purely a matter of circumstance. The weather is better or worse. The place you like is where your friends are.

Well, it's the best place, sort of, where I live. Well, the best place I think you could live in, but I'm sure there's lots more better places than where I live. I like visiting Wales and seeing all my friends and relations there. 'Cos that's where all my friends and relations live, really.   (girl, 8)

Cultural relativism can give a sense of tolerance. All have their own different points of view and habits. It can also give a strong sense of the idea of groups, of collective hegemonies of language or colour. It can also lead to a sense of such a fragile belief in the immutability of the status quo that any number of outside forces can be a threat. At the most immediate they can be a gang, a bullying peer group. They can be associated with a more generalized oppression: the collective control of social apparatus, the 'them' of teachers or the police. Finally, cultural relativism can be turned into the threat of the enemy, the nation against which it is possible to join in mutual self-defence.

The theme that there are places that are better, having, for instance, a superior climate, returns again and again. So does the pragmatic fact that people like to live where their friends are. The actual circumstances are secondary to the personal relationships. When children express their liking for the place they live there are few elevating or elevated ideas. They do not suggest any spiritual advantage, or the sense that the townscape or the landscape is the most wonderful in the world. Instead they home in on the everyday realities: they have friends, they are used to it, they like the street, or the school. Nothing could be at once more pragmatic and give more of a sense of the comparative than the fact that living where they do gives them the opportunity of using the same language, and communicating in a familiar way. They like where they are because of shops or friends, not because of any deeper moral advantage.

The consequences of the custom, or chance, of living in a particular place is simply the fact that there is where your friends are. The proximity of friends is more significant than the proximity of the family, for the latter will be with you always; they are part of the internal reality of things. A child has a taken-for-granted sense that parents are part of a personal sphere: not a case of 'belonging' but a case of their being close to the inner psyche. A child's outlook, they feel, is shared by the parents. They assume a unity. This does not mean that there are no quarrels or disagreements. Parents can be resented or fought against. But they are there, whether liked or not. Friends are a markedly different matter. They are the outside world coming closer. They are the means by which the purely personal connects with greater events. They are the entry into the social world, the 'zone of proximal equivalence'.[5] They are, rather than teachers, the conduits into the world of relationships, of friends and enemies, agreements and disagreements. Friends are the border zone of the outside world. They are also the reasons for liking (or not) the actual place you live.

I'd like to live in France, but I'd miss all my friends here.   (girl, 9)

Friendship defines what makes a particular place special or not. Children feel they could be transported anywhere, and make the assumption that their family, in those circumstances, would be transported with them. But friends are dependent on place and time; they are the chance additions to circumstance that give an extra quality.

It's a very quiet place. And there's not much cars. A lot of schools around the place. And there's lots of friends who I know round the place.
                                                                    (boy, 8)

In England it's quite nice because you've got nice lots of places and when you live down there you're not far from Brownies and Beavers. And you've got loads and loads of friends.   (girl, 8)

All other things being equal, a quiet suburban road and parks nearby, the real sense of being in the right place comes through friends. That is what would be missed if they lived elsewhere.

The hegemony of cultural amenities

There are some other factors that are appreciated and these are mostly to do with amenities, like 'parks and adventure places'. The fact that the children live on an island and therefore have access to the sea is also remarked on. So, in one case, is the wildlife, which accompanies other advantages.

I like England itself for the wildlife and nature, birds, for the water. And it's usually quite warm here in the summer. There are good footballs and bridle paths. I like the school. The roads are safe. I've got lots of friends. And that's all, really. Scotland is better, really – wildlife, the people up there. I like the accent. The waters are fresh up there.   (boy, 9)

Again and again, children appreciate where they are for the most parochial of reasons. They see no particular heroic virtues in the place they live, but any move elsewhere, perfectly natural and acceptable in itself, would deprive them of the friends they know. They would have to start from scratch. Nor would they have exactly the same amenities to which they have also become accustomed.

There's a fish shop and sweet shop just next to me. You just cross over the road and walk down a bit and then there's a grocery. 'Cos in the sweet shop there's bowls where, and these jars and there's these things to pick up. You push them down and it, and it grabs it. It's really good because it has all these sweet shops and stuff.   (boy, 6)

It does not need distractions for the children to appreciate what they like about where they live. They like the ordinary and the convenient, having a place like a park nearby, being able to go to shops, finding safe places to play with their friends. It all sounds like suburban bliss.

Because I like playing with my friend across the way from me. I like it here. 'Cos I like living here and I can walk to school with my mum's friend and her children. And every evening we always walk together and go round the shops.   (girl, 6)

The children's appreciation of places is parochial and everyday. It reflects the life they lead. If their own lives sound very ordinary this does not mean that they do not appreciate the possibilities of living somewhere more exotic. They might miss their friends, but there are other places to live which offer clear pleasures, especially in the United States, and, to a lesser extent, Australia.

I was born in London, really. But I would like to live in America. It's a healthy country. A free country. Hardly any bad things – well, some bad things.   (boy, 7)

If I could live anywhere in the world, I would prefer to live in somewhere like California. Because there's Disney World there and I really want to go there. And it's always quite hot.   (girl, 8)

Living in a place is not the same as belonging to a place. Whilst children realize that the nation they belong to is the place they happen to have been born, a matter of chance, they make a distinction between being an American and living in the place.

I like being English, but I'd like to live in America.   (boy, 9)

There are a number of children who have not only visited other countries but lived abroad and see where they live at present as nothing immutable.

I'd rather live in Sweden. Because I've got much more friends there and I can go to school with friends and you can wear private clothes. You can wear anything you like. I like that.   (girl, 8)

> I'd rather live in Ireland. 'Cos it's better. When I went over there, the weather was sunny and the houses and stuff were really nice and I like the mountains and the water everywhere. And it's got castles everywhere in it. They're quite happy over there. (girl, 8)

Children's strongly developed sense of the comparative is another aspect to their store of information. They might seem parochial in citing those features of their own environment they most appreciate, but they also reveal a great deal of awareness of other countries. Differences and contrasts abound and these include factors that are preferable. They do not assume that they live in the best country in the best of all possible worlds. They realize that there could be better places elsewhere, even if it is at the level of the weather. Children like the idea of travel and the possibilities of going on holiday.

> I'd like to live all round the world. I'd like to go to different spots I hadn't been to before. I'd like to go to Canada. My mum wants to live in Australia and I'd like to live in America for about twenty years and then come to England for about ten years and then I don't know where I might go. (boy, 9)

> If I was going to go there, then I would choose Spain, but only as a holiday. But if I was actually there and someone asked me which other country do you want to go to, I would say England. (girl, 7)

'England': naturally they wish to live where they do for the reasons that remain to them obvious: their friends and the familiarity of their circumstances. But when we say 'like', it does not follow that there is a consistent content, let alone patriotism or chauvinism. We have noted the comparative nature of children's awareness of other countries. Not only do they envisage the possibility of living abroad, they also express a pattern of discontent. They might appreciate the parochial benefits of where they are, but they also know that there are severe limitations. It is not necessarily the best place in the world.

> I came here when I was five. I don't like it. I don't like the teacher... and I don't like all the litter. (boy, 7)

> It's all right, but it's a bit rough. (boy, 8)

> I don't really know what's nice about it. (boy, 8)

> No. I dunno. You get all these kids beating you up every day. No. No. I want to move. (girl, 9)

I don't like my brother waking me up. He comes in and punches. Don't
like living here.   (girl, 7)

It's so horrible. I wish I was in France.   (boy, 8)

The list of discontents could go on. There is a pervasive sense that the place they live
is boring. Not only are there alternatives, but there is a palpable sense of disappointment. Whilst there are definite and everyday pleasures, as already outlined, this does
not mean that children rate where they live highly. The craving for space and security is met with the fact that the inner-city dwellers – and these are the most vocifer-
ously unhappy – do not have access to those things they most like. Having children
living in cramped conditions, under threat from bullies, does not make them accustomed to their circumstances. Instead, they learn to hate and resent them. This sense
of relativism does not lead to a sense of appreciation of other places so much as a
potential resentment of them. The threat of the outside world, and the enemies
within it, is the stronger for the essential insecurities of discontent.

In the context of close observation, comparison and discontent, the everyday
fabric of life is made clear. There are tracts of boredom as well as moments of pleasure. There are distractions and the everyday realities. Given such a feeling, it is not
surprising that children do not share any strong sense of the rightness of their
country or of its superiority over other nations. They are thankful that they do not
live in a poor country and thankful that they have their friends. But the
old-fashioned sense that belonging to a particular country has a virtue (or imposes
a duty) in itself is rare. Chauvinism is often associated with a generalized conception of some collective characteristic, superior to others.

I'm lucky to live here because it's a good country and it means we've got
good schools. But they might not, the other countries, they might not take
thing seriously. The English, they don't start much wars now. They only,
if there is a war, then England would only help whoever they think is the
best side. They wouldn't not just do anything about it. The selfish countries like Iraq.   (boy, 9)

This might give a kind of strength of moral virtue. The more common finding,
however, is a far weaker sense of place, of security at whatever level. Instead we
witness the as yet bewildered sense of comparison: against individual others at
first, as in academic success, and then in terms of the threat for the neighbourhood,
the peer group or the gang.

Children's views of their country and the circumstances they are in are closely
allied. There is little sign of political or national vision. It is all a question of where
they happen to be. At the same time, children want to be in a place that avoids
extremes and which does not put any extreme expectations on them.

It is the middle way, neither one thing nor the other. England is a 'medium' country. It is the place where your friends happen to be.

> I'm happy here at the moment in England. But if it had to be something different – I think here would be the best. It's not very crowded and it's not as crowded as America and I think it's a bit slower and steady. Unlike America, nothing's fast and loud or big or anything. It's just right. It's medium.
>
> (boy, 8)

The politics of nations

Children see themselves at the centre of the world, but this is not egocentricity. They see themselves as the observers; they accept that they are as they are, and live where they do. This might be a matter of chance, but it is also a matter of fact. At the same time, children see themselves as wanting to be in the middle between two extremes, as, for instance, between the academically very slow and the very quick. One of the extremes in which children wish to place themselves between is the extremes of the very rich and the very poor. They are quite clear that this contrast can be made between nations as between individuals. The world that they inhabit reveals enormous inequalities. It presents millions of famine-ridden people who possess nothing. And it presents the few who can own what they please.

When children attempt to make sense of the world as a whole, they need to put together all the images, the pictures that they have seen. This makes them understand the world in terms of binary opposites. They see that there are great imbalances. To an extent, they realize that this depends upon climate, upon the environmental circumstances in which people live. But they also know that there are inherent differences between nations, such as language. These differences are exacerbated by the apparent contrasts of circumstance. Underlying these contrasts is a sense that there is something politically inequitable about such unfairly distributed resources; and that something, like political charity, could be done about it.

> Some of them have got too much and they won't give it to anyone else.
> Sort of half of them are [rich] and half of them aren't.   (girl, 9)

Clearly the contrasts are also seen as circumstantial, depending on the weather, but they are embedded in circumstances that depend on human, as well as natural, resources.

> The southern ones [of Africa] they eat grains of wheat and some other
> parts of Africa are very, very rich and they get lots of chicken. They don't
> get bad droughts and they don't get lots of rain. And they hardly get any
> rain. And when it does rain they put buckets out and dig holes.   (boy, 8)

Whatever the reasons for or the symbols of the contrasts in wealth, it is the fact of
the contrasts that are significant, with the implication that there should be some
kind of redistribution.

> A lot of countries are poorer than others. Some countries are very poor
> and they haven't got very many houses and other countries are richer and
> they have a few houses and tents… on the news it showed what they were
> eating at the moment and what the trucks were bringing over to them.
> (girl, 8)

The contrast between rich and poor countries almost invariably leads to the
assumption that the rich have a responsibility to give to the poor. Just as the rich in
their own country are seen as being rich because they hold on to money that could
be helpful for other people, so by implication the rich countries, despite their charitable endeavours, are seen to hold on to those things that could alleviate suffering.
What happens at home is emulated elsewhere.

> Well, here it's like, it's mostly the same. There are some homeless people
> and starving people, but not nearly as many as Africa. In Africa it's just so
> different. There is one side that is very rich and one side that's very poor.
> (boy, 9)

As in the Robin Hood legend, there is a pervasive sentiment about the proper (but
voluntary) redistribution of wealth: a levelling out of income. When it comes to
other countries, this redistribution is symbolized by charities. The 'good' nation,
in this case Australia, is so because:

> They give food out to the other people that are poor.   (boy, 7)

Money, food and possessions are, however, just one symbol of contrasts between
countries. As with their awareness of the difficulties of communication between
countries so children are conscious of the significant differences between nations
at a variety of levels. There is no sense of a homogeneous world. On the contrary it
is countries, not their dictators or their political systems, that are branded as
responsible for certain acts. It is as if the nation were symbolic of all the people in it.
One of Brecht's plays begins with the statement: 'Hannibal crossed the Alps' and
the antiphon 'By himself? Where were his people?', and 'Alexander invaded Persia'

with the antiphon 'And didn't he have an army? What of them?' So are nations associated as a whole with particular actions or attitudes; some are rich and some poor, some good and some bad.

> Like some of them are violent and some of them are peaceful. Some of
> them are selfish and some of them are just unhappy.   (boy, 8)

What children find difficult to connect are the contrasts between countries and their relationship to political systems. This is because politics, the way that people organize their lives, is a subject that appears to be taboo. Children are assumed not to be capable of understanding politics. This is despite the fact that children see political realities and the results of politics around them every day, whether on the street or on television. As a result, they do their best to understand the societies they see and experience through their own interpretations, through sifting through the evidence, at first in terms of opposites and then in terms of systems.[6] So children, despite the attempts to hide realities from them – they are not aware of the real meaning of the term 'politics' – do their best to dissect the essential differences of systems in other countries.

Differences are most obviously experienced in looks and language, but there is an awareness that political systems vary from place to place. What these systems consist of, of course, is unclear, but they are seen to exist.

> Sometimes they make different rules than British people do. And they got
> a different prime minister.   (boy, 7)

Children struggle to define how political systems work, although they are aware that there are contrasts between them. They try to make sense of facts that are alluded to, but not explained; images that seem to carry potent messages, but stand by themselves. The attempts to make something intelligible out of this incoherence are, in fact, impressive.

> They're very strict there and before, they used to… there used to be a very
> nasty president who was shot I think or was beheaded and, anyway, he was
> not very nice and he made them do all kinds of things that, like, they were-
> n't free like us. We can do anything we like except murder people.
>   (girl, 9)

Even if children do not define what the differences are, they are, nevertheless, aware of them. The more images are presented that constitute their vision of different countries, the more differences become clear. Not only are there individual differences and group identities, but also large-scale contrasts. The world as a whole is one of barriers, of inequalities, of threats and dangers.

These perceptions are attempts to relate what is observed to what is experienced, to enter into the real possibilities of being inside another country. Whether they have personal knowledge or not, it is the sheer difference between people that the children insist upon.

> Like Mexicans. They're completely different. Just completely and utterly different to us. They speak different and look different. A lot of Russian people, they have like bushy types of hair. And they're big, lots of Russian people.
>
> (boy, 9)

The world is full of contrasts, and implied antipathies. We know that children would naturally enough not wish to live in conditions of deprivation, but we also know that they feel that such conditions are endemic.

> I'd like to spend my life in Africa, but I wouldn't like to be African. Because you'd have to stay black all your life and if an English person saw you – it's not very nice if you're black 'cos it's not a very nice colour, black. And when I went there I saw this black man and I saw these people go look at that black man. 'He's stupid.' 'He's black.' I think they are English. They keep on saying horrible things about you. I just heard that, when I was going to a hotel I just heard someone say that. It was just this old man walking along. They just said that. Because they don't like the colour or something like that.
>
> (boy, 6)

Politics consists of more than the work of governments. There is a politics of race, of stereotyping and prejudice. The idea of the differences between nations and between people is one of the most formative influences on children's shaping their understanding of the world. Differences also mean contrasts in culture, in the objects that define culture: milk shakes or rags.

> They speak a different language and they don't have personal stereos and televisions if they're poor. And coffee makers and milk shakes and things.
>
> (girl, 9)

These contrasts create a sense of universal, and not just personal, unfairness. There is a latent anger in the unequal distribution of wealth and power. The contrasts of the world, in terms of possessions, is always before them. This is abetted by the clear fact that little beyond charity is done about it.

> Some of them have got too much and they won't give it to anyone else...
> They're trying to help them. And they're arguing with the richer people.

> And they're being nicer to the poor than they are to the richer ones. They come from places like England and France and they went there to see if they could help.
>
> (girl, 9)

Political relations between nations seem to rest on two factors. One is the fact that each nation has its own system, and own independence. This implies that each nation is self-contained and does not depend on trade. The other is the traffic, not of trade, but of charity, as if relationships were distinctly ones of need and response to need. The journeys that children have experienced, of course, are mostly taken as tourists, which itself implies the views of the outsiders.

Despite the lack of a theoretical basis for understanding the concept of nationhood and the relations between people, children have extensive awareness of other countries. Occasionally, there is an opportunity to speculate at length about the way that countries differ, for reasons that include religion as well as conflict.

> The Kurds. They haven't got any homes. But there are about a few shops that they buy crops in and the crops don't grow because not any rain falls down. If I made the world I would make the Kurds not hungry and all the other people… 'Cos they don't have God, I don't think. They don't love him, I don't think and because they haven't got any homes they've been chasing – oh, I've forgotten the names of the people that are chasing them around – Turkey. The Kurds have gone into Turkey and they're a bit cross that Turkey has got a little bit of food that they could have.
>
> (girl, 6)

Again, we see the concept that the relationships between nations depend on food, even if it is not in the form of charity. We also note the knowledge that depends on stark and clear images.

There are, of course, children who have been encouraged to learn more about politics in one form or another. It is clear that they do not rate politicians at all highly when they do know about them.

> Not very good. I think they should consent to the doctors' work conditions. Well, I feel their policy towards Europe, I don't like their thinking. I agree with the monetary system. I don't really mind about the decrease of power towards Westminster and Whitehall.
>
> It would be better if they were sort of unified by two people from one country and then there's that overload, sort of high-up person. The politicians are not much different.
>
> (boy, 9)

Politicians might be the same all over the world, but children's abiding impression of the world is of its contrasts. People are not the same, in thinking or habits. Children accept these differences and they also accept the fact and the chance that has placed them where they are. They know that but for fate they could have been born in a different place with a different outlook entirely.

> I don't think I'd think the same. If I lived in New York maybe I might think that everywhere around the world is all big cities and all big, long streets and all power stations. (boy, 8)

Children's understanding of the contrasts of their perceived world is complex, ambivalent and ambiguous. No one can look with full empathetic insight into the conditions of others. We acknowledge that we do so from a particular cultural point of view. So children look at the rest of the world, defining themselves and their circumstances as they do so. The contrasts they see, and the acceptance of the arbitrary, give them a clear picture of distinction, of unfairness, of different points of view. This can present them with a sense of balance, of the acceptance of diversity. It can also lead to a strong sense of generalized injustice. *Why* should things be as they are is the pervasive question, mostly unanswered, mostly ignored. And deeper than that, *why* am I where I am? And what does it mean?

Children have to make sense of their world. They can define it as the actuality of what is, in contrast to others. Or they can resent it as being too much in contrast to others. They can take in the warmth of their own cultural familiarities, or they can dislike the inner poverty of their own lives. Their views of the world as a whole reveal how each individual can either go down the road of tolerance or end in the cul-de-sac of nationalism. The distinction between the two remains ambiguous.

References

1. This is an almost unique reference to something learnt in school, but it is learnt with a scepticism attached.
2. Habermas, J (1989) *The Structure Transformation of the Public Sphere: An inquiry into a category of bourgeois culture*, Polity Press, Cambridge
3. Podsnap and Veneering both patronize a visiting Frenchman by assuming that he would be overwhelmed by the wonderful British constitution as embodied in London – Londres – London.
4. Hofstede, G (1991) *Cultures and Organisations: Software of the mind*, McGraw-Hill, London
5. Vygotsky, L (1978) *Mind in Society*, Harvard University Press, Cambridge, MA.
6. Cullingford, C (1992) *Children and Society*, Cassell, London

8

Groups of identity: peoples, races, nations and cultures

Psychological institutions

In trying to understand the complexities of being human, we are constantly reminded of that earliest of organizational traits, categorization. Every word we use to define our thoughts is a symbolic definition; every act of communication a shared definition. Making sense of things and people is understood in terms of labels and distinctions. All our perceptions are dependent on categories. Sometimes we call them variables and sometimes characteristics. One of the most commonly used distinctions in mapping out society is between structure and agency, between the institution and the individual. This is one of the many distinctions that on the face of it is obvious. There is no doubt that organizations exist just as there are individual beings that belong to them. But the more we study them the less a simple distinction between structure and agency holds up to critical scrutiny if we try to enter into the experience of individual people. Institutions are reflections of the people in them, and the individuals formed by the cultural norms of which they are part. What they make of these norms varies. Organizations are cultural symbols that individuals share.

Prejudice, and its basis in forming either rigid or fluid boundaries, is a cultural phenomenon. People create their own psychological institutions. They create not just their own world but the way other people see them in it. They adjust themselves and define themselves according to other people and their implied perceptions. They long for things in common, matters that others will recognize and understand. In each person's efforts to justify him- or herself there is a need for recognition, for shared values, whether worldwide or more limited and immediate. There is a thirst for insights that only other people can give. What others see, or are perceived to see, is part of self-identity. Identity is never possible in isolation.

There is a need to belong to a culturally defined understanding. This neurotic rationality depends on seeing how the perceptions of others fit into the individual's own sense of identity.

The question remains: if all of us have to define ourselves in terms that certain others can understand, why do some have so much more difficulty in doing so than others? There are difficulties of place within the family, and within the community, that mixture of social hierarchy and social power. The tensions of self-consciousness and of personal worth on the one hand, and assertiveness and the ability to exert some kind of control on the other, are never completely resolved, although at the two pathological ends one might think they are. There are always conflicts between the sense of the self and the self as a part of some institution, some cultural set or habit, which is the true reflection of personal identity. This neurotic rationality, to find a justification for oneself, is what underpins every social community to which one belongs, from the family or club or school, to the nation. Thus we depend on psychological institutions, of which there are many.

The distinction, then, is between those who have the ability to possess many different kinds of psychological institution, and those whose definitions are narrower and more defensive. Intolerance is the result of personal subliminal threat translated into an absurdly crude self-definition. It is a flag of inconvenience thrown over the ontological insecurity that all feel, but some accept. Prejudice against others is more a psychological creation than a rational one. It might be rationalized after the event, and it might become a 'clubbable' value, but it is essentially a result of subliminal insecurity. The group, the gang, the club, the class can all mask that sense of loneliness. Some seem nothing more than the symbol of the place to which they belong. Others accept belonging as just another layer of self-definition. The underlying question, beyond the descriptions of nationalism or racism, is why some grow into the immaturity of prejudice and others into the maturity of understanding.

Note the word 'grow'. The limitations of intolerance and threat are not a natural phenomenon. They are learnt. They are cultural, not genetic. Personal characteristics have a part to play, but even these, in terms of relationships with other people, are dependent on cultural variables. Prejudice is learnt.

The desire for understanding by others, like sympathy for others, is a natural characteristic even in babies.[1] This entails not only sibling rivalry and the seeking of attention but the understanding of a family, of a group to which one belongs. Within the group are points of view, of antipathy and empathy, but the sense of a cultural group with something shared and understood is already strong. In early childhood, relationships are both natural and sought after. If there is a dawning realization that they either do not exist or are not fully reciprocal, then the ontological sense of self is already eroded.[2] Other senses of belonging and other group norms then come into play and foster a different, less personally secure, sense of identity. This creates a more strident seeking for individual attention. The individual cut off within family relationships seeks out larger definitions of the social self. The desire for warmth and understanding, if denied, provokes the heightened sense not only of different points of view, which all children recognize, but the threat, the enmity, of alternative points of view. The personal sense of isolation leads to the need to create groups of an enemy against which to define the self.

The less secure the feeling of personal identity, the more profound are the discriminations against others. Prejudice, in its manifestations of social intolerance, verbal or physical, is based on insecurity, or a lack of the sense of the complete, cultural, self. The first culture is that of the family. It is a matter of shared practices and shared assumptions, of understanding of behaviour and ideas. Every culture rests upon the unstated yet obvious commonalities of living, of nuances of language, of the sense of proxemics, the use of space and gesture, and the realization that out of this sharing comes belonging. There is a strong sense that personal relationships are within a framework of opportunity, of space, of the circumstance to which one happens to belong. The neutral realization that where one happens to be is arbitrary ironically reinforces that sense of belonging. We are where we are. The world outside, however immediate or large, is the world against which the self is defined.

There are layers of the 'world'. From the immediately enclosed circle of the family and its strangers, those who cross the threshold and those who do not, to the images of distance and unfamiliarity, these different levels of connection are perceived and analysed. So much of the embracing or the rejecting of other peoples depends on the vision that is developed at an early age. Certain phenomena, like being an only child with its concomitant self-centredness and all the consequences of the difficulty of sharing, are well recorded and recognized. But the deeper cultural estrangements formed at this time are less predictable. Other people can enter into a family as friend or threat; the neighbours can be friendly or be connected with the sense of the enemy. The unpredictability of what will happen throughout life can only be explained in these chance experiences. They can also be understood.

The family is not just a matter of the self-enclosed or the self-sufficient. Its warm emotional embrace is not enough. The family is also a symbol of looking outwards, of sharing collective identities in the face of a shared, anonymous world. Relationships with adults, with parents in particular, depend on the intellectual common ground of talking about other things. Agreement is not always complete. It does not need to be, for that form of false security in shared beliefs or monumental attitudes is the result not of intellectual insights or flexibility, but of fear and threat, of a retreat into a norm of thinking or behaviour. The complete family relishes differences of opinion. But it also shares views of what differences can be expressed. It is not so much uniting *against* the enemy, the physical, cultural and social world, as rejoicing in its shared observation of it.

If the family does not present a completely enclosed cultural case, then it is open to the outside world. If it does not have a coherent sense of itself, of shared values and the deliberate sharing of alternative values, then the peer group, the alternative sympathetic and more anonymous family, will. Within a family, or in any relationship, there is 'me' and 'you'. There is also the sense of the point of view, of 'us' against 'them'. Whilst this might be sibling rivalry, it will also embrace an insight into a world that is outside the family, different for reasons of circumstance, but different for reasons that can be obvious or guessed at. It is when the awareness of other people is developing that the crucial distinction between the person as a complete personality and the role, the person fulfilling a social function, is made. This is far more important than the artificial distinction between structure and agency, society and the people in it. Culture is the sharing of some aspects of identity. It is also the understanding of norms, of set expectations and collective habits, and their limitations.

Neurotic rationalities

The power of culture, that sense of shared values, is paradoxically strengthened by the sense of the neutrality, the arbitrariness of circumstances. Young children know that they could have been born elsewhere. They do not possess an atavistic sense of divine control, the curious chauvinism of 'God made me an Englishman' or whatever. That absurd notion comes later and the attribution of responsibility completely spurious. Instead there is, as we have noted, a strong feeling of the arbitrary. This does not lead of a sense of impersonality, or the multifariousness of cultures, but to the stronger feeling of one's place, one's time and one's identity. This is where I am, by chance, reflect children, with my *own* language, my own neighbourhood; and it could be so different. The sense of the possibility of being elsewhere, of being abroad, of speaking a different language strengthens the sense of cultural identity. The stronger the sense of self, the more easy it is to accept otherness. The more insecure the home, the more there is a need to mark the boundaries. All know their own cultural 'set'. Some resent it more, just as some relish it for its own sake. When there is a lack of identity it takes the form either of self-parody, of *being* the embodiment of cultural values, as in a 'class fix', or of aggressive self-assertion against others.

Everyone is 'branded on the tongue', is collectively programmed into a particular language and habit of mind. Between the individual and the shared manifestations of humanity come a whole host of traits, learnt and imbibed, inevitable and so deep we take them and their consequences often completely for granted. Every culture, after all, considers itself normal: it is all the others that are strange. But then there are multifarious cultures. Just to take some examples, there are the religious constraints of exclusiveness – 'There is only one God, Allah, and Mohammed is his prophet' – there is the 'American Dream' or the Protestant work ethic, the creed of communism, the idea of the gentleman, and the deep fear of losing face. These are all-powerful social forces that mark people in some way, that dominate some and inform others. All this is both inevitable and understandable, until the moment such cultural values are turned into prejudice, into a jihad, hatred, bigotry or destructive snobbery.

Personal identity depends on circumstances. It might not *feel* like that but it is recognized as being so. To create new identities therefore is always possible. We belong to a new school or a new club. Indeed, group psychology has long shown us how adaptable we are, how we have multiple identities.[3] Each individual is defined according to gender, age, class, religion and ethnicity, let alone the more lubricious notions of language and culture. There are individual and collective identities. It is the way that people chose to identify themselves, and how they distinguish between role – the individual in a foreign country – and themselves – the person trying to communicate – that counts. Personal identity is a matter of circumstance.

That there are shared cultural habits both at the level of group and at the level of nationhood is clear. Richard Lewis provides a typical anecdote.[4] A group of Finns, Italians and Japanese all learning English in Wales have planned a trip to Snowdon. It becomes clear the day before that the perpetual rain will not cease. The Finns suggest calling the trip off. The Italians protest. They have counted on it. The Japanese don't mind whatever happens. In the event the coach for the trip turns up. The Finns climb in, fuming. The Japanese do so smiling. The Italians are nowhere to be seen; they have stayed in bed. What are the cultural phenomena of the connections between thought and speech; and speech and action? Are these different cultural actions typical? Those who went on the trip, out of a sense of duty, having had a premonition that it would be uncomfortable, had a bad time. Those who had insisted that it went ahead since it was paid for, changed their minds. Cultural boundaries, the gentler side of prejudice, are also observed between towns and cities, their football rivalries and their accents, and even between the clearly defined differences between Oxford and Cambridge colleges. Superciliousness, the most controlled of all forms of prejudice, abounds.

Culture has many levels. It is of course, as Hofstede reminds us, both a refinement of the mind and, more to the point, a form of what he calls mental software.[5] It is about categories, and about distinction.[6] It is not just a self-indulgent sense of superiority but a value that can celebrate distinctiveness or be employed as a weapon against others. Culture forms people. It civilizes. But it is also both the height of humanity in all its understanding and the force that causes such hatred of *other* people's cultures that the very variety of human collective endeavour can be turned into destructiveness. The list to illustrate this could be endless. It strikes the consciousness day by day, year by year in different places. Culture is what forms us as individuals. In the way it is used it also can enable us to destroy each other.

Familiarity and ontological insecurity

It is often suggested that familiarity with other people's cultures, through visits and through dialogue, promotes tolerance and understanding. Many of the initiatives to create a more harmonious and united Europe are centred on this premise. But mere visits do not in themselves end in understanding. Often there is no attempt to enter into a real dialogue with the locality; on the contrary, the sense of the reinforcement of one's own identity can be stronger than the glimpse into other people's lives. Football supporters following their team into foreign capitals reassert their own nationality rather than appreciate where they are. Tourists in popular resorts, drinking their imported beer, watching videos of their home team and going to discotheques are hardly imbibing local colour. Even sending groups of youths abroad to learn the language has as great a tendency to bond them with each other as isolated groups as to open their eyes to other possibilities. The close observation of children abroad, or of the images of television, can lead to as much distaste as appreciation. The familiar of the home neighbourhood is reinforced.

There is also a counter-argument that distance from other groups avoids tensions, as if that peaceful world of the past, where people were so isolated that any stranger was indeed so strange that they could be welcomed, were still possible. Surveys of householders asked whom they would object to as next-door neighbours reveals depth of racism – Gypsies being most resented and feared – and reinforces the notion that many people yearn for the ghettoization of their culture. Differences cause tensions, but only at times. The example of Bosnia is but a recent one where after years of ordinary neighbourliness people who know each other well to the point of close friendship suddenly turn into the most barbaric of enemies.

The term 'culture shock' is often used to describe the difficulties of meeting the unfamiliar.[7] The need to understand how others operate, in business and communication, is assumed to rest on insights into certain cultural habits, like the relationship of thought to word and word to action. Approaches to business, as is the case of the Finns, the Italians and the Japanese, are therefore delineated. This is seen as the gentle, constructive side to the overcoming to prejudice. But there is still an assumption made about the difficulties, the barriers to really entering into other people's modes of consciousness. The shock of the different, the close proximity to other people's habits of thought, is supposed to cause strain.[8] Much more important than this, however, is the loss of the familiar. In analysing the experience of students studying abroad for a considerable length of time, it is found that whilst they appreciate the kindliness and practical friendliness of the host country, what causes them most distress is the absence of their own familiar cultural habits, from food to modes of thought. The tendency to cling together, to reinforce each other's sense of identity, becomes paramount.

Being in a different country, or in an alien group, often has the effect of reinforcing the sense of cultural identity, even to the point of self-parody. Even people who choose to go abroad to study find it far more difficult and far more alienating than they expect.[9] It is the loss of the sense of shared personal meanings and understandings that is significant. When cultural values are never questioned or compared, the unspoken assumptions of superiority, or at least distinction, are reinforced. Studies of migrants demonstrate not only the mental difficulties that they have in adjusting to different styles of living and different expectations, but how much they miss sharing the familiar.[10] Even tourists undergo a certain amount of stress, and businessmen feel psychological distance. But it is not so much the shock of learning new social skills, or being faced with the need to change, or to understand different modes of thought that is so crucial, but the sense of loss. The familiar, those things taken for granted, that make up and reinforce the cultural sense of self is what is missing, however well the migrant is prepared. Of course some merely take their own collective identities with them and live in cultural isolation.

Even those who choose to travel become aware of what they miss. This is usually experienced in an inability to understand the language, but it is actually deeper than that and is dependent on shared understandings, on gestures, on assumptions, on interpretations. Any 'foreign' experience will, unless the language and culture is fully imbibed, contain the sense of what is missing, as well as covering it up with an unfamiliar contrast. Homesickness is not so much due to shock as to the sense of the unfamiliar. It is a matter of depression rather than anxiety.[11] Being in a host country not only demands analysis of how the people behave and what they expect, but reinforces the traveller's sense of personal identity and territoriality.[12]

Culture, of the group or the nation, of a class or a religion, is both a powerful notion and hard to determine in its effects. It always has in it a sense of definition, of preferring one object or statement or means of expression to another. It is possible to argue that taste is an artificial matter and not only that but a means of self-perpetuation and even dominance over others.[13] But culture is more pervasive; it affects everyone. The shared values and understandings might not be 'high culture' or matters of deliberate taste, but they are the kind of information through which people identify both themselves and their relationships to others. There are many dimensions of culture, brought to the fore by comparisons not only between what is desired as valuable by some and not by others, but between what is taken for granted by some and not by others. In the 'collective programming of the mind', there are some clear distinctions to be made between alternative approaches to relationships.[14] Hofstede describes different people's attitudes to power and authority, from dependence to independence. He talks of some people's ability to accept uncertainty, and other's strenuous attempts to avoid it. And he notes the distinction between the sense of the individual holding on to his personal values, and the alternative stress of a collective belief.[15] Each nation, or tribe, or group goes about its business differently.

Young children are able to appreciate different points of view. They understand distinctions between truth and falsehood.[16] They are therefore well equipped for the comparative, for the avoidance of prejudice. But prejudice grows over the years as certain personal habits of thought and shared assumptions become hardened. It is only when the habits of mind are so encrusted with familiarity that the notion of cognitive dissonance sets in.[17] The fluidity of the mind, in absorbing all kinds of new notions and ideas, gradually becomes hardened, not into a sense of self as much as a into a collective identity, a sense of belonging. This means that what is taken for granted at one stage only later becomes a revelation of difference, when the unfamiliar is looked at not with curiosity but with a sense of threat.[18] The construction of personal frameworks of thought can either be on a constantly comparative basis, a recognition that where one happens to be, and what one happens to believe, is arbitrary as well as powerfully individual, or on a basis of threatened self-justification or assertion against others. In young children's views of other countries we see both. They could develop either way. Social groups define themselves by comparisons.[19] It is only if a norm is recognized as a collective habit of thought that the assertion of a gang, or a peer group, has any symbolic meaning. From flags to nose studs, the assertion of identity is *against* others. Relativism, neutrality, objectivity and reflection of the facts are the basis of all understanding, as young children interpret the world in which they find themselves. This is the basis for tolerance. It can also be, by the same sense of personal neutrality, a means of potential threat. Insecurity of one's own position strengthens assertiveness.

Bahktin reminds us that however hard we try to enter into a foreign culture, and however long one lives in it, it is impossible to forget one's own.[20] This does not mean to say that understanding is impossible: on the contrary. But it does recognize the profound hold of those artefacts of shared culture developed when we are young, and usually ignored, or taken for granted by the education system. Points of view, both individual within the home, and collective, like arguments between nations, are understood. They are also used, consciously or subconsciously, in the assertions of self.

Nationhoods and nationalism

The self only has meaning in relation to some other, which can be a person or a place. It is not in a vacuum. Definitions of others, of differences, are therefore crucial. Whilst there are many different levels and types of distinction, the most obvious and possibly the most destructive is that of nationalism. Whilst there are many sides to the feelings of patriotism, often noble – *dulce et decorum est pro patria mori* – it is essentially an expression of antipathy towards the other. The effect of these collective feelings in action translates self-interest and self-protection into profound harm. Nations are not altogether artificial. They are not only political entities but, exploited as this is by politicians, large groups of common interests and, more significantly, shared identities. They give sustenance to the collective self, transcending ethnicity and class. They are an emotional support that gives meaning to the single identity.

The sense of a shared identity is given substance by ascribing certain characteristics to other nations. These can be comparatively benevolent or neutral, as well as harsh. Thus the stereotypes associated with different people have both a banal symbolism – the bowler hat or the kilt – or a more pervasive ascription of character, like coldness and reserve or emotional flamboyance. That people do have shared characteristics is clear. The Poles, for example, are shaped by their language and their history, their territorial position and by their religion. The Finns see themselves as gloomy, pessimistic, honest and understated. The idea of the 'stiff upper lip' was one that was for a long time deliberately fostered as a part of the British self-image.[21] In times of conflict those relatively benign attributions to others can become dangerous, when the characteristics are so widely shared that people are no longer seen as individuals but as a type.[22] There is always a difficulty for some people to distinguish between the role and the personality, so that police officers doing their duty are perceived as having a *personal* grudge, and expressing personal enmity. In conflict the 'other' nations are not just a collection of people but deemed to give expression to a shared personal characteristic.

There are always comparisons being made between 'in groups' and 'out groups'.[23] The attributions of identity include not only images but emotions. Thus there is a polarization of different characteristics by which some of the tensions of the north/south divide – rich Northern Italy versus the backward south, for example – crosses national boundaries. Germany is linked with efficiency, Italy with emotion.[24] Each nation is viewed in terms of contrast; the familiarity and the empathy of one's own kind seen in terms of the threatening alternative.

Many collective attitudes have an historical base. It is no surprise that Germans should be looked on with undiminished suspicion in other European countries. Despite the fostering of European understanding and cooperation, there are deep suspicions that remain more than 50 years after conflict and occupation. The

Dutch and British have far more negative views of the Germans than any other nation, associating them with arrogance and dominance.[25] It is clear that such views are not based on considered examination of the present evidence, or on personal experience, but on a shared collective view that is formed by the past, through the passing on of attitudes by parents and by images.[26]

Cultural bias and stereotypes are pervasive. They are seen clearly in school textbooks. The justification given for this is to foster the sense of patriotism, to create a positive image of a nation. When the National Curriculum in Great Britain was being debated much was made of the idea of history as triumphalism, with the result that the celebration of the 'finest hour' is contrasted to images of mindless instinctive aggression by Germans.[27] A glance at Irish school textbooks, on the other hand, gives such an interpretation of Great Britain, as a constant focus of attention as the great defining enemy, that it is difficult for a native to recognize such an interpretation or to believe that the only significant events in Irish history were the struggles against the Protestant ascendancy. But then school textbooks have always shown bias. Despite attempts to foster international understanding, from the League of Nations to UNESCO, by examining the way in which history is presented, in schools, textbooks remain rooted in historical bias.[28]

School textbooks demonstrate the close association between history and mythology. Whilst nationalism is a comparatively recent phenomenon, it is a collective feeling that is not only thriving but consciously fostered, for example in the aftermath of the break up of the Soviet Union. It is a result of the desire for a shared identity, a collective belonging to a particular community which has a collection of myths and shared memories, often associated with particular places.[29] Beyond the concept of the nation-state lies a deeper desire for ethnic attributions, for the creation of the collective self defined against others. Kosovo is an example both of the sense of shared memories and its bitter outcomes in murder and revenge. The sense of the enemy goes deeper than the sense of outside threat. One can understand the suspicion of the Turks felt by Greeks.[30] But there are also deeper atavistic insecurities at work, an intolerance born not out of fear or threat as much as a sense of inarticulate rage.

The problem is that the concept of shared identity can be at once an image of the positive, and a collective journey into violence. George Orwell defined the difference between patriotism as something which meant no harm to others and nationalism which sought to dominate. It was taken for granted by Green in England and Renan in France that a love of one's country was a positive virtue to be fostered.[31] How then does this turn sour? The distinction between the definition of nationhood and nationality is an important one. In the French Revolution the concept of citizenship meant that people belonged to a cultural community, without any dependence on birth.[32] Nationality is a sentiment, a feeling of unity which contains all kinds of factors. It is a pride in a collective self, a sense of assertion that is stronger for being understood by others. That it does not depend purely on race is clear from the example of the United States. That it is not dependent on language is shown by Switzerland.[33] There is also a distinction to be made between the state, like Austro-Hungary, and the nation.

Nationality is a given cultural factor, sometimes positive and sometimes negative. The distinction is when through ontological insecurity the sense of the personal, with its realization of neutrality and chance, leads to the need to foster the influence of others, in a more collective will. Young children have a phlegmatic unbiased view of their own position in society. They understand the contrasts and the fact that whilst they are who they are, and where, they could have just as easily been somewhere else. They are given a language, but they are also given views of other people. This can be neutral or positive or negative. Their view of other nations is a mixture, but they soon develop the mental maps that create contrasts in attribution. The extent to which these become powerful is dependent on their feelings of insecurity both in the home and at school. It is when the general hurly-burly of school, the bullying and teasing, get out of hand that gangs are formed and vulnerability turned to self-assertion. It is then that there grows a need to hate, beyond particular individuals. Groups of enemies are formed: the snobs, the rich, the police, the others who define the contrast with themselves.

The most extreme forms of nationalism are often associated with collective self-doubt. Explanations of the rise of Hitler often include the German sense of the world disintegrating and having to find something to hate.[34] The Jews were hated for their symbolic destructiveness, as in the cases of Marx on society, Freud on the psyche, Schoenberg on harmony, even Einstein on Newtonian mechanics. The question remains whether the holocaust is actually an example of nationalism. Nationalism takes all kinds of forms and is hard to define. It is an 'imagined political community'.[35] The people do not know each other but feel they belong together. Nationalism is both an attachment that people feel to a state – tombs of the unknown soldier symbolizing collective sacrifice to the flag – and a cultural celebration of the vernacular, in language or in music, using folk traditions and the demotic in the assertion of distinct identity. Whilst nationalism can be traced to the French Revolution and the consequences perceived in collective assertion, as Herder defines it, it is also something constantly being reinvented. It is argued that the idea of the nation-state was fostered by colonization, creating a grammar of nationalism that defines itself against the imposition of other national consciousness, like the uprisings against the Dutch in the Far East.[36]

What is the hold that nationalism has so that even in Marxist states the international ideal is replaced by assertions of cultural autonomy? Class warfare is replaced by people's wars of liberation. Territorial conflict or competition is replaced with the singing of national anthems and the flying of national flags at sporting events. Whatever the level, nationalism is one of the most revealing of group identities, since it is both artificial and a recent phenomenon. Billig, in describing 'banal nationalism', points out that it is not an age-old primordial condition but it is a powerful form of identity or ideological consciousness, even a banal mysticism.[37] Children only slowly acquire the sense that their own language has some kind of national identity. Having witnessed the multiplicities of language they learn that there is something defining about their own as if they were naturally associated with certain peoples.

Roots of prejudice

Nationalism in its virulent form surfaces when there is a crisis, a sense of threat or insecurity.[38] But this sense of the reversion to a group assertion is true at a number of levels. It is true of the peer group or the gang in school. There needs to be an enemy beyond personality. The enemy then is not an individual teacher but the impersonal school system in which all teachers are demonized, even if the point of attrition is a particular individual. The enemy is the person who shows differences of taste or interest, who works hard and or is a swot, who is in some other way different, by reason of wearing glasses or having different coloured hair. The sense of distinction, of race or belief, is one that grows and develops throughout the experience of school.[39] All have multiple identities. Young children realize this. But they also choose to discard some of the more complex ones, just as they learn to ignore the complexities in the interests of a simpler less chaotic understanding. Identity is 'situational'.[40] Thus children slowly learn to simplify their maps of the world, from their own small place in a neighbourhood to the sense of larger boundaries and more particularly those potent images of the 'other'.

The process of assimilation of information is paralleled by the need to make a coherent structure out of it. To that extent the idea of stages of understanding makes sense, not because of children's limitations but because they need to accumulate not only their factual knowledge but their sense of emotional association.[41] No acquired knowledge is without its affective attributes. As fast as the concept of different countries is understood so is their association with matters they like or do not like.[42] The approval of the United States rather than Germany begins early, and certainly earlier than any mention of them in the school curriculum. An emotional attitude to 'others' also begins early. The complexities of sibling rivalry demonstrate this. But it then becomes more formalized by information. There are labels to be attached to the emotions.

The problem is that in insecure self-definition, in the psychological institutions that each person creates, there are all kinds of choices of the other. The enemy can be a personal rival or a tribe. It can be the criminal, the threat to the neighbourhood, the burglar.[43] It can be taken from a whole menagerie of possibilities: the class bully, the changeable friend or soldiers generally.[44] This formulation of the 'other' is important because it is a matter not only of self-definition but of the contextualizing of the self. This essential habitation is a matter of more than taste.[45] It is a constantly changing re-definition which can be fluid with irony or hardened into prejudice. And the sense of the other is complex. There are distinctions of class, and of gender, of any number of groups by which people choose to identify themselves. What happens, for example, to the ethnic minorities within nations? The patterns of movement, of migration and international communication, point up all the difficulties and complexities, and the hope. The more convoluted the argument of identity, in a sense, the closer we get to the real essence of being human. The more confusing the picture, the less stereotyped.[46]

The reason that nationalism is such a potent concept is both its artificiality, even absurdity, and because it crosses the boundaries of other cruder distinctions. Children know they are born in one place, but does that make them special? Their own cultural distinctiveness depends on language. They know that. They are equally identified with one *part* not only of the country in which they live, but also of their town. Before they extrapolate the differences of cultural and mechanical inheritances, like the use of refrigeration, they are aware of their own social circumstances. They can accept that or they can begin to worry about the disparities. They do not have to make larger distinctions. Some, not all, find this the most attractive way of making some kind of sense of themselves.

There is an almost arbitrary choice of what kind of enemy is created. It can be a rival gang. It can be a class, like the rich or the very poor. It can be the neighbourhood drunk or the person who is exceptionally strange. Or it can be people who look different, and who can be easily labelled. We sometimes think that both nationalism and racism are simple (and that those who hold such attitudes should be eliminated). But what, after all, are these concepts? Young children have very equivocal views of what it is to have 'blood'. Their complex and comparative view, objective as it is, sees themselves in relation to others. They know that they have friends from all kinds of backgrounds. They know they are part of an overall culture with its internal rhythms of language and understanding. And yet they talk of blood, of inheritance; of having to relate to a particular line of ethnic identity. This is arbitrary. It is there. It is a fact, not of great importance in itself. After all the blood line could be almost any. Young children talk about it as openly as any other given fact, like parents' behaviour or characteristics.

When it comes to national identity young children remain unsure. This is an uncertainty that is far more positive than negative. Chauvinism has to be learnt. To take one example of ethnicity and nationalism, what does one make of the distinction between being English and being British? It has become a habit to associate Britishness with some kind of alienation: the 'lesser breeds' of Welsh, or Irish, or of a minority ethnic group. Yet those who live in England, let alone those born and bred there, are English. The concept of Britishness is at once complex and double-edged. It both crosses and undermines ethnic/national boundaries. It crosses them since all kinds of groups with different accents and national inheritances are British, as rich a display of stereotypes as the scenes before battle in *Henry V*. At the same time the term is used as a demarcation line; 'here, but not white'.[47] Young children find it very hard to label themselves English or British until such time as there are political significances attached, until there is a sense of identity that is created by having demarcation lines.

Being British or not is an accident, like the colour of one's skin. Long before there is any sense of belonging there is a notion of place that only gradually becomes a matter of symbolic boundaries. There is no deep-seated sense of patriotism.[48] The tension between different forms of definition within minority ethnic groups and the majority comes later. The question is how marginal people feel to a collective group identity; the former sense of the marginal depends on their perceptions of the latter, the notion of a people at large.[49] It is only when there is a clear sense of a strong cultural hegemony that it is possible to feel estranged from it. In the multiplicity of identities, however, it is also possible to feel a part of more than one culture. Thus Asian girls are both wedded to the idea of their inherited society and pleasing their parents, and fully part of the immediate culture in which they are being embedded.[50]

Ethnicity and patriotism

Nationalism, as a simple concept, is rapidly undermined by the mixture of ethnic identities that make it up. There has been a tendency to associate race and nationalism, but even fascism with its fierce sense of racial hatred is quite separate from real nationalism, that sense of belonging to an ideal of cultural and historical as well as ancestral strength. It is possible to identify closely with a particular group without being ethnocentric.[51] Ethnicity, for young children, younger than 11, is of low salience. It can be fostered, nurtured and elaborated, but that comes later.[52] It is only gradually that prejudice against others is formulated into single categories. In all the profusion of experience of the immediate kind, the sense of otherness, of belonging to a group, of oneself as a social not just an individual being, or of others no longer as mere personalities but representatives, is something that is gradually learnt.

In attempts to classify racist attitudes there are assumptions that there is such a strong sense of a cultural hegemony that any intruders will be easily rejected. Studies of young children, however, suggest that the sense of self is far more complicated to start with, and only gradually becomes simplified into prejudice. There is no simple sense of cultural hegemony. If there are colour lines, by which ethnic minorities slowly become accepted through the levels of political rights, followed by economic rights and finally private contacts, then that is descriptive of adults, not children.[53] The idea that ethnic groups are a threat to the culture of the group depends on the notion of a well-identified and complete group to which a person belongs. The group replaces the personality. The insecure individual needs the group.[54] Whilst there are different levels of prejudice, these are learnt. The feigned sophistication lies in how to narrow the demarcation lines, how to be able to identify the enemy as such as the particular 'other' in a uniform of one kind or another. Young children do not know about uniforms. Such knowledge has to be consciously fostered.

The steps in the acceptance of ethnic minorities, like rank orders of discrimination, depend on the notion of a cultural standard and a shared norm.[55] For young children working out their perceptions of meaning according to experience there is no such one hegemony. They see the world as fluid and complex. They have to make sense of it. The idea of discrimination, of national or ethnic or cultural distinction is therefore not natural. It is the deliberate outcome of self-assertion, either self-protective or self-projecting.

Racial prejudice is also a complex construct. Given the mind sets of young children it is no surprise that it is an artificial matter. That might be a challenging statement. Nothing is more apparent, or as skin deep, as colour. But does it matter, compared to cultural understanding? The research reported here concludes that culture rather than looks matter. But we live in an age when we cannot easily accept this fact for reasons that could load another book. There is a received wisdom that young children are racially aware and prejudiced by the age of four.[56] At the same time the research shows that they are also indifferent to it, whilst recognizing where power lies. The crucial difference is the influence of teachers: how they influence the minds of the very young. Of course, teachers do not try to influence. That is ostensibly not their job. It is not part of the National Curriculum.

When fostered, racism is a very powerful form of self-identity and prejudice. In all the choices for distinction and teasing in school, looks are as easy an object of derision as cleverness or behaviour. The colour of skin can be a tool for hurting but it is usually only manifest in gang form. Racism is not a *natural* phenomenon in that whilst young children soon learn about demarcations and differences, ethnicity does not have any particular meaning. The cultural factors that bound people together in the same class are far more important. It is when the idea of a group is formed within the society of school that borders on ethnic grounds are formed. It is a desire to seek out a collective victim as well as a sense of threat that informs the development of racism. Racism is a complex phenomenon since it involves both personal and individual relations and attitudes, and more collective generalized ones according to the circumstances. It is not a coherent attitude but discriminates differently according to the particular ethnic group, from Jews to Gypsies – the latter being consistently most resented – and it changes according to opportunity and conditions.[57]

Overt racism is quite different from more subtle assumptions formed by imagination rather than experience. Name calling or racist bullying can be easily measured, but studies of attitudes within the classroom show how children first form their own interactional dialogues before turning this into the cruder attitudes of discriminating against others according to their colour.[58] The complex series of relationships, very personal and intense and at the same time part of the social reformulation that is the changing of friends, are far more important than the labels that are used later and in a more superficial way. That there are differences in culture and sometimes language is obvious, but not significant compared to the more dominant and shared social circumstances of school. This is why differences in aspiration attract so much attention.[59] Sometimes such concern draws interest away from the individual lives of the pupils, even to the extent of questioning whether some minority groups *should* have strong aspirations, but it does demonstrate something about the school. There are many more attitudinal and cultural assumptions in common than the distinctions according to background. This suggests that there is a choice for some pupils to foster or to develop racism. It is something that can be nurtured. Only certain people do so.

The ways in which attitudes to other groups are formed often have more to do with superficial associations or peculiar attributes than more blanket assumptions of difference. The association of some with the ability to speak a different language, or a habit of dress, or a style of talking can be powerful and interesting long before they are threatening. The insecurities of those who will form an identity of a group against others do not have much to do with these cultural artefacts. Insecurities are to do with failures of relationship, not failures of judgement or understanding. The codes of behaviour are far more important than the way they are presented, in dress or language. Later, the associations might be used – associations of the Jews with being rich, or of the French with frogs – but they are not in themselves important.[60] The sequence of the forming of prejudice is first the development of fear or threat, and only afterwards the projection of this into seeing the differentiations as an excuse.[61]

Racism, as expressed in extreme right-wing groups, also says more about those who express it than those to whom they refer. For it is impossible to maintain the cruder distinctions of ethnic groups in terms of black or white, in terms of real cultural labelling. The race card is used, like the term 'black', when it is deemed useful. But there is no cultural hegemony in the terms. What is the similarity of those who are Muslim with those who are Hindu or Sikh? Is there any culture that fits a label? After all, there are many different versions of 'British' culture, from roast beef and Vaughan Williams to fish and chips and discos. [62] Racism in its manifestation is the outcome of a sense of threat to an insecure identity, which is why it is so closely linked to nationalism.[63] The fear of losing the familiar is again a more powerful emotional force than the threat of the new or the strange. What will the presence of others do to one's own *modus vivendi*? It is only a question that is significant if the hold on one's own cultural identity, that connection between relationships and their modes of expression, is weak.

Identity as a form of hatred

The links between all forms of prejudice, against other nations or regions, against other ethnicities or classes, are close. They are all an expression of a particular manifestation of identity against others according to the context. They are all born in some form of insecurity and only really achieve full expression when the individual has developed beyond the early years of schooling. Of course some can have prejudice forced upon them early, like an army uniform, but this is still an expression of adult attitudes. The manifestation of prejudice is normally clear in adolescence, but the conditions for its formation lie earlier. They then find expression according to circumstances, against another group of peoples. Sometimes the overlap between nationalism, xenophobia and racism is so close that some, like the Hungarians, find that nationalism is *almost* as important as hatred of Gypsies.[64]

In certain circumstances as in tribal wars one might have thought that shared hatreds would include all people of all ages. But even in continuing conflicts children still rely on interpersonal models, they seek individual relationships rather than immediately seeking their identity within the aspirations of a group.[65] The development of shared generalized attributions is one that follows from the earliest desires to explore identity within a series of groups. The personal sense of self in terms of a generalized image is a sign of atrophy of the mind, a retreat into self-stereotypes rather than an essential or innate human characteristic. Children observe at once the sense of the inevitability of war and realize that it is actually a choice being made; there is nothing that really explains its recurrence.[66]

The judgements that young people make of the world around them include some simple prejudices which are not necessarily taken altogether seriously or examined by them. At a deeper level their judgements are far more complex, understanding the relativity of their lives and the importance of making sense of their own lives as well as those of others.[67] Children are not driven by simple ambitions or by a sense of crude cultural self-assertions. They therefore can consider carefully the nature of prejudice, both understanding its existence (as early as truth and falsehood) and its limitations. If it is possible to have a more carefully considered view of others, the question is, given the importance of early relationships, whether people overcome prejudice by contact with others, through visits or mass communications, or by a more considered view of themselves. Clearly information in itself does not make a difference, since the mind set, say of the soccer fan, will not even delve into the actual point of view of the other. The 'other' is merely an enemy, an object of hate or derision. Contact in itself makes little difference.[68] But those who are not already prejudiced, who have not set out to be in circumstances where prejudice can have its stage, are clearly influenced by the reality of other people and their relationships with them. They can be taught to see the dangers of generalization.[69]

In the studies of different conflicts and their impact on children a great deal is made of stress.[70] How this is dealt with by different children varies enormously. There is no automatic representation of others as enemies. The stability or instability of the individual is paramount. Some see political violence as personally directed aggression. Others understand it in its context, a representation of circumstance rather than inappropriate personal hate. Of course for those adults giving expression to *their* feelings, the personal anger is an important part of their emotional uniform, and a feeling deliberately fostered in armies.

Children are confronted by masses of information both public and private, and have to make sense, through their observation, of what meanings they carry. They see the state in its intervention, for good or bad, as in wars, and they see the people who enact and embody this impersonal force. They see abstract market forces at work on people, and they see the personalization and personal attributes within the anonymity of the mass media. Someone particular, even if a disembodied voice, is telling you what to think, is asking for trust in the delivery of facts. In all events the public and the individual are bound up. This has an impact on the privacy of isolated individuals; they cannot take all the information in. Do they make it their own interpretation and select what they need, or do they follow a given line? They live in what Habermas calls 'floodlit privacy'.[71]

The perception of the self is a matter of definition against others. The desire and the need to be independent, to be *unlike* others is closely embroiled in the counter-need to belong, to be *like* others. The question is always the extent to which personal identity is dependent on others. This is a cultural matter, as well as an emotional one. The self in its experiences is a matter of the environment in which it is placed. At the same time the way that the environment is viewed rests on emotional attitudes. In the work of the 1940s and 1950s, now seemingly forgotten, a great deal of attention was paid to the way that the perceptions of children were altered according to factors such as hunger, or a hint of attribution given before seeing someone.[72] Even an individual's private and personal perception and therefore the expressed attitudes depend on the cultural icons that are presented to them, the shared or expected norms.[73] The desire to sympathize is one aspect of this; the need to conform the other.

Personhood can be argued to be essentially a cultural phenomenon.[74] The sense of self, of entity, of each being as unique is not something held in a kind of separating aspic. It cannot be separated from the locality of other people and their perceptions, any more than we can think of individual beings as merely products of some mass consciousness or psychological norm. The self looks out at others, and has its own temperamental characteristics. It is also a totality of the impression made upon others as well as a way of relating to them. Most of this is so instinctive that we forget how deeply imbued we are with the standard rules or expectations of our society. Searle, drawing on Wittgenstein, notes that following a rule is not the same as acting in accordance with a rule.[75] Conforming to rules is not the same as knowing them, and the distinction is emulated in that between prejudice and tolerance. The more we are aware of how culturally located we are, the more we are able to accept the self and shared definitions of others. The irony is that such cultural relativism, strong in the young, depends on a sense of self-worth. And the tragedy is that this is knocked out of some people, especially around the age of eight where personal effort is no longer automatically linked to personal success.[76]

The overlap between the sense of personal worth and its recognition by others is so close that in some societies the distinction is very difficult to make.[77] The sense of the global village is based on the attributes of the enclosed and communicating tribe. Communication in the past was with those with whom one was in talking distance; the outside world was a matter of indifference, rather than enmity. The essential system of communication depended upon a shared and collective memory, with stories following a similar, familiar pattern. Personal identity was of one within the group.[78] But now the whole world is communicated in a particular way through a point of view. Real access to it, rather than oblique reference, is difficult.

Shared consciousness gives strong personal as well as cultural identity. When it is disturbed, the sense of the skill needed to create a larger, more general belonging is the more strong. Fragile personalities who have missed the relationships that give shared values are the more likely to cling to the uncomplicated ones which are negative and which depend upon polarization. In prejudice we see the desire for self-assertion against all restraint. We see general relationships interpreted as personal. We see people judged not by who they are but what they do and where. And all relationships become specific and simple, especially collective ones.

In this context it should be recalled that whilst *all* people share cultural values of their own, and have a sense of both distinction and difference from others, it is in only a small proportion that ethnocentricity turns to violence. It is also significant that such assertive action – 'getting retaliation in first' – is a male phenomenon.[79] Some would argue that girls are less likely to discriminate against others having some experience of it themselves. Hostility, whether born from insecurity or self-doubt, is the pathological form of self-assertion. It does not *look* like a sign of weakness. But that inner sense of insecurity developed before there is a recognition that personal worth is not correlated to personal success is what drives people into the assertion of difference. The 'habitus' is in fact not just shared taste but a definition of the self as a result of others.[80]

It is perhaps odd to conclude that the development of prejudice and nationalism, in its virulent forms, begins by the age of eight or so. Of course that is not the last turning point. Those curious simplicities of understanding, the habit of collecting the simple sense of virulent right or wrong without perspective, are manifested later.[81] But an understanding of the whole world, a sense of the self in relation to groups of others are all formed early. These 'closed loops of thought' are early ones, and shared by all but only become pathological in some.[82] What children do notice and what concerns them the most in the end are those smallest of groups and the relationships within them.[83] What happens afterwards to their developing world-views depends upon what they make of these.

References

1. Dunn, J (1987) *The Beginnings of Social Understanding*, Basil Blackwell, Oxford
2. Cullingford,C (1999) *The Causes of Exclusion: Home, school and the development of young criminals*, Kogan Page, London
3. Smith, A (1996) The resurgence of nationalism? Myth and memory in the renewal of nations, *British Journal of Sociology*, **47** (4), pp 575–98
4. Lewis, R (1998) *Cross Cultural Letters*, Hants Institute of Cross Cultural Communication
5. Hofstede, G (1991) *Culture and Organisations: Software of the mind*, McGraw-Hill, London
Hofstede, G (1980) *Culture's Consequences*, Sage, London
6. Bourdieu, P (1997) Cultural reproduction and social reproduction, in *Power and Ideology in Education*, eds J Karabel and Halsey, Oxford University Press, New York
7. Furnham, A (1993) Communicating in foreign lands: the cause, consequences and cures of culture shock, *Language, Culture and Curriculum*, **6** (1), pp 91–109
8. Furnham, A and Bochner, S (1986) *Culture Shock: Psychological reactions to unfamiliar environments*, Methuen, London
9. Osler, A (1998) European citizenship and study abroad: student teachers' experience and identities, *Cambridge Journal of Education*, **28** (1), pp 77–96
It should be added that any new grouping that makes an intellectual demand, even of experienced professionals or an 'in-service' development course, can be emotionally difficult. Salzberger-Wittenberg, I, Gianna, H and Osborne, E (1993) *The Emotional Experience of Learning and Teaching*, Routledge and Kegan Paul, London
10. Furnham, A and Bochner, S, op cit
11. Thurber, C (1995) The experience and expression of homesickness in pre-adolescent and adolescent boys, *Child Development*, **66** (4), pp 1162–78

12. Boekestijn (1984) Intercultural migration and the development of personal identity: the dilemma between identity maintenance and cultural adaptation. *Seventh Annual International Congress of Cross-Cultural Psychology*, Acapulco, Mexico
13. Bourdieu, P (1984) *Distinction: A social critique of the judgement of taste*, Routledge, London
14. Hofstede, G, op cit, 1980
15. 'Gemeinschaft' and 'Gesellschaft'.
16. See earlier chapters.
17. Festinger, L (1957) *A Theory of Cognitive Dissonance*, Stanford University Press, Evanston
18. Fishbeirn, M and Ajzen, I (1975) *Belief, Attitude, Intention and Behavior*, Addison-Wesley, Reading, MA.
19. Tajfel, H ed (1978) *Differentiation Between Social Groups*, Academic Press, London
20. Bahktin, M (1986) *Speech Genres and Other Late Essays*, University of Texas Press, Austin
21. Cullingford, C (1996) *Children's Literature and Its Effects*, Cassell, London
22. Hoffman, M and Bizman, A (1996) Attributions and responses to the Arab–Israeli conflict: a developmental analysis, *Child Development*, **67** (1), pp 117–28
23. Tajfel, H (1981) *Human Groups and Social Categories*, Cambridge University Press, Cambridge
24. Linssen, H and Hagendoorn, L (1994) Social and geographical factors in the explanation of European nationality stereotypes, *British Journal of Social Psychology*, **33** (2), pp 165–82
25. Dekker, H. and Jansen, B (1996) Attitudes, Images and Stereotypes of Young People in The Netherlands with respect to Germany and Other European Union Countries, Leiden University
26. Du Bois-Reymond, M (1998) European identity in the young and Dutch students' images of Germany and the Germans, *Comparative Education*, **34** (1), pp 27–40
27. Coman, P (1996) Reading about the enemy: school textbook representation of Germany's role in the war with Britain during the period from April 1940 to May 1941, *British Journal of Sociology of Education*, **17** (3), pp 327–40
28. Berghahn, V and Schissler, H. eds (1987) *Perceptions of History. An analysis of school textbooks*, Berg, Oxford
29. Smith, A, op cit
30. Lister, I and Paida, S (1997 and 1998) Young children's images of the enemy: an exploration into mental mapping, *New Era in Education*, **78** (3), pp 81–84, **79** (1), pp 13–17
31. Green, J. A (1874) *A Short History of the English Peoples*, Macmillan, London
Renan, E (1882) *Qu'est-ce que'une Nation?*, Calmann-Levy, Paris
32. Scharma, S (1989) Citizens: A chronicle of the French Revolution, p 6, Viking, London
33. Appardorai, A (1968) *The Substance of Politics*, Oxford University Press, Oxford
34. Stone, O (1980) *Hitler*, Hodder and Stoughton, London
35. Seton-Watson, H (1977) *Nations and States: An enquiry into the origins of nations and the politics of nationalism*, Westview Press, Boulder
36. Anderson, B (1991) *Imagined Communities: Reflections on the origin and spread of nationalism*, Verso, London
37. Billig, M (1995) *Banal Nationalism*, Sage, London
38. Smith, A, op cit
39. Toivonen, K and Cullingford, C (1998) Racial prejudice in a liberal democracy: a case study, *Politics, Groups and the Individual*, **7** (1 & 2), pp 45–56
40. Smith, A (1979) *Nationalism in the Twentieth Century*, Martin Robertson, London
cf. Harré, R (1998) *The Singular Sell*, Sage, London

41. Piaget, J and Weil, R (1951) The development in children of the idea of the homeland and of relations with other countries, *International Social Science Bulletin*, (3), pp 561–78
42. Tajfel, H et al (1970) The development of children's preferences for their own country. A cross-national study, *International Journal of Psychology*, (5), pp 245–53
43. Cullingford, C (1999) *The Human Experience: The early years*, Ashgate, Aldershot
44. Lister, J and Paida, S, op cit
45. Bourdieu, P, op cit
46. Rattawi, A (1995) Just framing ethnicities and racisms in a 'post-modern' framework, in *Social Post-Modernism: Beyond identity politics* eds L Nicholson and S Seidman, pp 250–86, Cambridge University Press, Cambridge
47. Carrington, B and Short, G (1995) What makes a person British? Children's conceptions of the national culture and identity, *Educational Studies*, **21** (2), pp 217–38
48. Phoenix, A (1995) Difference and differentiation: young Londoners' accounts of 'race' and nation, in *Growing Up in Europe: Contemporary horizons in childhood and youth studies* eds L Chisholm et al, pp 173–88, Walter de Bruyter, Berlin
49. Tizard, B and Phoenix. A (1993) *Black, White or Mixed Race? Race and racism in the lives of young children of mixed parentage*, Routledge, London
50. Barker, C (1997) Television and the reflexive project of the self: soaps, teenage talk and hybrid identities, *British Journal of Sociology*, **48** (6), pp 611–28
51. Davey, A and Mullin, P (1980) Ethnic identification and preference of British primary school children, *Journal of Child Psychology and Psychiatry*, **21** (3), pp 241–51
52. Bennett, M, Dewberry, C and Yeeles, C A (1991) Reassessment of the role of ethnicity in children's social perception, *Journal of Child Psychology and Psychiatry*, **32** (6), pp 969–82
53. Blumer, H (1965) The future of the color line, in *The South in Continuity and Change*, eds J McKinney and E Thompson, pp 35–59, Seeman, Durham
54. Kleinpenning, G and Hagendoorn, L (1993) Forms of racism and the cumulative dimensions of ethnic attitudes, *Social Psychology Quarterly*, **56** (1), pp 21–36
55. Myrdal, G (1968) *Value in Social Theory*, Routledge and Kegan Paul, London
56. Jeffcoate, R (1977) Children's racial ideas and feelings, *English in Education*, **11** (1), pp 32–46
57. Toivonen, K and Cullingford, C, op cit
58. Troyna, B and Hatcher, R (1992) *Racism in Children's Lives*, Routledge, London
59. Tomlinson, S (1984) *Home and School in Multi-Cultural Britain*, Batsford, London
Tomlinson, S (1987) *Ethnic Minorities in British Schools*, Gower, Aldershot
60. Carrington, B and Short, G, op cit
61. Horowitz, L (1941) Some aspects of the development of patriotism in children. *Sociometry*, (3), pp 329–41
62. Milner, D (1975) *Children and Race*, Penguin, Harmondsworth
Milner, D (1983) *Children and Race. Ten years on*, Ward Lock, London.
63. Troyna, B and Hatcher, R, op cit
64. Tóth, Q (1995) Political-moral attitudes amongst young people in post-communist Hungary, in Chisholm, L. et al, op cit, pp 189–94
65. Hoffman, M and Bizman, A (1996) Attributions and responses to the Arab–Israeli conflict: a developmental analysis, *Child Development*, **67** (1), pp 117–28
66. Selman, R (1980) *The Growth of Interpersonal Understanding: A developmental and clinical analysis*, Academic Press, New York

67. Du Bois-Reymond, M (1998) 'I don't want to commit myself yet': young people's life concepts, *Journal of Youth Studies*, **1** (1), pp 63–79

68. Troyna, B and Hatcher, R, op cit

69. Short, G (1993) Prejudice reduction in schools: the value of inter-racial contact, *British Journal of Sociology of Education*, **14** (2), pp 159–68

70. Cairns, E and Dawes, A (1996) Children and ethnic and political violence – a commentary, *Child Development*, **67** (2), pp 129–39

71. Habermas, J (1989) *The Structural Transformation of the Public Sphere: An enquiry into a category of bourgeois culture*, Polity Press, Cambridge

72. eg Bruner, J and Goodman, C (1947) Value and need as organising factors in perception, *Journal of Abnormal and Social Psychology*, (42), pp 33–42

73. Katz, E and Lazersfeld, P (1955) *Personal Influence*, Glencoe Free Press

74. Harré, R. op cit

75. Searle, J (1995) *The Construction of Social Reality*, Allen Lane, London

76. Stipek, D (1981) Children's perceptions of their own and their classmates' ability, *Journal of Educational Psychology*, **73** (3), pp 404–10

77. Liberman, K (1989) 'Decentering the self': two perspectives from philosophical anthropology, in *The Question of the Other*, eds A Dallery and C Scott, SUNY Press, New York

78. Ong, W (1982) *Orality and Literacy. The technologizing of the word*, Methuen, London

79. Vollebergh, W (1995) Inter-ethnic violence: a male youth problem? In Chisholm, L. *et al*, op cit, pp 243–56

80 Bourdieu, P, op cit

81. Plato. See Egan, K (1983) *Education and Psychology: Plato, Piaget and scientific psychology*, Teachers College Press, New York

82. Rapport, N (1993) *Diverse World Views in an English Village*, Edinburgh University Press, Edinburgh

83. Erricker, C *et al* (1997) *The Education of the Whole Child*, Cassell, London

Towards conclusions

There are two incontrovertible facts about the human condition. One is the immutable individuality of each person, unique in looks, voice and mind. The other is the fact that each individual sensibility is moulded by culture, manifested in language, social attitudes and beliefs. These facts might be incontrovertible but they are also in tension. Prejudice emerges from the way in which the ambiguities of existence, both individually self-centred and culturally moulded, are dealt with. There are two pathological extremes, attempts to withdraw from the cultural environment as much as possible, and basing as much of one's existence as possible on being subsumed within it.

If there are extremes of engagement and disengagement there are also extremes of interpretation. Environmental determinism, from the psychoanalysis of Freud to the domination of language over thought, is recently less favoured than genetic determinism. In either case the explanations suggest the helplessness of the individual. This book deals with those things for which the individual is responsible. It is not about the cultural milieu or about personality. It is about behaviour. Whatever genetic or environmental influence moulds the temperament, propensity to illness, taste and means of communication, the individual is still responsible for the manifestation of understanding and behaviour. This is why education is so important. There are still good and bad actions, however expressed in tone and language.

All empirical research needs to be based on accepting the importance of every piece of individual evidence and drawing from it those things that can be communicated, even if it cannot consistently reach this standard. There can be no communication without some degree of generalization. There would be nothing worth communicating. Respect for the inner voice of the individual is also a recognition of that individual's connection to others, to shared cultural understandings. This ethical question of research – how do you really listen to the evidence rather than try to find a hypothesis, like a policy, to be proved – is also at the heart of analysing prejudice, of understanding collective motivation and attitudes. Prejudice is individual, but can become a shared bias, or at its most extreme pathological form, a whole movement of shared cruelty.

There is a need to understand what we have in common, but generalization, the stuff of nationalism, can be dangerous. There are too many examples of collective antipathies demonstrated in dire action, from racism to snobbery, from ethnic cleansing to exclusion. These are the result not only of shared strong beliefs but also of the loss of a sense of individual identity. We know the complexities of our own character, but assume other people are simpler to understand. When we know our own complexities and can accept them with confidence, it is easier to accept others and theirs, including those marks of identity that are their cultural banners.

It is too easy to assume that prejudice, in its most primitive and extreme forms, is part of the human condition. We witness the phenomenon often enough. Politics is the science of trying to deal with it, either manipulating or using it, or fighting against it. But if we confronted ourselves with the notion that we would act in the same way as those who have carried out the most violent of acts, if we were able to admit to ourselves the vicious comfort of thinking of others as less complete or less civilized than ourselves, we would surely be as easily offended as comforted. The very same people who were party to a policy of extermination were shocked at the very idea of what they were doing. Those behaviours taken for granted at the time become terrible on examination. This contradiction lies at the heart of prejudice. Whilst one point of view can replace another, it is more common to see them held, even in contradiction, at the very same time. This ability to be ruled by instinct as well as reason, and to hold opinions based on rationally defined absurdities, needs to be understood. Education is not so much about knowledge as social insight.

The distinction between those who indulge themselves or defend themselves in prejudiced actions against others, and those who refuse to cross that line of wrong behaviour, is a subtle one. The moral pressure on the individual to conform is strong. People are not supposed to 'foul their own nest' or be 'unpatriotic'. The marks of distinction are proudly presented, like an awareness and knowledge of a type of music, or the command of an arcane academic subject. Taste is identity. At which point is that essential perception of personal difference and taste turned into prejudice directed against others? When is a display of cultural distinction shadowed by the atavistic demeanour of exclusion?

It might seem that the most public manifestations of collective prejudice – mass rallies to share patriotic values, or to hate the enemy – are a long way from the intimate relations of the home. The circumstances are completely different. And yet the two are connected. The first means of making sense of the world is through categories, including those of people who are preferred and those who are not. Discriminating between what different people say, their tone of voice and their motivations is as essential as understanding the physical actuality of the world. Categories are not just words, generalizations of shared understanding, of communicable phenomena, but individuals and groups of people. There are those for us and those against us, those who agree with us and those who do not.

We are concerned here with the experience of prejudice, and not just its manifestation. We have explored the phenomenon, as a matter of feeling as well as action. We have sought the reasons for the way in which people develop, in their own and in their collective ways, ways of seeing others that create false as well as real demarcation lines. To understand the ways in which prejudice develops in all its forms we need to be sensitive to the inadvertent effects of other people and experiences. The individual's personal coming to terms with the world is often ignored. It remains hidden and deliberately obscure within the weighty information that is the formal curriculum, the generalized knowledge that is deemed both uncontroversial and, to many pupils, ultimately meaningless. What takes place on the surface, like an isolated stimulus, can have all kinds of unforeseen and different effects. Giving the individual a voice, listening to it, and hearing it, is the only way to understand, in all the complexity of experience, which are the influential moments that leave their mark.

Intentionality, the awareness of what one is doing, in terms of having responsibility for having an effect on others, is important. A deliberate act of cruelty is that much worse than an anonymous, accidental misdemeanour. The intention to hurt is so much worse than the accident from the point of view of the perpetrator. From the experience of the victim, however, many significant actions that influence and harm are inadvertent. It is the effect that matters, not the intention. In order to develop a form of education that deals with social issues like bias, taste and prejudice, we need to be able to listen to the individuals, to include their own perspectives on what they experience.

The home is usually depicted as a safe haven, a model of security. The family, like motherhood, is associated with stability and all that is socially most acceptable. This ideal remains important, for the home has such an influence for good or bad that it creates the emotional conditions, the strengths and vulnerabilities, that mark the rest of people's lives. Unfortunately even the best regulated of households provide circumstances of inadvertent damage, the overheard quarrel or the careless remark.

Children are from the earliest times essentially social beings. Their powers of observation, combined with their personal emotional needs, mean that they are seeking to make discriminations both between those who are close to them, who care for them, and those who do not, and between the different manifestations of the same phenomena, in the same person. 'How will he or she react to me? Can I influence them?' are two of the earliest questions children ask themselves, years before they can articulate them.

The awareness of how other people might react to them and the adapting to different moods and tones of response is an essential part of the two-way process of relationships, of wanting positive responses or wishing to please. The interactions of children with their parents and other adults are complex and unique. On these relationships depend developing attitudes, not only to other people, but also to the ways in which other people can be related to. Insights, as well as discrimination, and an understanding of motivation, as well as emotional bonding, are at the heart of the interaction of the child with others. Critical thinking is an essential ability that needs development, not just in terms of abstract thought but in the application of conscious scrutiny of social phenomena.

Relationships, even at the earliest stage, can be benign or malign. There can be as many threats to emotional stability as there are securities. The emotions involved in relationships can be extreme, but that should not obscure the fact that intelligence is also at work. An emotional world-view is being developed long before it is expressed in language. The sense of personal identity defined against the threat of others has its basis in these early years.

Those homes that seem to work well, putting aside the inadvertent events that cannot be helped, are those that are both disciplined and loving. In these homes discipline is authoritative and consistent, but not angry or spiteful. Love is not a desire for emotional response or sentimentality but a disinterested concern for the well-being of others. There are two opposite ways in which stable relationships can go wrong. In one type of home, the laissez-faire, there are no real close personal relationships. Whatever the children do is of no particular concern to the parents.[1] In the other type of home the parents are over-strict, wanting their own way without negotiation, by creating their sense of blanket authoritarianism that allows little sense of identity in the young. We see in these homes the essential ontological insecurities of either being left too much alone or being subsumed in other people's wills. The laissez-faire home is one in which the individual child has to see his or her own connections with other people, and where society as a whole appears in its more formal aspects not only an alienating absence, but peopled by those who not only play their roles within it, but are seen as some form of enemy, of having a bias against the individual, of not treating the individual with respect. The lack of critical relationships with their dialogues of mutual repositioning and negotiation means that emotion, suppressed anger, and the longing for recognition dominate everyday transactions. This leads to an oversensitive awareness of the way in which society operates, a society from which the individual feels estranged. Over-awareness of social norms also results from the extreme of too much parental dominance, on the insistence that certain things are carried out in certain ways because that is what others expect, for their sake rather than that of the child. Again, this has an alienating effect on views of society when it is inevitably discovered that it is possible to say no, to rebel against those things that have never quite been taken for granted.

Prejudice in the permanent form of the threat of others can emerge from either of these pathological extremes. When there is a sense of carelessness, when there are no firm boundaries or rules, children seek relationships elsewhere. They turn to a peer group as a type of collective authority. They learn to conform with an alternative shared will. In the absence of discriminating dialogues they look for the most obvious forms of control and discipline, and these lie in the actions of others. They will easily become prone to being manipulated by others in order to fit in. Ironically this conformity is a result of a lack of discipline, a lack of will. The behavioural and anonymous authority of the school is nothing like as powerful as the tempting certainties of the group. The desire for social meaning, that connection between emotional attachment to others and a shared intellectual understanding and point of view, can only be found in peers, if it cannot be developed in the home.

Indifferent parents, caught up in their own emotional problems, create children vulnerable to, and seeking, control. This control is of a collective kind that social institutions attempt to provide. If there is a failure to include all who are part of it, the control will instead be provided by the group, at first by a small one, and later, as a larger and essentially impersonal group, like a political party. There is nothing as emotionally comforting for some as a nationalistic anthem. Being made to feel that there is a sense of belonging, an emotional warmth that is part of a collective endeavour, replaces the insecurities, the ambivalences and the uncertainties of home and school.

Over-authoritarian parents might mean very well but have similar effects to those who are careless. Often because of their own self-absorption, they effect the same ends: a lack of recognition of a separate and demanding person who impinges on their own lives. There is a wish for control, to make their children conform and obey. No individual can conform entirely without question. If power lies in authority and obedience then personal identity lies in rebellion. The more powerfully complete the social structure of authority appears, the more extreme is either the adherence to it or rejection of it. When parents or social institutions frame themselves as over-zealous authorities, they also create the notion that there must be a personal identity to be sought elsewhere. The questioning of authority is often the questioning of authoritarianism. Children seek discipline: rules, order and understanding. They also seek an emotional and personal basis for it, the kind that is supposed to be provided by parents.

Those homes that for one reason or another do no more than let their children find their own solutions to social questions, like relationships and understanding the ways in which groups of people work and understand each other, provide the basis for a belief in a collective social discipline. The longing for stability results in a willingness to follow the norms of peers. Those who seek to impose a social discipline without understanding force children to seek an emotional alternative.

Children see distinctions, and perceive differences in others, of points of view or attitude. This is at the heart of all relationships. If the understanding of the inevitability of differences is denied then some other solution will be sought. Adults provide not just food and warmth but fulfil intellectual needs. These are just as important. Children seek the chance to *share* the world, to talk about it, to be helped to make sense of it. They want to discuss, which they do with each other, and want to internalize all the most essential and obvious questions about the meaning of life, like those underlying this book: why are we as we are?

In many an education system (using the broadest interpretation to include the early years through to lifelong learning) this most essential, even primitive, of human intellectual questions is denied or ignored. In the home one can see why. Questions take up time. They are a challenge to all that is taken for granted. In the educational system it is more difficult to see why the essential questions are ignored, but one has to conclude that they are thought not to matter, or they are already understood or they are already covered in the curriculum.

Those who are concerned with the curriculum are in the habit of adding pieces to it that are supposed to address issues of civics and citizenship, or personal and political socialization. The problem is that the addition of more knowledge, whatever the subject, does not address the issue of the purpose of school. Young children, in their observation of social relationships, and in their ability to discern points of view, develop a world-view. They ask fundamental questions. These are rarely addressed seriously. One of the first experiences of the breakdown of relationships is the brushing aside of children's interests, on the grounds that they are supposedly not yet ready to understand them, or finding it easier to derive pleasure from making fun of their earnest entreaties. 'Seen and not heard' remains the standard for undeveloped relationships.

The inability to cope with normal relationships leads to intolerance. This can be the result of the mixing up of roles and personalities. The vast majority of people seen, let alone interacted with, remain anonymous. They remain strange as well as strangers. They are assumed to have their own collective norms, understood as being either like one's own or as being distant and alien. What is sought is the possibility of relationships. If the person then does strike up a dialogue are they doing so as an individual or as part of a job or routine? Is it their duty, like a teacher, to ask limited questions? The muddle of personality and role is something most people take for granted, whilst making their own discriminatory judgements. For some, each interaction has the potential for tension, so that the action taken by the other, whether the person at the checkout or the police officer, is attributable to some characteristic from their ethnic origin or class.

The lack of knowledge about how to deal with normal relationships is a result of not knowing how to balance emotion and intellect. There is a tendency to believe that emotional warmth and security is all, or even that intelligence is cold and threatening. Emotion alone, out of control, is changeable and unreliable. Intelligence can be full of curiosity, of interest and concern. Children need both.

Relationships in the home are an essential influence on subsequent negotiations with the social world. The ability to argue a point of view, to detect what others are saying and to understand the nature of real conversation all stem from the earliest of dialogues. There are some children who find that the kind of language used at home is completely different from that used in school.[2] They are not deprived of language in terms of emotional warmth or in the amount they use. They are deprived of the language of analysis and discussion. Much has been made of the different levels of language, private and public, of the differences between dialects, the marks of a distinctly local group, and the formalities of public utterances. Academic language is contrasted to the everyday vernacular. These distinctions have often been ascribed to class, as if learning were some kind of veneer or social rash.[3] They are far more important than that, because everyone needs to be able to cross the boundaries of these distinctions, to understand the different uses of language, in themselves and in others.

Language, as children have noted, can be a barrier to as well as a means of communication. Social relationships all depend on the understanding of language, not just for a shared point of view but for an ability to accept differences. Those children who are unaccustomed to the sharing of definitions will always find school difficult. This is not a matter simply of socio-economic circumstances. The lack of a full and developed argumentative and negotiating capacity is a form of intellectual deprivation.

It is also a root cause of prejudice. The inability to engage with other people's points of view leads to the oversimplification of differences. Young children have an innate grasp of points of view, of truth and falsehood. This sophistication can be overridden by the difficulties involved in depersonalizing the standpoint of others. If there is nothing more to language than interpersonal relationships, then it is difficult at once both to understand and to accept the distinction of others. Either they are ignored, or they are strongly embraced or confronted.

Prejudice comes about because it is the extreme, the pathological form of the inability to use language as critical dialogue. Others are either strongly 'for' the individual or against; they either show them 'respect' or do not. Most people are not permanently and consistently prejudiced. They are prejudiced at times and in certain conditions. Prejudice is one of the chosen identities. It is not against everything all the time. It is intermittent. The inner dislocation of discontent finds a cause against which, or whom, it can be explained. Intermittent prejudice, like the vagaries of taste, is quite different from institutionalized prejudice. Individual teachers might be liked or disliked; it is when they symbolize a system that the difficulties really begin.

Those who are unable to strike the balance of accepting both appreciation and disagreement find themselves therefore under greater psychological pressure. The explanation of stress and how to cope with it centres on the lack of psychological space. The social world and the demands it seems to make become far too pressing. Terms used like 'pressure' suggest that sense of oppression, of demands from which it is easier to run away. Attention on stress tends to concentrate on its extreme forms, but it is a condition encountered at certain times by everyone. Some people are not able to deal with it as well as others: they feel beleaguered, that they are being unfairly singled out. They feel picked on, indeed they feel prejudiced against.

The need for psychological space, for the freedom of intellectual understanding, is paramount. If it does not exist fully, then the essential unfairness of the social world becomes a dangerous juxtaposition to someone's own circumstances. Whilst poverty itself is not an explanation for antisocial behaviour, it is associated with the lack of this psychological space. The sense of personal unfairness becomes a structural one. All children understand and witness the imbalance of circumstances, the contrast in standards of living, just as they perceive the differences in points of view. They accept the facts of relativity. When they are confronted with the relationship of their own circumstances to those of others they can be forced to protest, to react against the pressure of oppression. This is when they seek not just definitions of their own differences but links with others in similar circumstances.

Groups are an important part in the development of chosen identities. They provide a sense of belonging as well as a sense of rejection. They provide definitions of the self against others. Young children's moral understanding contains the same sophistication as that of adults, including a sense of their own limitations and faults.[4] Ambiguities are accepted. Only later is the sense of outright demarcation lines of acceptance or rejection simplified, by some, into attributions of right and wrong.

The home, and what takes place in it, with its psychological spaces and symbolic boundaries, is the seed-bed on which the tendency to prejudice can be grown. It is the school that sees this tendency grow and flourish. Schools are unusual institutions in many ways and probably more influential in what they present of social order than in developing the minds of pupils. Schools are perceived as the centre of social groups and relationships. They rely or groups, both formal and informal. The very concept of a group is presented every day, within the class and outside it. There are formal rules and defined places. It is here that the psychological institutions are first created.

Underneath the formal groups in the organization of the school are more intense informal networks which are more fluid and more searching. For some children, attachments are like a security blanket, something to turn to for comfort, just as a flag or a badge can become. The perception of schools rests on the juxtaposition of the hierarchies of position and the detection of where real power lies: they do not always agree. The symbolic boundaries of the group depend on choice, both of what to be attached to and what to avoid.[5] The stranger the collective identity, the less the sense of personal security and self-belief. The comfort of the gang is like the comfort of being noticed, just as drawing attention (and approval) to oneself is carrying out some act of defiance. Without the tacit admiration of others such disobedience would be meaningless.

The problem with schools in the way in which they are made to operate is that they easily become associated with all the insult and the anguish of failure. The batteries of tests and the hierarchies of achievement are inevitably going to cause comparisons in which some people do badly. The very structure of the curriculum, and the demands of finding out what the teachers want so that the pupil can please him or her, undermine the sense of personal well-being and autonomy. The significant majority of pupils somehow survive this. They are equipped with adaptability. They know how to adjust to or manipulate the emotional and intellectual system.

Schools are places that are inadvertently successful at creating a sense of enmity. This can be against individuals or against groups, against particular demands or styles of organization. The school can even become the symbolic representation of the state, the organized social world. Underneath that sense of an overarching hierarchy come the groups, generalized into those that are 'for' and those that are 'against'. Just as teasing and bullying find trivial starting points in the way someone looks or dresses, so generalized enmities can arise from simple demarcations.

Groups are identified against each other and against authority, which is also seen as a collective, a system of combined interests. A view of the world simplified into symbolic boundaries is enhanced by the experience of school, with its rituals of herding and different hierarchies of power. The psychological impact of being told what to do and where to go can prove too much for some. They take it personally and need some group in which to foster the recognition of their own identity. In school the prevailing ethos is the avoidance of choice. The pupils are expected to accept the will of those in authority, whether it is in terms of behaviours or in terms of the formal curriculum. This can foster prejudice, because in the place of a critical engagement with what is presented and collectively agreed comes the sense of submission, of outer obedience.

It is within schools that collective attributions are developed. There are many issues of distinction, of knowledge and ability, of different motivations and alternative behaviours. Schools depend on the acceptance of authority, not just in terms of physical obedience, but in defining the territory of the curriculum, those parts that are most important rather than those which connect with the sense of purpose in the pupils.[6] In the absence of critical thinking, or of the fostering of discussion about controversial issues, pupils learn about those matters that most interest them, like their own personal relations with society, from each other. It is as if there were two worlds of schooling, that laid down formally by statutory orders, even to the point of telling teachers how to teach as well as what to teach, and the other more intense social world of the real lives of pupils.

Schools, in their juxtaposition between the public and the private, the overall organizing of large groups and the intense and volatile testing of relationships, are essentially the places where attitudes to the social world and towards others, individually and collectively, are formed. They underline distinctions, putting people into sets, or classes, or groups or houses. Competition abounds. The formal and the psychological institutions go side by side. The experiences of strong belonging or strong rejection are both provided. Schools offer the extremes: of loneliness and of belonging; of withdrawal from collective endeavour and of complete reliance on it.

Individual pupils bring into school their incipient ability to cope, although this is not always manifested until later. Some cannot accept the mixture of attachment and anonymity. They withdraw from the demands. Or they seek out alternatives. Again there are the pathological extremes, of those who do not wish to make any connection with others. What do we make of the following negativity, constant and repeated in a girl of eight?

Q: Do you like living here?
A: No... I don't like the houses and I don't like the cars. I don't like living here. Because the houses are uncomfy. And the roads... 'cos there's this naughty boy. He doesn't go to school... He throws stones. And he's rudeness.
    When I have assemblies I like running away... They're boring.
Q: Do you like anything about yourself?
A: No.
Q: Nothing at all?
A: No... I just don't like the other children... They pick on me... They're rude. They say naughty things.
Q: If I could wave my magic wand and change something about you, what would you like to change?
A: A horse.
Q: You'd like to be a horse?
A: Yeah... 'cos they're nice creatures. They're nice animals.
Q: Do you like being you?
A: No.
Q: What don't you like?
A: I never do nothing when I go home... I just watch telly... I don't like watching telly... we've nothing to do in our house... I always get told off...

And so it continues. Is it a mood? A deliberate attempt to alienate? A desire to shock? Or is it a single case of essential disengagement, of the negativity of not wanting to make normal relationships, or being accustomed to doing without. In her mind there is, in fact, a better environment than the one she lives in: 'America... because it's a richer country'.

At the other extreme from this disengagement and dislike of the immediate environment is an example of someone far too interested in and wrapped up in the actualities and the possibilities of the everyday. Instead of linking riches and a better life with a distant dream, better things are within reach and can be acquired.

Q: Do you like being you?

A: Yeah, but I wish I was rich and stuff. Really, a rich kid or something. I could get the things I want really... I'd like to be rich, because, like I said I'd like to have like computer games and really good bags and stuff and good shoes and clothes and things, really... there's some things like in supermarkets that you really like and you really wanna get, but you can't afford it...

Q: Why do you think that your dad and your mum are poor?

A: I don't know really. Because sort of they say 'I can't afford it', and things. And sometimes I think they are lying or something... I used to steal as well, so he used to say, 'Come on, let's have my money back'. And sometimes he used to take, I had loads of pens and stuff and he used to say 'Where's all my money?' I said 'I can't give you the money back', so he took all my money and I say 'Hey, I only took a few of your money'...

Some things make me sad like people being horrible and saying 'No, you can't have this'. And I say, 'Well, they mustn't like me or somethink'. Like, you say like 'No you can't have that' and then I just feel a bit upset... And shout and things. I get a bit upset 'cos I don't really like it, so I just do the things back. And I really want things, like 'Oh, please' and they don't let me...

If I was rich I could get the things I want, but some people might not like me if I'm rich, but I like being really rich. Except some people might not like it. So I might as well spend it on things I really wanted...

Q: What job do you want to do?

A: Taxi thing or something because sometimes, or a cash till man, like shopkeepers. Sometimes you can like sometimes steal the money. Not steal but take some and put it in your pocket... I'd take just a tenner because I could get something, like a computer game or something...

(boy, 8)

Here the immediacy of the sense of acquisition places other people in a different light. Others have the possessions that are desired. Relationships are a matter of transactions. Far from displaying a sense of distance from people we are offered a sense of mechanistic closeness, equally impersonal but depending on the transactional. Others, whether family or not, are also a generalized group, there to provide.

Both of these glimpses into styles of thinking reveal the potential bases of prejudice, of wanting to be far from the immediate social institutions with their demands, or wanting to be in complete personal control. Both suggest patterns of attitudes that could easily be turned into patterns of behaviour. Both have consistent reasons for their positions.

Prejudice is a form of neurotic rationality. Each type has its reasons. It rests on the over-simplification of categories, the personal identity consisting not of irony and complexity, but of definitions of belonging and rejecting. Sometimes collective identities are fluid. Certain groups, both within school and outside, can become accepted. In the United States, for example, the definitions of different 'races' in terms of acceptance has changed over the years.[7] Being 'white' only means something generalized enough to have meaning when juxtaposed against the opposite. Within the term there can be any number of distinctions, between Jews, Armenians, Italians, Irish and Slavs, each with their own ethnicities, and each only slowly absorbed in the United States into the generalized concept of 'Caucasian'. The underlying concepts of 'us' and 'them' might change according to personal or social self-interest but it is always at the heart of categorization.

There is a tension between the moral imperative of complexity and irony, and the atavistic tendency to simplify, to create a sense of belonging. The symbolic value of shared taste is not to be denied, but its attribution as a defining cultural icon leads to the prejudice of insecurity. The desire to break away from that narrow intellectual space of the self, not to be 'cabined, cribbed and confined', can lead either to a freedom of understanding of others in their otherness, or the expansion of an emotional sense of belonging through the collection of others who have the same narrow concepts. The 'isms' can include a variety of individual or group identities in dialogue, each distinct, or a more primitive and less articulate definition of the shared and collective self. All political 'isms' are the pathological extremes of necessary discriminations.

The most obvious manifestations of prejudice, of ethnic cleansing or tribal decimation, evoke horror and indignation. How could people behave like that? To understand that we need to understand the relatively normal, relatively benign manifestations of discrimination, of defining the self through shared interests, through a collective self, as well as relying purely on difference. It is a human tendency. It is also a simplified form of self-protection against the sense of normlessness and estrangement in and from others.

Some questions remain. Is the relationship between individual prejudice and the collective groups as manifested in nationalism so close that the two will always overlap? Are personal and cultural identity so akin that there will inevitably be some atavistic reversion to the actions of distaste? Or can necessary prejudice be contained? Can it become a part of the understanding of cultural hegemony? In a world of global politics we see the possibility of even larger cultural blocks, of conflicts between larger civilizations.[8] We also see the clearer definitions of regionalism, of closer and smaller communities vying for more particular recognition. In all we see the needs of personal identity translated into the fluid, changeable but always significant boundaries of collective definition. There is always the possibility of a kind of cultural atomization as a consequence of the proliferation of cyber-societies. The family, the school, the community, the region and the nation are all vulnerable to new modes of thinking and communicating. Prejudice will then take new forms, or be more profoundly understood.

At the root of prejudice is the personal or collective insecurity of the person or people. The definition of difference is essential. The act of its power against others is unnecessary. It is not inevitable. The extremes of prejudice are learnt. Notions of race, ethnicity and nation will go on existing as categories that foster understanding. They are part of conceptual understanding. But they do not make a good basis for any action.[9]

The last question is this. If prejudice is born out of ontological insecurity, and if it can be so destructive, then why do we collectively allow life, in the sense of our institutions, to remain so essentially insecure? We know about the influence of the home and the nature of schools. We realize the profound and unattributable influences that are brought to bear on each individual. We understand the inadvertent traumas of the early experience of being human. We also see that whilst in the broader sense prejudice, in terms of collective action against others, looks inevitable, it is not necessary. Prejudice in terms of categories, or stereotypes, is part of experience. But it can be contained. It can be understood, and it can be controlled.

This book began in wondering what and how people think of each other. It also concentrated on a more difficult question: Why? If the answer to that question were the focus of attention for education, in the broadest sense, then it would have implications for policy that are both profound and practical.

References

1. Cullingford, C (1999) *The Causes of Exclusion: Home, school and the development of young criminals*, Kogan Page, London
2. Heath, S B (1983) *Ways with Words: Language, life and work in communities and classrooms*, Cambridge University Press, Cambridge

3. eg The arguments around Bernstein, B (1975) *Class, Codes and Control*, Routledge and Kegan Paul, London: to what extent is thought dependent on extended linguistic ability? Labov demonstrates sophisticated thinking in young New Yorkers, but this is not the same thing as the social argument.

4. Webb, C (1998) *Young children's understanding of morality and social relationships*, University of Huddersfield, Huddersfield

5. Pollard, B (1985) *The Social World of the Primary School*, Holt, Rinehart and Winston, London

6. Cullingford, C (1991) *The Inner World of the School*, Cassell, London

7. Jacobson, M (1999) *Whiteness of a Different Color: European immigrants and the alchemy of race*, Harvard University Press, Boston, MA

8. Huntingdon, S (1996) *The Clash of Civilisations and the Remaking of the World Order*, Simon and Schuster, New York

9. Hirschfield, L (1996) *Race in the Making*, MIT Press, London

Index

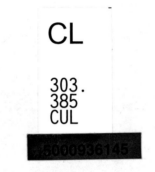